CITY & SUBURBAN GARDENS
BY TOM RIKER

FRONT YARDS
BACK YARDS
TERRACES
ROOFTOPS
WINDOW
BOXES

Prentice-Hall, Inc.
Englewood Cliffs, N. J.

CITY & SUBURBAN GARDENS by Tom Riker

Copyright © 1977 by Tom Riker

Printed in the United States of America

Prentice-Hall International, Inc., London
Prentice-Hall of Australia, Pty. Ltd., Sydney
Prentice-Hall of Canada, Ltd., Toronto
Prentice-Hall of India Private Ltd., New Delhi
Prentice-Hall of Japan, Inc., Tokyo
Prentice-Hall of Southeast Asia Pte. Ltd., Singapore
Whitehall Books Limited, Wellington, New Zealand

10 9 8 7 6 5 4 3 2 1

Library of Congress Cataloging in Publication Data
Riker, Tom
   City and suburban gardens.

   1. Gardening. 2. Roof gardening. I. Title.
SB405.R48   635.9'671   76-58532
ISBN 0-13-134544-3
ISBN 0-13-134536-2 pbk

ACKNOWLEDGEMENTS

To my good friend Will, a fighter for the good life. . .
W. Atlee Burpee Company and especially Jeanette Lowe,
Horticulturist, for her assistance and material provided,
The Lord and Burnham Co., Manufacturer of Fine Green-
houses, The U. S. Dept. of Agriculture and the Year-
Book Staff, Harris Seed Co., and the many artists of
the past for the fantastic archive engravings.

CREDITS

Other Books Edited
and Designed by
Tom Riker

"THE GARDENER'S CATALOGUE",
the nationally best selling
how-to-do-it, where-to-find-it
guidebook for gardeners,
"FOOD GARDENS
Indoors, Outdoors, Under Glass",
the critically acclaimed
most definitive guide
to home grown food available,
"THE GUIDE TO BUYING
PLANTS, and International
Plant Collectors Handbook",
"SEX IN THE GARDEN".

This book was designed by Tom Riker and
Michael Edstrom at Dovetail Design Works,
95 Fifth Ave., New York City
The Mechanicals by Michael Edström
Photographs by Tom Riker
Manuscript and Rewrite by Lars Skattebol
Photographed Archive Engravings, Photo
Conversions and Darkroom Work by
Karl Bruning

CITY & SUBURBAN GARDENS

TABLE OF CONTENTS

8

Building a garden for ornamentation or the harvest of food is a very special task. If the owner of the property supervises the work to be done, or calls on the professional, a plan is needed. In this case the plan is a book, this book. A garden book should not only be used as a decoration for the table, but also as something to carry into the garden along with the other tools. A book on garden planning and garden building can help you a great deal and also save you money—if you have the right questions to ask.

Most of my work in the horticultural field has been strictly in city and suburban areas and I have dealt primarily with the problems of the small-plot gardener and the weekend leaf rakers. I have heard the questions come as the seasons change and most of the questions have to do with the change of seasons and the work that one needs to accomplish to make the spring and summer seasons a colorful success.

We have all seen the garden calendars and the note-pad books that insist that we jot down our ideas and observations as the season passes and try to make a little sense out of the complex and often confusing systems that even the smallest of gardens have. I adhere to a logical methodology and have myself noted various rates of growth of certain plants under certain conditions, be it climatical or soil, be it bright sunlight or dense shade, be it high humidity (due to lack of sunlight) or baked out there in the open field where tomatoes like to ripen. I have seen, being a professional landscape designer, how certain broadleaf evergreens like some of the hybrid rhododendrons or boxwood do in conditions that are not noted for their broadleafs and found that the soil was not acid enough and so had to feed them more often.

1.

2.

1. A window completely framed by perennial vines and annuals growing in the window box.

2. On a northern exposure, but in full light, umbrella plant, centaurea, geraniums, vinca, and asparagus thrive.

The growth rate of foundation plants is especially important and can be solved just by proper spacing. I have included in the Back of the Book a section that deals with spacing requirements for plants in the ground and proper container sizes for the terrace and big-city backyards where most of the plants are in boxes and tubs. I want this book to be used as a tool and hopefully save you some money and aggravation. The lists and tables are important. I know that modern technology is rigid and tables and charts are sort of a pain, but it is

1. The awning is rolled back most of the time so that sun-loving plants can be flowered there. Later the cannas in the jardiniere will be a blaze of red.

2. A prize porch decoration. Coleus, Vinca major, geraniums, Asparagus Sprengert and Boston fern are in the boxes. The tall plant in the basket is Dracaena indivisa. Aspidistra, on the steps, is the toughest of all house plants; seems to stand anything but hard frost.

3. A porch box with vines connects the house with the garden. The Virginia creeper (Ampelopsis quinque-folia) overruns both porch and window box. The plants used in this box, Asparagus Sprengeri, Boston fern and tuberous begonias are among the best for a north exposure.

1.

2.

3.

easier to list certain procedures this way than in the text of the book. A book with plenty of charts, tables, drawings and visuals that are easy to read, easy to understand, and handy, seems to me to be the best way of getting the information across.

I can remember the best textbooks I had when studying ornamental horticulture and commercial floriculture were those with lists of plants, names of soils and lots of pictures to help me identify the garden. So in this book I am helping to keep alive a tradition which helped me. Use this handbook and grow, grow, grow.

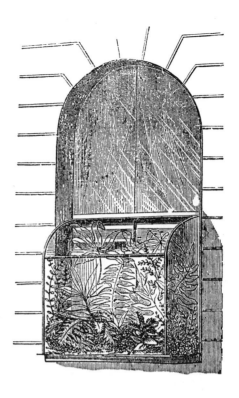

1. Palms, rubbers, dracaenas, and other foliage plants that have been indoors all winter must not be put outdoors in full sunshine during summer. If plunged in the ground and covered by an open lath frame and syringed daily for red spider they will be stronger by fall.

1.

SOIL AND SOIL MIXES

Soil Mixes

Proper inspection of the grounds before attempting to plant is probably the most important aspect of a successful garden. If the soil has not been used for many years, or if the previous owner did not garden properly, you can expect little or no organic matter. The soil may also be poorly drained and contain debris that will harm the plants, such as oil spills and other toxic chemical substances. Inspect the soil, turn it over with a spade, and if you find it poor I suggest the following.

1. Recondition the soil with peatmoss or other types of soil conditioners such as cow manure (dried).

2. Buy a load of good topsoil from a local nursery or landscape outfit.

3. Use an artificial mix (in containers). This mix consists of perlite or vermiculite, peatmoss, some limestone and a garden fertilizer (5-10-5).

All of the above mixes and soil types can be used in window boxes, larger containers, and in the yard. It probably will depend on the availability of material. Topsoil by the yard (truck loads) are almost impossible to get in larger cities, but you can buy bags of clean soil from most nurseries or garden centers that do planting as well as run a retail operation. Ask the store operator if the soil has been sterilized, for if it has not, and you plant indoor plants in containers, you may bring insects and plant diseases into the house. There are national brands that do pack soil in bags and most of the common names are equally good.

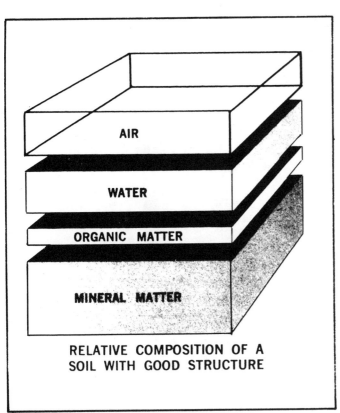

RELATIVE COMPOSITION OF A SOIL WITH GOOD STRUCTURE

I have found that if you have access to a local grower of green plants (a greenhouse operation), sometimes they will sell you mixes designed for tropical rain forest plants but then can be used for container material as well. If you do end up using a common garden loam, and find it is too heavy, you can mix perlite or vermiculite into the container to lighten up the soil and help the drainage. When you put a heavy soil in any container drainage is number one in importance. Gravel or broken pots in the bottom will help, but be sure to drill holes in the tub or box and lift the container off the deck. A block of wood on each side or a couple of bricks will do the trick.

When you are mixing the soil spread it out on a ground cloth or plastic sheet and mix well until the vermiculite or perlite is equally mixed with the loam, sand and peatmoss. I have found to be an overall reliable mix for most plants: One part a good clean garden loam, one part peatmoss, two parts sand (the kind you find in sandboxes in play yards). Add some fertilizer (a regular 5-10-5) for every 50 square feet of area and if you are planting bulbs some bone meal will help the development of the new bulbs. The best time to improve the soil is in the fall of the year (I know about spring fever), but a new mix will allow bulbs, perennials, and shrubs to develop new roots for a more vigorous spring season. You must remember to keep the soil in shape, for every year plants take nutrients out of the soil. I might add that instead of using a commercial fertilizer organic gardeners use cow and sheep manure along with other organic materials to recondition the soil. Whether you choose organic or non-organic, prepare it properly. Take your time for good soil produces healthy plants.

Mulch

A mulch is any organic material such as peat-moss, wood chips, coco shells, used to cover the soil and protect the area. The protection and advantage of mulching are as follows:

1. A mulch keeps the soil in the beds moist and the garden requires less maintenance and watering.

2. A thick mulch such as peatmoss will prevent the germination of weed seeds and even smother weed plants.

3. Mulch prevents soil runoff. The rainfall slowly filters down through the layer of mulch and does not directly hit the soil surface and break the top soil.

4. Mulching in the fall helps to protect the perennial beds and bulb plants from freezing.

5. When a mulch is applied in the vegetable garden, the low-growing vegetables such as melons and tomatoes rest on the mulch and not on the soil. This prevents staining of the fruit.

If you use mulch in vegetable gardens, and I suggest that you do, apply late in the spring after the soil has warmed up. If you apply too soon after the frost the soil will remain cool and thus prevent the rapid growth of new seedlings. When you are sure of warm weather apply the mulch about two inches in depth around the base of the plants. Depending on the growth habit of the plants to be mulched, you must not spread too much peatmoss or other type of mulch around low-growing plants. For example, if you mulch vine crops such as melons, spread the mulch throughout the bed. If you are mulching lettuce or radishes, spread only a few inches deep. You probably know the growing habits of most of the common vegetables and use the mulch accordingly.

When mulching permanent ornamental beds such as foundation plantings in the front of the home or backyards, try and use a stronger, longer lasting mulch such as wood chips or possibly stone. The problems of stone, such as white marble chips, is keeping it out of the lawn area, and if any soil shows through the layer it looks terrible. I personally like wood chips and peatmoss.

If you only mulch to prevent freezing this should be done in the fall. The purpose of this mulching procedure is to prevent a continual freezing and thawing. Usually roses are mulched as are perennial beds and strawberries.

Mulch List

Peatmoss, wood chips (redwood bark, pine bark), dry leaves in sheltered places, straw or salt hay, marble chips, and black plastic.

Black Plastic Mulch

As the use of black plastic mulch becomes more and more popular, a short discussion is in order.

MULCH

Lupine, *Lupinus polyphyllus Ada*

This material is used for exactly the same reasons as other mulches and has advantages and disadvantages. The obvious advantages are permanence and as a work saver. Nothing will grow under the plastic, thus reducing the maintenance in a vegetable or ornamental bed to almost zero.

The disadvantage is caused by the loss of water in dry regions by the plants. You must water through the plastic under such conditions. In heavy rich soil in temperate climates where the rainfall is above average the moisture content under the black plastic mulch is too great and may cause damage to the plants because of lack of aeration.

PLASTIC MULCH FOR FLOWER BEDS

STEPS IN PLANTING

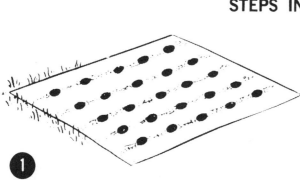

1 Prepare the planting site in the fall. Dig planting holes 4 to 6 inches wider and deeper than the plant root ball. Mix peat moss and organic matter in the planting holes. Space plants evenly over the site.

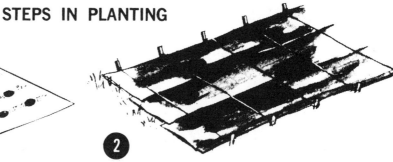

2 Place rolls of black plastic over the area to shade out weeds and retard water loss. Use three or four wide strips slightly overlapping. Tie down the plastic with rocks, wires, or stakes. You may cover the area with a mulch of organic matter instead of using plastic if you wish. Keep the mulch moist to keep it in place.

3 Cut an X slit in the plastic over each planting hole. Enlarge the slits to the proper size hole and set the plants through them.

4 Set the plants at the same level they were growing before they were transplanted. Fill the hole with good soil and pack the soil firmly around the roots. Leave a slight basin at the top to hold water. Water thoroughly after planting.

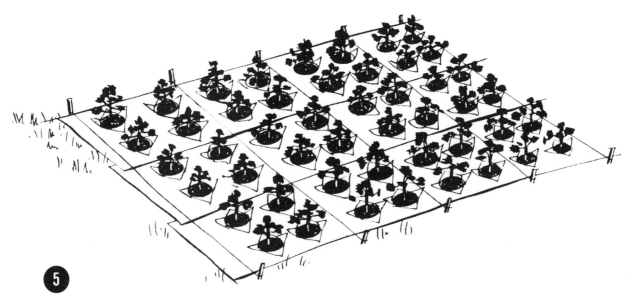

5 Keep the plants in place with an organic mulch over the plastic until the plants are established. Use a mulch of pine bark, wood chips, or hulls. Pull weeds by hand if they grow.

The most common method of laying the black plastic is to fertilize the garden and turn the soil. Level the area to be covered with the black plastic. Anchor the ends of the plastic by digging trenches and covering with soil. You can then measure the garden area and work out a plan where the plants are to be set. You can get directions from the nursery or seller of the black plastic to the spacing requirements for various crops. Usually this mulch is used for plants that are grown in hills like melons, peppers, squash, cucumbers, strawberries, and rhubarb.

1. Compost ready for use in the garden.
2. Using a soil compost mixture under and around the plants in the garden.

COMPOST

The continual use of commercial fertilizers does not improve the soil in the garden. If you are growing annuals either as flowers or vegetables try and utilize the compost pile. It is very easy, and instead of throwing away the vast amount of stored-up nutrients that are to be found in waste materials of organic make-up, use them as a source of fertilizer. Chemicals do not put anything back in the soil but composting does. You can improve the soil make-up and have healthy food plants as well as beautiful ornamentals.

Compost is a combination of soil and organic matter that is used as a soil conditioner and a source for plant nutrients. The humus that is the result of the mixing of green waste material such as grass clippings, kitchen green waste, weeds, and even dead leaves, is used then as a top dressing for lawns, a mulch around trees and shrubs and a fertilizer around vegetable or flower beds.

Briefly, the chemistry of the compost pile is the conversion of organic waste to a very rich humus by several bacteria and fungi. The fungi begin the process by breaking down the complex structures of the plants. As the decay takes place the fungi reproduce at a very rapid rate. The temperature of the pile begins to rise and reaches a high of 160 to 165 degrees F. This temperature reduces the weed seeds and harmful organisms. In a few months the temperature of the compost pile begins to decrease and bacteria take over, breaking down the organic material to a rich humus. If you live in a region with a lot of acid in the soil you can add a little limestone or wood-ash to prevent excess acidity.

CONSTRUCTION OF A COMPOST BIN

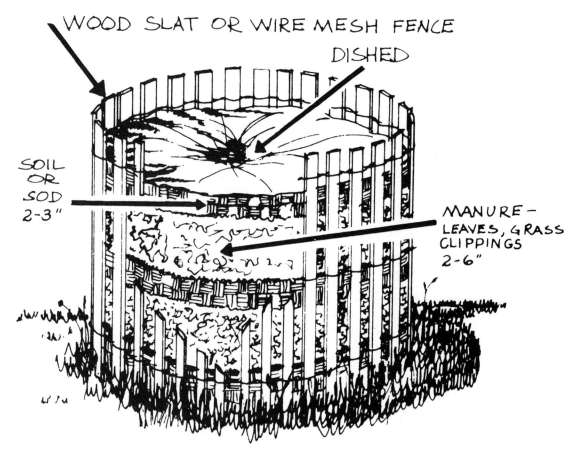

WOOD SLAT OR WIRE MESH FENCE

DISHED

SOIL OR SOD 2-3"

MANURE - LEAVES, GRASS CLIPPINGS 2-6"

CUT-AWAY DIAGRAM SHOWING LAYERING OF WASTE MATERIALS INSIDE THE ROTO-CROP 'ACCELERATOR' COMPOST BIN.

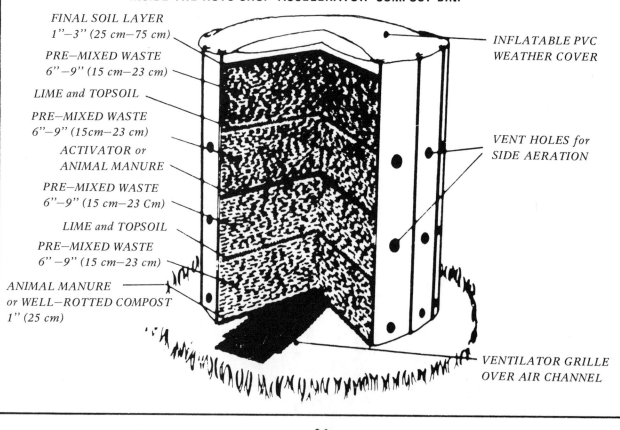

FINAL SOIL LAYER 1"–3" (25 cm–75 cm)

PRE–MIXED WASTE 6"–9" (15 cm–23 cm)

LIME and TOPSOIL

PRE–MIXED WASTE 6"–9" (15cm–23 cm)

ACTIVATOR or ANIMAL MANURE

PRE–MIXED WASTE 6"–9" (15 cm–23 Cm)

LIME and TOPSOIL

PRE–MIXED WASTE 6"–9" (15 cm–23 cm)

ANIMAL MANURE or WELL–ROTTED COMPOST 1" (25 cm)

INFLATABLE PVC WEATHER COVER

VENT HOLES for SIDE AERATION

VENTILATOR GRILLE OVER AIR CHANNEL

Location of the Compost Pit

Build your pit in an out-of-the-way location in an area where water does not accumulate. Remember you have to carry green waste to the pit so locate in a relatively handy place. A compost pit should not smell and if constructed in a location that is visible make it as attractive as possible.

It is possible to just let the pile of waste stay out in the open but the rain will leach away the nutrients and it is just as simple to build a structure. There are as many ways to build a compost pit as materials found in a lumber yard or in the back lot. One good method is a snow fence (wooden slat with wire) forming a circle with a plastic lining. The plastic will keep the temperature up during the process and help keep the rain out.

You can build a permanent structure out of cinder blocks of lumber. Any kind of box-like structure will do.

The size of the compost pit depends on your needs. I suggest building one about five by eight for the average city garden or small plot garden. If you use the snow fence, about seven feet in diameter will do. I have always tried to make the pit in two sections, the first section being the one in use and the second being the one I am building up.

How to Build the Compost Pile

The beginning step in building a compost pile is to line the bottom of the pit with sandy soil about three feet deep. Then add the grass clippings or other finely textured green waste. You can hasten the process by adding manure or, if you like, a commercial fertilizer. I only use manure but you can use the commercial chemicals. The idea of the manure is to feed the bacteria now in the process of turning the organic material into the humus that will end up in the garden.

This sequence is repeated over and over and water is added each time a layer is added. Keep the center of the compost pile lower to prevent the water from running off. If the weather gets dry keep the pile moist. Dry compost is of little value. A new compost pile should be ready for use in four or five months. As the decomposition takes place there are signs to look for as the humus is formed.

1. The pile should get smaller.
2. Never let it get strong in odor and beware of an ammonia smell. This is caused by over watering. Let the pile dry out some and ventilate.
3. After a few weeks if the process is working right the pile should be hot in the center.
4. After the process is completed the pile should be half the size of the original material. It should smell like rich earth and moldy leaves.

Instant Compost for Those in a Hurry

You can hasten the process by adding technology to the garden and plugging in machines. First the structure must be tightly closed with plastic. Second all the green material going into the heap must be finely shredded. Of course you now need a shredder, or a grinder. You then add all the material as used in the slower method but you mix it all together. This process usually takes three to four weeks.

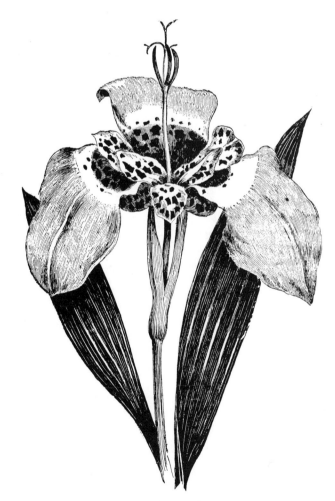

TIGRIDIA FLOWER

Salts in the Soil

When a soil or water has too much salt in its makeup the results may be hazardous to plant life. Salinity may cause the foliage to burn, dwarf the plants or in some cases even kill the plants. There is a danger of salt buildup in many parts of the country where irrigation is practiced and a large amount of fertilizer is continually used on the soil. You can solve the soil problem in regard to your indoor plants by using packaged soil from the local garden center but you must still use the water. Outdoors you have to contend with both soil and water.

The accumulation of salts in water and soil is usually the direct result of the following sources.

1. Various soil mixes.
2. Irrigation water.
3. Commercial fertilizers.

Salt is the result of the decomposition of rocks and minerals. The biggest problem of salinity is to be found in semi-arid regions like the southwest, where nature in the form of rainfall does not wash out the salt. In the southern California and southwest desert regions the gardener must learn to wash out artificially these salts by leaching. All inorganic fertilizers are salts and plants absorb salts for survival. The levels must be kept at the requirements of the plant life, for excess salts may and will do a great deal of damage.

A time-table or measuring stick for salt buildup is sometimes rather difficult if you do not have the sophisticated laboratory equipment of a university or commercial grower. You can send samples of water and soil to your state extension services for analysis. Very seldom do garden-center operators talk about salt buildup in relation to unhealthy plants. Test a container for about two months by just passing water into the soil without letting the water run out. Fertilize a few times with a commercial fertilizer, nothing special. In that time the salt buildup will be harmful enough to damage most flowering plants and foliage plants. The fertilizer and water must continually pass through and out of the container to properly leach out the salts that accumulate.

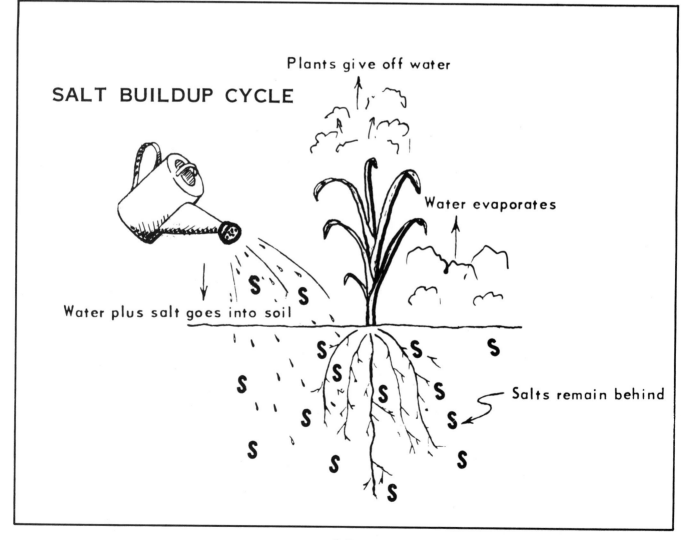

SALT BUILDUP CYCLE

Plants give off water

Water evaporates

Water plus salt goes into soil

Salts remain behind

20

TOOLS

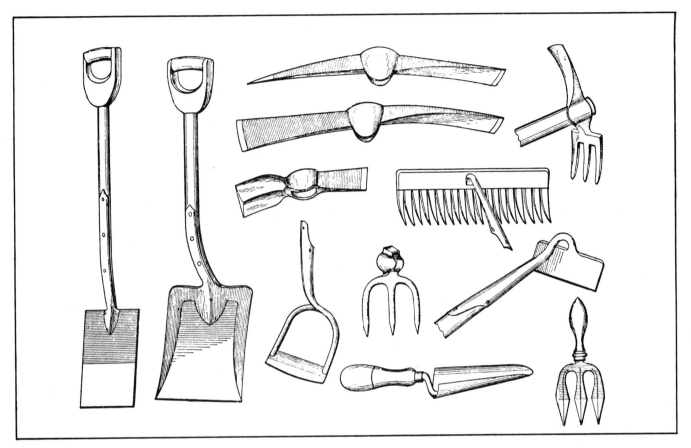

GARDEN BASICS—TOOLS AND WORKSHOPS

Anyone gardening has to have a workshop, just as do the woodworker and the shipbuilder. This place must be equipped with the proper tools. If you live in a city apartment, try and keep your tools in a box or closet and have a portable potting shed. Good tools cost money, so don't let the kids play with them or leave them in the rain. I can think of nothing to replace a trowel or pruning shears. If you need one or both you can't use something else from the kitchen or car trunk. The size and the kind of garden you have will determine the kinds of tools you will need to do what you have to do. You would not buy a grass rake if you have no lawn but you might buy a small pair of shears for miniature roses. Only what you need.

If you go into a garden center or hardware store and look at the rack of tools you might faint or feel you need one of each. You only need four tools. The first is the flat spade with a short handle and good grip. This is the professional gardener's right

arm. This tool is used for cutting beds, digging plants and any heavy work related to the above. The next is the small trowel. This is used for planting the seedlings and bulbs and this operation is done on your knees, or if you have a strong back, on the balls of your feet. Next is a hard-grass rake or soil rake to smooth the soil and clean up the loose ends. The hoe or cultivator is the last and this is used to keep out the weeds and move the soil around. You can garden with the above tools.

The next level of tools comes when you start to shape and spray, transplant larger trees, or move plants around the garden. This list includes a wheelbarrow or cart. Wheels beat heels and bad backs are death for gardeners. Next, a hose.

If you have a lawn you need a mower. I will not get into the machinery of cutting, raking, bagging, mulching and whatever else you can do with some of the new models of lawn equipment. The most important thing to remember is replacement parts and the availability of competent mechanics for repairs. I have seen very expensive riding mowers with plastic gears that break every

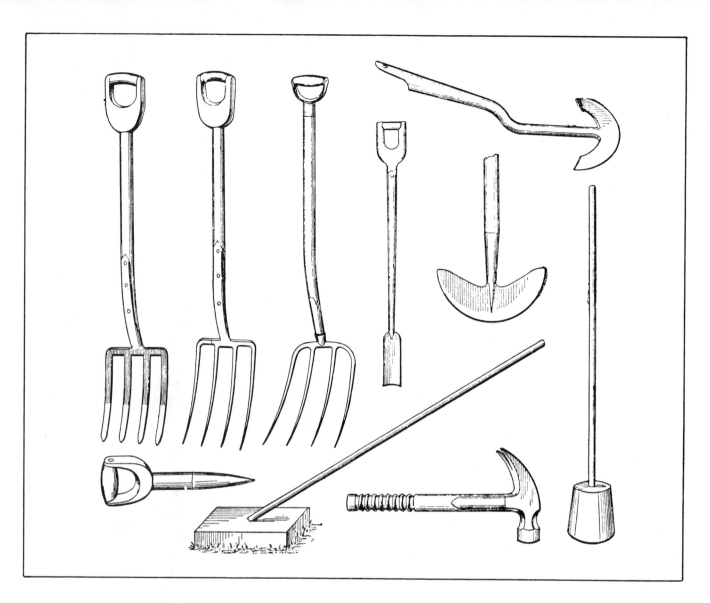

time the grass gets over two inches. This is a tough item and all I can say is: "Buyer, beware." Buy a national brand with a good guarantee. You get what you pay for.

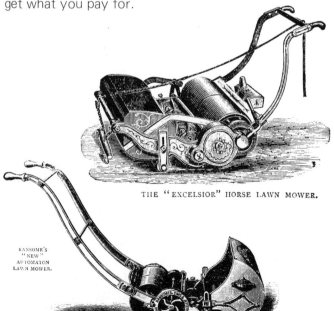

THE "EXCELSIOR" HORSE LAWN MOWER.

RANSOME'S "NEW" AUTOMATON LAWN MOWER.

If you have a hedge you need hedge clippers. I have always used the manual kind. Pruning shears are important. Get a good pair that permits the blade to be replaced, and a larger pair of lopping shears to prune fruit trees and clean out dead wood on over-grown deciduous shrubs and trees. The hedge shears can be used to shape evergreens like yews and junipers. So here's what we have.

1. Spade.
2. Rake, soft steel and hard soil.
3. Small hand tools (trowel).
4. Hoe or cultivator.
5. Wheelbarrow or lawn cart (preferably wheelbarrow).
6. Hose (rubber) with good brass fittings with a fan nozzle and shut-off switch.
7. Lawn mower (your choice), power or manual.
8. Pruning tools—hedge clipper, pruning shears and lopping shears.

PRUNING ORNAMENTAL TREES AND SHRUBS

Pruning is a necessary chore in any garden. It should begin when you purchase the plant from the nursery, or when you transplant from another part of the garden. Pruning not only increases the ornamental value of the tree or shrub by shaping it to meet your demands for the type of garden you have, but it also keeps the plant healthy. Nothing looks as bad as an over-grown shrub that badly needs removal of dead wood and the elimination of branches that block windows or interfere with the texture and growing habits of the surrounding plants. Every spring or fall you should remove dead wood, cut off diseased or damaged branches and shape the plant to its natural growing habits. If you are growing a formal hedge or if you shape evergreens in an ornamental fashion, you still must follow a regular cleaning procedure to keep the plant healthy.

PRUNING

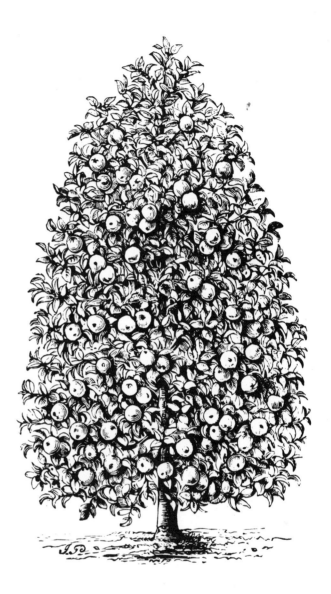

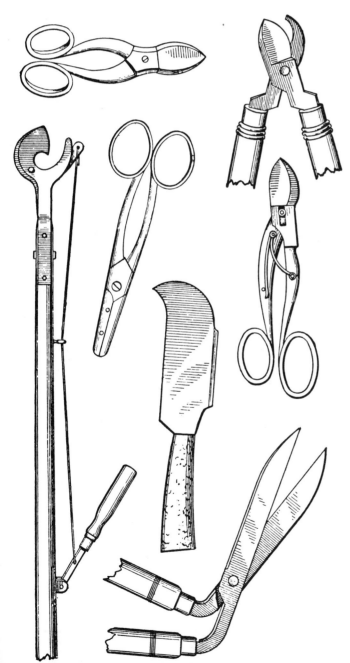

DECIDUOUS SHRUBS

Deciduous shrubs drop their foliage in the fall. If a plant is part of the landscape you must keep it under control by pruning. If you prune for direction of growth, be sure the cut is in the right place. A new shoot will grow in the direction the bud points. Think ahead and try to visualize the final result by drawing a picture of the new shoots in the direction that the buds point. It is very easy to cut to order if you follow the rules of normal growth. The picture on the next page indicates the proper angles to cut and the proper distance to cut from the bud. When you remove an entire branch, prune flush with the stem. If you prune off dead wood always cut a little into the green wood.

PRUNING SUMMER SHRUBS

The flowers of this grouping produce flowers on the wood that grew this eason. Always prune in the off or dormant season. That could be late fall into the winter and very early spring.

Abelia. Prune to shape and keep the sucker well cut back.

Beautybush. I usually cut this plant way back in the off season. If you prune down to ten inches you will do no harm.

Bladder senna (Colutea). Cut back to the ground every year.

Bluebeard (Caryopteris). Cut back to the ground every year.

Bushclover. Like most summer producing shrubs you can prune quite heavily. Prune to shape and top every few years.

Butterflybush. Cut way back every year. Some gardeners and even non-gardeners cut them back to the ground every year.

Chastetree (Vitex). Cut way back to about 10 in. every year.

Coralberry (Symphoicarpos). Prune back to about the third bud and clean up dead wood.

Crape myrtle. Heavy pruning is required to produce full flowering. This is another ornamental shrub that is often turned into a small tree by pruning.

Elder, Red berry. Prune to the natural shape of the plant.

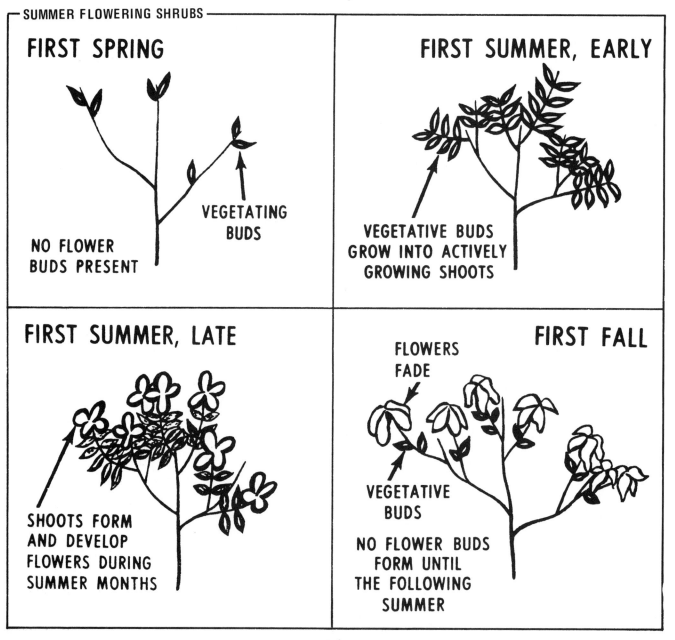

SUMMER FLOWERING SHRUBS

FIRST SPRING

NO FLOWER BUDS PRESENT

VEGETATING BUDS

FIRST SUMMER, EARLY

VEGETATIVE BUDS GROW INTO ACTIVELY GROWING SHOOTS

FIRST SUMMER, LATE

SHOOTS FORM AND DEVELOP FLOWERS DURING SUMMER MONTHS

FIRST FALL

FLOWERS FADE

VEGETATIVE BUDS

NO FLOWER BUDS FORM UNTIL THE FOLLOWING SUMMER

Eleagnus. Every two or three years give a good thinning out and remove dead branches, cutting well into the green wood every year.

Heather. Never prune in the winter or in the summer. This will kill the plant. Prune back in the spring to the ground and cover in northern regions with a heavy mulch.

Hibiscus. Leave two or three buds on each branch each spring.

Honeysuckle. This is a very fast growing shrub and can be pruned way back in the spring. It tends to get out of hand in the landscape but if you need a good screen plant, this is it.

Hydrangea. May kill back to the ground. Clean out all dead wood and cut back heavily in the spring.

Indigobush. Keep thin and clear of all dead wood.

Jersey Tea. Cut way back every year. It can be pruned back as far as ten inches without any trouble.

Magnolia (Virginiana). Do not prune except to shape plant. It does not need to be pruned to promote new growth or produce flowers.

Mintshrub (Elsholtzia). Cut back to the ground every year.

Raspberry. Cut back just after flowering to promote new growth.

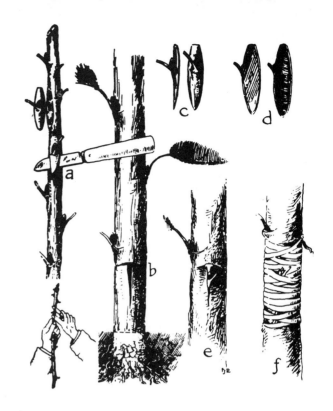

Budding or bud grafting, using the T-bud or shield bud technique.

a. Bud-stick. Proper method of holding knife and cutting bud is shown in lower left-hand corner.
b. T-cut on stock.
c. Side and front view of a "bud."
d. Inside view of bud with and without wood.
e. Stock with bud inserted.
f. Bud in place and tied with rubber band.

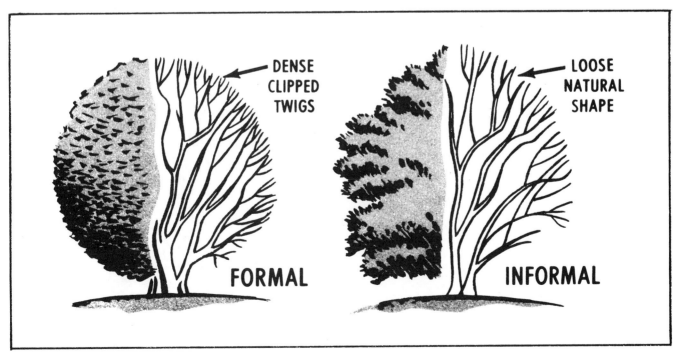

DENSE CLIPPED TWIGS

LOOSE NATURAL SHAPE

FORMAL

INFORMAL

Rose. Look in the rose section and graphic display on how to prune roses.

St. Johnswort (Hypericum). Prune back to about two buds each spring to promote new growth and full flowering.

Snowberry (Symphoicarpos). Thin out older wood and remove dead wood. Prune back to two or three buds in the spring.

Spirea (false) (Sorbaria). Remove seed pods each year and cut back every two or three years.

Spirea. Flowering types of this family include Anthony Waterer, bumalda, Japanese, and billiard. Remove seed pods and cut back to a few buds.

Stephanandra. Remove dead wood and thin in the spring.

BEDDING-ROSES.

A Good Background For Low Shrubs

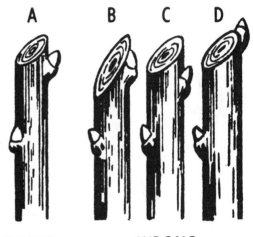

PROPER PRUNING ANGLE

A   B   C   D

RIGHT   WRONG

When possible, cut back to a side bud and make the cut at a slant. A is cut correctly. B is too slanting. C is too far from the bud. D is too close to the bud.

Sumac (Rhus). This plant is now so common in the cities that it is replacing the brick as the new image of the city. This plant can be pruned back to the ground in the spring and formed into a single tree if all the suckers are kept down.

Summersweet. Prune to shape and remove all dead wood.

Tamarisk. Remove seed pods and when the plant gets out of hand cut back to the ground.

CHINESE WISTARIA (*Wistaria sinensis*).

SPRING FLOWERING SHRUBS

The flowers that appear on the shrubs during the regular blooming periods are produced on the growth of the year before. If you prune in the fall or winter months you probably will remove most of the stems that will give your garden the color. All spring flowering shrubs should be pruned as soon as the flowers fade in the late spring. This will give the plant plenty of time to produce the branching and buds for the next season's color. The general rule for most spring flowers regarding pruning is that larger flowers can be expected if you prune in season and prune correctly. Following is a good list of spring flowering shrubs and their pruning requirements.

Azalea. Prune to the shape of the plant and remove all sucker shoots from the base of the plant.

Almond. Prune to the shape of the plant and remove all dead wood. Almond does have a tendency to kill back in some northern regions.

Beautybush. Prune all dead wood and old growth. Let the shrub have a lot of new growth over the summer months. This will promote a good flowering period the following season.

Barberry. Remove all dead wood and cut back old wood. This is a fast growing plant and removing old wood will stimulate new growth and develop a healthy plant with a lot of new growth for color.

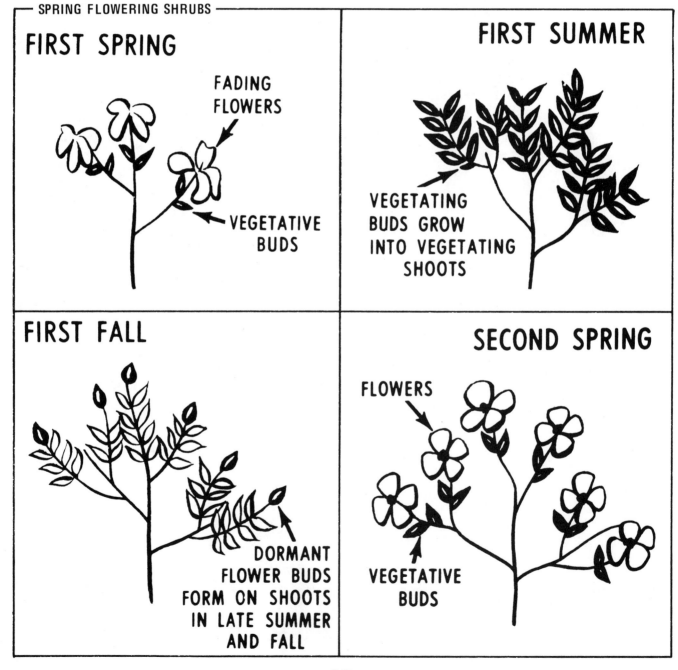

SPRING FLOWERING SHRUBS

FIRST SPRING
FADING FLOWERS
VEGETATIVE BUDS

FIRST SUMMER
VEGETATING BUDS GROW INTO VEGETATING SHOOTS

FIRST FALL
DORMANT FLOWER BUDS FORM ON SHOOTS IN LATE SUMMER AND FALL

SECOND SPRING
FLOWERS
VEGETATIVE BUDS

Blueberry. Prune the smaller branches that are not strong. This plant is also a beautiful fall foliage plant and this sort of pruning will promote new foliage for fall color as well as providing a stronger plant for the spring flowering season.

Broom. Remove old dead wood and cut back somewhat to keep size down.

Burningbush. Prune to shape of plant and thin out crowded branches. This is also a beautiful fall foliage plant and should be planted in the landscape with evergreens to stimulate the color balance in the late fall months.

Crab, Flowering. You can treat all the flowering crabs in the same manner. Shape the plant so branches do not cross and this will provide a perfect plant for the corner planting or the middle of the lawn. I have grown crabs in very dark backyards in the city with good results. They tend to

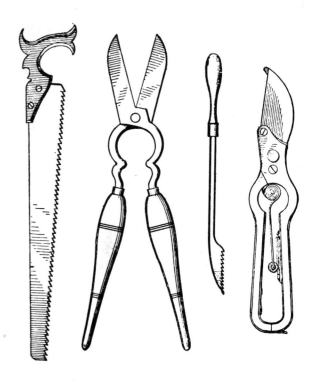

BEST WOOD TO PRUNE FOR RAPID REGROWTH

- ■ NEW WOOD
- ■ LIGHT COLOR
- ■ SMOOTH BARK
- ■ NEW BUDS

shoot straight up looking for sunlight so I suggest you keep them down on top and remove all suckers from the base.

Current. Remove all older wood and prune to shape of plant.

Deutzia. Remove old wood to promote new stock for flowering period but do not destroy the natural shape of the plant. This is a graceful plant and heavy pruning without regard for this will destroy the shape.

Dogwood. Remove three-year-old wood to promote flowering. Do not over prune dogwood but let them grow in a natural way.

Elder. Shape the plant around the original form and remove all dead wood.

Enkianthus. Prune very moderately, only removing dead wood.

Firethorn. Heavy pruning may damage the plant's ability to produce berries in the late fall months. Just control the shape and size.

Forsythia. This plant can be pruned very heavily. Many times I cut back to the ground for good new growth.

Fringetree. Controlling the size is important with this plant. Remove dead wood and prune to the shape of the plant.

Garlandflower (Daphne). This plant can stand heavy pruning.

Heath. Prune heavily to promote new growth.

Honeysuckle. Prune old wood and remove dead wood. This plant tends to grow very tall without proper care. If you live in the city and want to keep this plant for the sweet smelling flowers, and use it for a screen, I suggest you prune every spring.

Hydrangea. Never prune this plant in the winter or early spring. Many times winter damage causes the flower buds to be damaged and the results are nice green foliage but no flowers. Prune in summer after the plants have completely flowered.

HEDGE PRUNING

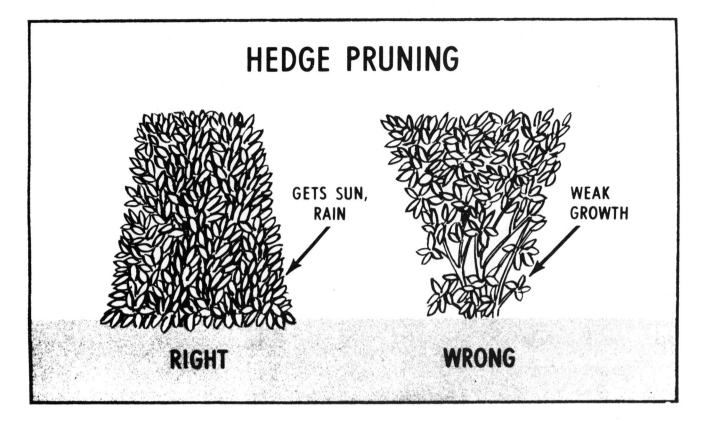

GETS SUN, RAIN

WEAK GROWTH

RIGHT

WRONG

Kerria. Prune old wood and remove dead wood. Try and keep the natural shape for like other plants of this type any attempt to cut to a special shape does not work well.

Lilac. Remove the flowers and base suckers.

Magnolia. You can shape the plant after you remove the seed pods.

Mock orange. Prune older wood (three to four years) to promote new growth.

Ninebark. Thin plant every year to develop new growth and encourage flowering habit of shrub.

Pearlbush. Thin the shrub, removing dead wood and any older branches that do not promote new growth.

Privet. This is the common hedge plant and needless to say will stand a lot of pruning and shaping. Do what you will, the privet tree and hedge will remain.

Quince. New flowers only appear on last year's wood, so keep thinned out each year and remove dead wood that the winter has killed back.

COMMON PURPLE LILAC.
(SYRINGA VULGARIS.)

JAPAN QUINCE (*Cydonia Japonica*).

SHAPING PLANTS

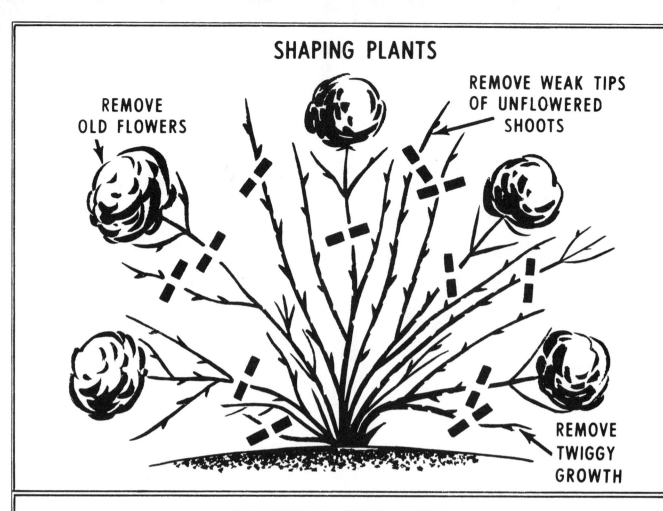

REMOVE
OLD FLOWERS

REMOVE WEAK TIPS
OF UNFLOWERED
SHOOTS

REMOVE
TWIGGY
GROWTH

REMOVING SEED PODS

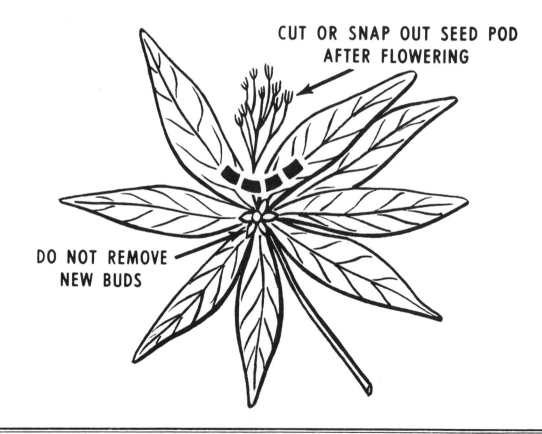

CUT OR SNAP OUT SEED POD
AFTER FLOWERING

DO NOT REMOVE
NEW BUDS

Rockspray (Cotoneaster). Thin out every few years to promote growth. The low rock garden varieties may be treated the same as the upright kinds.

Shadbush. Controlling size is of most importance, for this plant will take off after a few seasons. Keep the old wood under control.

Snowball. The ornamental method of a snowball tree is just removing all the shoots except one and treating like a tree. Thin out every few years.

Spirea. Always prune to the shape of the plant. There are many kinds of spirea but the above applies to all forms. Never try to shape a plant that has a distinct form.

Sweetshrub. Keep down by thinning every two years. If you want a screen only take out the dead wood and those branches not producing good young branches.

Tamarisk. Never let any shrub get leggy and this applies specially here. Remove older branches to promote new growth.

Viburnum. This again is a very large family of very beautiful flowering shrubs. The grouping of shrubs that you have in your backyard and could not name probably is some sort of viburnum. Prune to shape and thin out dead wood.

Weigela. This shrub tends to get thick in the middle section like many of my more inactive friends. Prune older wood and keep nice and thin.

Witch hazel. Prune every few years to the shape of the plant. Remove old and dead wood every year.

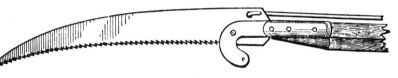

GOLDEN-BELL (*Forsythia viridissima*).

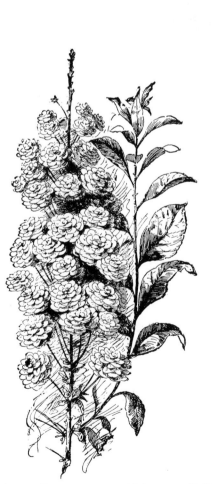

BRIDAL-WREATH (*Spiræa prunifolia*).

WEIGELA (*Diervilla rosea*).

EVERGREENS (BROADLEAF)

All broadleaf evergreens such as rhododendron that produce flower buds in the fall for spring color should be pruned just after the spring flowering period. Those plants that produce the flowers on the new spring growth can be pruned any time during the dormant seasons.

Andromedia (Pieris japonica). Prune to shape with pruning shears and not hedge shears.

Aucuba. Remove damaged wood in the spring and shape plant with pruning shears.

Blueberry, Box (Vaccinium). Prune to promote new growth.

Boxwood (Buxus). A common evergreen hedge used in formal places. A close compact plant is the best. Cut with hedge shears.

Camellia. Cut out older wood and remove dead wood to promote new growth.

Cherry laurel. Every year cut back old wood.

Holly (Ilex). Prune to shape with pruning shears.

Hollygrape (Mahonia). Prune back old wood to keep from becoming leggy.

Holly (Osmathus). Prune to shape of plant.

Inkberry (Ilex). Prune to control the shape and remove all winter kill.

TAXUS BACCATA DOVASTONI.

Leucothoe. Thin out plant of older wood every few years.

Mountain Laurel (Kalmia). Remove older wood to promote new growth.

Nandina (domestica). Older wood and dead wood must be removed every few years to keep the plant healthy.

THUYA GIGANTEA.

PINUS CEMBRA.

Oleander. Prune the top and keep the original shape.

Privet. The evergreen types of privet can be treated just like the deciduous types.

Rhododendron. Prune after flowering periods. Take off the leggy branches every spring.

Skimmia. Cut like box for hedge or prune to the natural shape in the spring.

PICEA SMITHIANA.

Prune pines in late spring by removing one-half of the candle, or new shoot. Do not damage needle tips because the tips of cut needles tend to turn brown.

You can reduce open spaces on spruces by cutting off one-half of the leader, or terminal shoot, in the spring when the new needles are about half developed.

Keep side branches from growing out of bounds by removing the terminal bud. This not only slows outward growth but also helps to make the plants more bushy.

You can replace a lost leader by tying one of the branches in the top whorl to a vertical brace.

Trees that have already grown too wide can be narrowed by cutting the branches back to an inner bud.

If the tree develops two leaders, remove the less desirable one in early spring. Trees with more than one leader are weaker and less attractive than trees that have a single, strong, central leader.

Basic Pruning Steps For Espalier

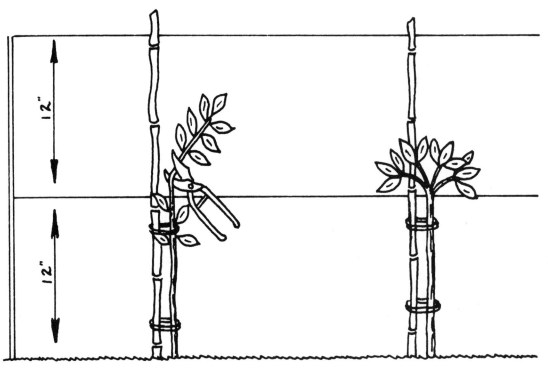

12"

12"

cut to height
of first cordon

wait for
new shoots

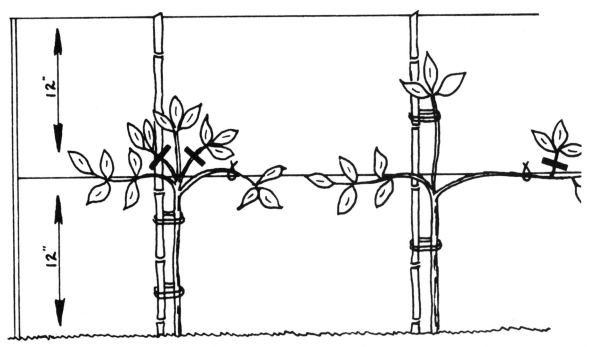

12"

12"

train three best
shoots on bottom
cordon; prune excess

allow one center
shoot to continue;
pinch offshoots on
horizontals

Single

Horizontal Cordons

Double

CONTAINERS

The growing area in most city gardens is usually a combination of small back yards, side terraces, rooftops, window gardens and an occasional hanging basket. All of these areas need containers except the yards, and usually pots and tubs can be found there too. Most commercially sold containers are suitable and it is not worth your while to build boxes out of ordinary lumber for they will rot and have to be replaced after a few seasons. They are also very difficult to make waterproof and they lose their shape. Stick to redwood boxes, barrels (usually oak sold at city garden centers that originally held brandy or whisky), clay pots and some of the new fiberglass containers (some are expensive) but the longevity is remarkable. If you buy wooden boxes of common lumber then paint the inside and outside with a wood preservative and finish the inside with some sort of tar paint. Never use mildew-proof paints for they are toxic to plant life. If you wish to paint the outside I suggest darker colors for shady areas and brighter colors for bright sunlight. Dark colors absorb heat and bright colors reflect sunlight.

If you want to build permanent structures on the terrace or rooftop, drainage is a problem. You have to construct drainpipes under the stone or cement work. The problems that result from accumulation of excess water under such structures could result in flooding or dead plants due to rotting of root sections. I cannot over-stress the importance of good drainage for any type of container. Before you build anything of a permanent nature you should check with the owner of the property, for many buildings do not allow such construction. Portable containers are the best. They can be moved about into the sunlight and all of the problems of build-ins are eliminated. Take the easy way and the best way.

Method of using Tourniquet

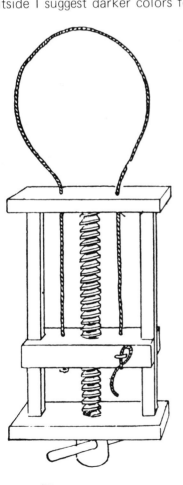

Tourniquet

41

CONTAINERS

Proper watering is essential for container gardening success. Plants dry out much faster than when grown in the ground, especially in a hot, sunny, breezy spot. Try to shelter containers from strong wind.

Water plants thoroughly whenever the planting material feels dry to touch. This may be more than once a day in hot bright weather, or less often during a cloudy, cool or rainy spell. In a very hot spot it often helps to insert the pot in which the plant is growing into the next size larger pot and pack the space in between them with damp sphagnum moss or Vermiculite. This keeps the plant from drying out so fast, and perhaps wilting if you are not home all day to watch the watering.

Control Insects and Diseases with a safe spray or dust. Follow manufacturer's directions carefully.

Water plants thoroughly whenever planting material feels dry to touch. This may be more than once a day in hot, bright weather, or less often during a cool, cloudy or rainy spell.

Feed container plants about once a week with a water soluble fertilizer according to package directions. Since the frequent watering washes nutrients out of the growing medium, it is necessary to apply fertilizer regularly and often.

Pick off faded flowers and seed pods to extend period of bloom. Harvest vegetables at their peak for ripeness and flavor; this also helps keep plants productive.

Control insects with one of the many excellent all-purpose sprays or dusts on the market. Prevent or control most diseases by growing disease-resistant varieties; by removing and discarding any "sick" plants; or by using a safe spray or dust containing proper fungicide when trouble is first noticed.

HANGING BASKETS

Hanging baskets are as old as gardening and are still being used to display hanging vines and other trailing plants. The old style baskets were made of wire frames and lined with various kinds of moss. The water ran through them, but plastic liners can be put between the frame and the moss to prevent run-off.

I personally like the look of an old style basket with the moss and wire frames but I have to admit that the new plastic hanging pots are much more practical and not bad to look at. You can buy them in various colors to match your interior or garden. Clay pots still seem to be popular for they do have a feeling of greenhouses and are handsome enough to be put anywhere. The only problem with clay is the growth of moss and algae but if you keep the pots clean and control the growth with an ammonium compound that you can buy in most garden centers the problem is eliminated. If the clay pots are in the garden, moss growing and algae seem to be natural enough not to worry most gardeners.

HANGING BASKETS

Hanging baskets of flowers and vegetables are both attractive and useful to decorate walls, lamp posts, porches, balconies and trellises. Line mesh baskets with sphagnum moss or use plastic hanging pots. Eight or nine inch diameter baskets will hold two or three Sweet Alyssum, Begonia, Impatiens, Trailing Lobelia, Nugget Marigold, Nasturtium, Pansy or Petunia plants (or combinations thereof). Loosehead Lettuce, Herbs, Parsley and Malabar Spinach can also be grown in these size baskets, but larger ones (11 or 12 inch diameter and 12 to 18 in. deep) are necessary for pixie Hybrid, Basket Pak, Red Cherry and Yellow Plum Tomatoes (1 plant per container). Tomato baskets can be "prettied up" with a few Sweet Alyssum or Nugget Marigold plants around the edges.

**Tomato Hanging Basket
1 Tomato Plant, Basket Pak or Red Cherry gives "good picking" at arm's length in a hanging basket.**

Several Impatiens plants in a pretty ceramic container beautify a shady spot all summer.

Use a suitable growing medium

Plants in containers need a growing medium which doesn't pack hard; drains well, yet doesn't dry out too fast; and supplies sufficient nutrients for good growth. A potting mixture of two thirds Burpee Planting Forumula to one third sieved garden soil is satisfactory. To reduce the watering requirement use Burpee's new Special Potting Mixture in place of the Planting Formula. Plants can also be grown entirely in Planting Formula, Special Potting Mixture, Vermiculite or similar materials.

These planting materials not only promote good plant growth, but are relatively light—an important plus for container gardening. Pots, boxes and hanging baskets can be heavy to move around or suspend and are much easier to handle if weight is kept to a minimum. Even so, you should put large containers in their permanent places before filling and planting. Use strong supports and hooks for hanging baskets.

WINDOW BOXES

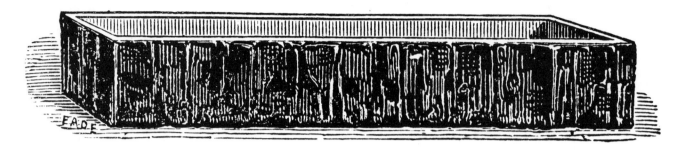

Windowboxes

A windowbox, well placed and cared for is an added attraction to any landscape and sometimes is the landscape. But I might add that there is nothing so bad as a windowbox, placed in view for all to see, that is neglected and overgrown. A garden on the window in the summer months adds beauty to the indoor room, charm and attractiveness to the outside and if you plan ahead, pleasant odors or perfume that only flowers in boxes on the window can add to a sitting room.

Windowboxes do exceedingly well in areas not shaded by overhanging porches or other buildings. The idea of the windowbox is to add color to the architecture of the building and bring a little of the outdoors in. This being the case, place the box in as much sunlight as possible. Many plants that are too tender to grow in the open may do well in windowboxes. Ferns, fuchsias, caladiums and tuberous-rooted begonias, like the angel's wing, all do well in the box. Rubra and most of the begonia family do well in the north light. Where the window faces the street or sidewalk the main idea is to show off some color either in the foliage or the flowers. Hanging petunias (cascade) in combination with vinca vine or ivy make a real show. If you are growing any of the annuals that have been developed for their bright flowers you must have good sunlight. If the window is shaded, grow begonias, coleus, impatiens and possibly ferns. A box with all green (vinca, ivy) does sure give a brick wall some green.

One of the most common plants for windowboxes is of course the geranium. The geranium likes to dry out and small containers do have a way of getting dry in the summer months. I have seen perennials, evergreens (low growing junipers) and even holly in windowboxes. Of course everyone is entitled to his or her opinion but it seems to me that the main purpose of the windowbox is to provide summer color and summer green. This is only achieved by the wide range of annuals and some hanging vines. If you live in a mild climate where you have a very long growing season you can modify the boxes to a more permanent nature but by and large annuals are the perfect plant for the windowbox.

You can buy good windowboxes from any garden center or nursery almost as cheaply as you can make them. Some of the more expensive boxes, say the redwood planters, do last a long time and as they weather they seem to pick up a lot of character. The fiberglass and plastic boxes are a little cheaper and will serve the exact purpose. The tin boxes that were very common years ago have a short life for they rust (even when they are painted). Stick to wood and plastic or fiberglass.

Try and order the boxes to fit the entire length of the window casing and they should be at least ten inches wide and over six inches deep.

PREPARING CONTAINERS FOR PLANTING

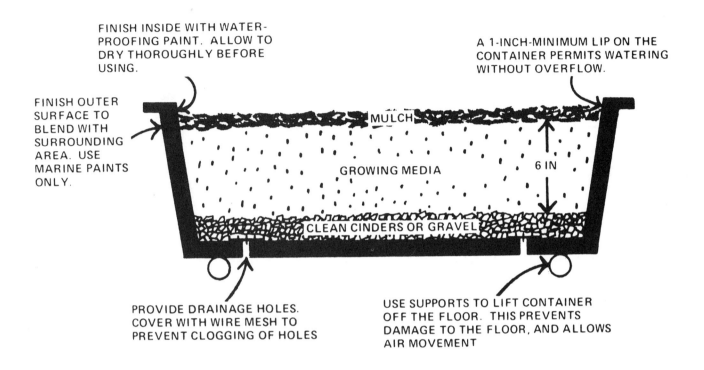

FINISH INSIDE WITH WATER-PROOFING PAINT. ALLOW TO DRY THOROUGHLY BEFORE USING.

A 1-INCH-MINIMUM LIP ON THE CONTAINER PERMITS WATERING WITHOUT OVERFLOW.

FINISH OUTER SURFACE TO BLEND WITH SURROUNDING AREA. USE MARINE PAINTS ONLY.

MULCH

GROWING MEDIA

6 IN

CLEAN CINDERS OR GRAVEL

PROVIDE DRAINAGE HOLES. COVER WITH WIRE MESH TO PREVENT CLOGGING OF HOLES

USE SUPPORTS TO LIFT CONTAINER OFF THE FLOOR. THIS PREVENTS DAMAGE TO THE FLOOR, AND ALLOWS AIR MOVEMENT

Most of the "ready made" windowboxes are designed and constructed to fit most window casings. The sizes run from 12 inches all the way to 48 inches. If you have a special size casing, most landscape services and city garden centers specializing in terrace and penthouse planting can have them made to order. Of course every time something is done that is not off the assembly line it costs more. Be prepared to really pay for custom boxes of any kind.

There are several kinds of hardware made to fit most casings. These are usually made of wrought iron or some sort of steel and are designed for safety for the people walking on the street or the folks that live on the terrace below. If there is no danger of a box falling on the street then any type of strap or wooden brace will do.

All boxes should have drainage holes in the bottom for run-off in rainstorms or just regular waterings. I would place a piece of broken pot over the hole to prevent soil from clogging up the drain. The hot air of summer will tend to pull the soil back from the sides of the boxes. If you leave the center of the box a little lower in soil than the sides this will be prevented. You will soon determine how much run-off will occur. It is trial and error depending on the root sections

of the plants and the kinds of plants in the boxes.

Do not crowd plants in the container. I understand that when one only has a couple of windows, and the boxes are the only place you can grow a few geraniums, the temptation is to get as many as possible in the space. You will be further ahead, and save money, if you plant the proper number of

plants in the boxes and allow them to grow in the right way. Four healthy plants look a lot better than six sparce, yellow-leafed geraniums. Do yourself a favor and limit the planting to what the box can hold.

The following is a listing of the various combinations of flowers you can grow successfully in windowboxes, taking into consideration your exposure.

Plants for Low Temperature (50-60 degrees F. at Night)
Australian laurel
Azalea
Babytears
Black pepper
Boxwood
Bromeliads
Calceolaria
Camellia
Christmas Begonia
Cineraria
Citrus
Cyclamen
Easter lily
English ivy cultivars
Fatshedera
Flowering maple
Fuchsia
Geraniums
German ivy
Honeysuckle
Jerusalem-cherry
Kalanchoe
Miniature holly
Mother-of-thousands
Oxalis
Primrose
Sensitive plant
Spindle tree
Vinca
White calla lily

Sweet Potato Vine in vase.

Plants for Medium Temperature (60-65 degrees F. at Night)
Achimenes
Amaryllis
Ardisia
Avocado
Bromeliads
Browallia
Chenille plant
Christmas cactus
Chrysanthemum
Citrus
Copperleaf
Crown of thorns
Easter lily
English ivy cultivars
Gardenia
Grape ivy
Hibiscus
Hydrangea
Norfolk Island pine
Palms
Peperomia
Pilea
Poinsettia
Rose
Shrimp plant
Silk-oak
Ti Plant
Tuberous begonia
Velvet plant
Wax begonia
Wax plant
Yellow calla lily

—Dieffenbachia.

Plants for High Temperature (65-75 degrees F. at Night)
African-violet
Aphelandra
Arrowhead
Australian umbrella tree
Banded Maranta
Cacti and succulents
Caladium
Chinese evergreen
Croton
Dracaena
Episcia
Figs
Gloxinia
Golddust plant
Philodendron
Scindapus (Pothos)
Seersucker plant
Snake plant
Spathyphyllum
Veitch screwpine

Plants for Extremely Dry Conditions
Bromeliads
Cacti
Crown of thorns
Ovalleaf Peperomia
Snake plant
Scindapsus (Pothos)
Wandering Jew

Plants for Hanging Baskets
African-violet
Anthericum (Spider plant)
Asparagus fern
Begonias (some types)
Black pepper
English ivy cultivars
Episcia
Fuchsia (some cultivars)
German ivy
Goldfish plant
Grape ivy
Honeysuckle
Italian bellflower
Ivy geranium
Peperomia (some species)
Philodendron (some species)
Saxifraga
Scindapsus (pothos)
Syngonium
Trailing-coleus
Wandering Jew
Wax plant

—Agave Americana.

49

For Special Exposures

South or West Windows
Amaryllis
Azalea
Begonia (in winter)
Bloodleaf
Cacti and succulents
Calla lily
Coleus
Cyclamen
Easter lily
Gardenia
Geranium
Lily
Oxalis
Poinsettia
Rose
Sweetflag
tulip
Velvet plant

North Window
African-violet (in summer)
Anthericum
Arrowhead
Australian umbrella tree
Babytears
Cast-iron plant
Chinese evergreen
Dracaena
Dumbcane
Fern
Ivy
Mother-of-thousands
Norfolk Island pine
Peperomia
Philodendron
Piggyback plant
Pleomele
Rubber plant
Scindapsus (Pothos)
Snake plant
Tuftroot
Wandering-Jew

Suggestions for Large Tubbed Specimens
Australian umbrella tree
Dracaenas
False-aralia
Fatshedera
Fiddle-leaf fig
India-rubber plant and cultivars
Palms
Philodendrons
Silk-oak
Tuftroot
Veitch screwpine

Plants That Will Withstand Abuse
Arrowhead
Australian umbrella tree
Cast-iron plant
Chinese evergreen
Crown of thorns
Devil's ivy
Fiddle-leaf fig
Grape ivy
Heartleaf Philodendron
India-rubber plant
Jade plant
Ovalleaf Peperomia
Pleomele
Snake plant
Spathyphyllum
Trileaf Wonder
Tuftroot (D. amoena)
Veitch screwpine
Zebra plant

Vines and Trailing Plants for Totem Poles
Arrowhead
Black pepper
Creeping fig
English ivy cultivars
Grape ivy
Kangaroo vine
Pellionia
Philodendron
Scindapsus (Pothos)
Syngonium
Wax Plant

50

East Window

African-violet
Banded maranta
Caladium
Dracaena
Fatshedera
Fern
Gloxinia
Ivy
Peperomia
Philodendron
Rubber plant
Scindapsus (Pothos)
Serissa
Silk-oak
Tuftroot
Veitch screwpine
Wandering-Jew
Wax Plant

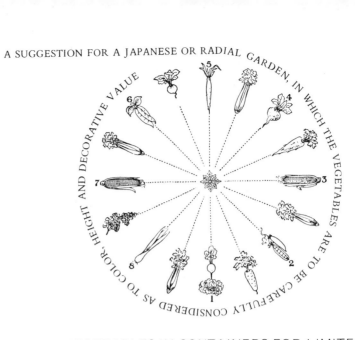

A SUGGESTION FOR A JAPANESE OR RADIAL GARDEN, IN WHICH THE VEGETABLES ARE TO BE CAREFULLY CONSIDERED AS TO COLOR, HEIGHT AND DECORATIVE VALUE

VEGETABLES IN CONTAINERS FOR LIMITED SPACE OR NO SPACE

Everyone wants to grow herbs or tomatoes and probably would like a hill of corn, but if you live in the city and have no space except a windowbox or front step, try to grow in containers with a synthetic soil. This is not a new idea; many commercial growers of large greenhouse crops now grow in synthetic mixes to prevent insects and plant diseases.

First you need some containers. In the section of the book on growing in containers you will find the various types and structures suitable for growing plants. As I said in that section I prefer wood outside but in the house plastic or clay pots will do fine. All you have to remember is a pot should be large enough to hold the mature plant. Most seeds packages will give you mature sizes and even basic directions on how to grow. In the Back of the Book section you will find cultural requirements for all common garden vegetables.

A synthetic soil is a mix of several kinds of inert material that is just needed to hold the root sections of the plants and support the top. There are several commercially available mixes now being sold in the marketplace and as far as I can determine they are much alike. The biggest advantage of a synthetic mix is the elimination of many soil-related diseases and insects. It is also very light and easy to move around in and out of the sunlight. Most top soil has weed seeds and organic organisms but synthetic mixes are free of them.

The disadvantage is that when using such a mix, you must use a fertilizer—usually of a chemical nature. The 5-10-5 formulation is probably the best but I prefer an organic cultivation method for food crops, and chemicals in the synthetic soil is not my cup of tea. There is of course fish emulsion and liquid manure that can be used. Depending on your situation and philosophy you must make the decision.

FERTILIZERS PESTICIDES AND HERBICIDES

Insecticides for Organic Gardeners

The following is a list of substances frequently used or recommended by organic gardeners, although purists do not rely on any pesticides. Instead they pay meticulous attention to horticultural and non-chemical control methods, taking pains not to disturb their crop's environment.

Users of pesticides should read the directions on the labels carefully. Pay particular attention to possible hazards, the concentration and amount of pesticides to use, the days to harvest and the possibility of pesticide injury to the plant (phytotoxicity).

NICOTINE

Nicotine is an alkaloid derived from plants in genus Nicotiana and is well known as a greenhouse insecticide. It is usually found as a 40 percent alkaloid formulation; used as a fumigant, dust or spray, and can be used on many crops and ornamentals.

Pests Controlled. Aphids, thrips and mealy bugs.

Environmental Impact. It is highly to moderately toxic to man, especially if inhaled; has a rapid breakdown (little residual effect), is not harmful to bees and most beneficial insects.

RYANIA

Ryania is a botanical derived from Ryania speciosa roots and stems, is a contact and stomach poison, and is not commonly found.

Pests Controlled. Cranberry fruit worms, European corn borers and caterpillars (codling moth) on apple.

Environmental Impact. Slightly toxic to mammals.

PYRETHRUM

Pyrethrum is a botanical derived from certain dried flower heads in the genus Chrysanthemum and comes in dust or liquid formulation. It is a contact insecticide with rapid knockdown that affects the nervous system of the insect. It can be used on most fruits and vegetables.

Pests Controlled. Ants, aphids, asparagus beetles, cabbage loopers, cheesemites, crickets, fleabeetles, flies, fruit flies, gnats, horseflies, leafhoppers, leafrollers, psyllids, roaches, spiders, sodwebworm, wasps and ticks.

Environmental Impact. It is slightly toxic to man, not hazardous to birds and other wildlife with extremely low toxicity to mammals. It is nontoxic when used on pets (dogs, cats, birds), and can be used in food areas. There is a broad spectrum of insecticidal activity, and lack of persistence and biomagnification in the food chain. Because it irritates insects, it acts as a flushing agent, making them leave their hiding places. There is rapid breakdown when exposed to sunlight and alkali.

MILKY SPORE DISEASE

Milky spore is a bacterial disease that takes about three years to become effective but once effective the bacteria resist heat, cold, dryness, and moisture. The disease remains in the soil for a long time and is spread to adjacent areas by birds and other predators of the grubs.

Pest Controlled. Specificially for Japanese beetle grubs.

Environmental Impact. Harmless to other organisms.

ROTENONE

Rotenone is a non-phytotoxic botanical derived from derris or cuberoots. It is primarily a contact insecticide but also acts as a stomach

poison and inactivates an enzyme system causing death from lack of oxygen. It is registered for most fruits and vegetables.

Pests Controlled. Aphids, cabbageworms, Colorado potato beetles, asparagus beetles, ants, bedbugs, cucumber beetles, cockroaches, European corn borers, bean beetles, fleas, flea beetles, Japanese beetles, lice, greenhouse white flies, houseflies, pepper maggots, rose chafers and squash bugs. It has some acaricidal (kills spiders and mites) action.

Environmental Impact. It is moderately toxic to man, extremely toxic to fish and other cold-blooded animals, and is reported highly toxic to swine. The hazard to birds and wildlife is low. It has a short residual life, usually less than one week; is not compatible with alkaline materials; and is broken down in the presence of light and alkali to less toxic insecticidal compounds. It has a low environmental pollution level.

OILS

Most frequently used oil is petroleum (60 to 70 second superior oil) but oils derived from plants and animals are also used. Toxicity may be due to suffocation of eggs and insects or to the toxic properties of oil.

Do not use when frost is anticipated, but for best results use immediately before bud break when weather is dry, mild and sunny. Do not use on Douglas fir, blue spruce, sugar maple, Japanese maple, beech, birch, hickory, walnut or butternut.

Pests Controlled. Some aphids, mealy bugs, pear psylla, some armored scales, soft scales, and white flies.

Environmental Impact. It is safe to man and animals and exempt from tolerances on food. It may be toxic to some plants.

SABADILLA

Sabadilla is derived from seeds of Schoenocaulon officinale, but is not readily available. Alkali and heat treatment enhance its insecticidal activity.

Pest Controlled. True bugs such as chinch, harlequin, squash, and stink bug, and also thrips when used in sugar bait.

Environmental Impact. There is slight toxicity to mammals but it can cause irritation to eyes and respiratory tract. It has rapid breakdown in the presence of light.

BACILLUS THURINGIENSIS

This is a bacterial disease that produces a poison in the gut of certain lepidoptera larvae.

Pests Controlled. Many lepidoptera (caterpillars); cabbage loopers, hornworms, cankerworms, gypsy moths, and tent caterpillars.

Environmental Impact. It is harmless to mammals and soil organisms, and is exempt from residue tolerances on food.

Primary Nutrients Contained in Organic Fertilizers
(Average Analysis of Fertilizers Without Losses from Leaching or Decomposition)

	Percent Nitrogen* N	Percent Phosphorus* P_2O_5	Percent Potassium* K_2O
Bulky Organic Materials			
Alfalfa hay	2.50	.50	2.10
Alfalfa straw	1.50	.30	1.50
Bean straw	1.20	.25	1.25
Cattle manure (fresh)	.55	.15	.45
Cotton bolls	1.00	.15	4.00
Grain straw	.60	.20	1.10
Hog manure (fresh)	.50	.35	.45
Horse manure (fresh)	.65	.25	.50
Olive pomaces	1.20	.80	.50
Peanut hulls	1.50	.12	.78
Peat and muck	2.30	.40	.75
Poultry manure (fresh)	1.00	.85	.45
Sawdust and wood shavings	.20	.10	.20
Seaweed (kelp)	.60	.09	1.30
Sheep manure (fresh)	1.05	.40	1.00
Timothy hay	1.02	.20	1.50
Winery pomaces	1.50	1.50	.80
Organic Concentrates			
Animal tankage	9.0	10.0	1.5
Bat guano	10.0	4.5	2.0
Bone charcoal and bone black**	1.5	32.0	.0
Bone meal	4.0	23.0	.0
Caster pomace	6.0	1.9	.5
Cocoa shell meal	2.5	1.5	2.5
Cotton seed meal	6.0	2.5	1.5
Dried blood	13.0	1.5	.8
Fish meal	10.0	6.0	.0
Fish scrap	5.0	3.0	.0
Garbage tankage	2.5	1.5	1.5
Hoof and horn meal	12.0	2.0	.0
Sewage sludge	3.0	2.5	0.4
Soybean meal	7.0	1.2	1.5
Steamed bone meal	.8	30.0	.0
Tobacco dust and stems	1.5	.5	5.0
Wood ashes**	.0	2.0	6.0
Wool wastes	7.5	.0	.0

* Based on dry weight except for the fresh manures which contain about 65 to 85% water.
** Burning eliminates organic matter and forms inorganic compounds.

Common Sources of Fertilizer Nitrogen for Gardens

Name	Grade	Nitrogen
		Percent
Chemical		
Ammonium nitrate...33–0–0		33.5
Ammonium sulfate...21–0–0		21
Sodium nitrate.......16–0–0		16
Urea 45–0–0		45
Urea formaldehyde...46–0–0		46
Organic		
Dried blood........11–0–0		13.3
Castor pomace......5–2–1		5.5
Cottonseed meal.....6–3–0		7.0
Dried manure.......varies		varies
Activated sewage sludge 6–3–0		varies

Common Sources of Potassium Fertilizers

Material	Grade	Potash
		Percent
Muriate of potash..0–0–60		60 – 63
Sulfate of potash...0–0–50		50 – 53
Sulfate of potash- magnesia 0–0–22		22 – 23
Nitrate of potash...13–0–44		44 – 46

Common Sources of Phosphate for Gardens

Material	Grade	Available phosphoric acid
		Percent
Rock phosphate	—	
Normal superphosphate .	0–20–0	20
Triple superphosphate .	0–45–0	45
Ammonium phosphate	variable [1]	14 – 53
Steamed bonemeal	2–27–0 [2]	18 – 34

[1] 11–48–0, 13–29–0, 16–20–0, 21–53–0 and 27–14–0.
[2] Averaged values from State fertilizer control officials.

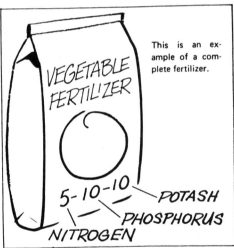

This is an example of a complete fertilizer.

VEGETABLE FERTILIZER

5-10-10 — POTASH
— PHOSPHORUS
NITROGEN

Primary Nutrients Contained in Inorganic Fertilizers

Fertilizer	Formula	Percent Nitrogen N	Available Percent Phosphorus P_2O_5	Percent Potassium K_2O
Ammonium nitrate	NH_4NO_3	33.5	0	0
Ammonium sulfate	$(NH_4)_2SO_4$	21	0	0
Calcium nitrate	$Ca(NO_3)_2$	16	0	0
Nitrogen solutions	(Varies)	20 50		0
Sodium nitrate	$NaNO_3$	16	0	0
Urea	$CO(NH_2)_2$	45	0	0
Ammonium phosphate	$NH_4H_2PO_4$ mostly	11	48	0
Diammonium phosphate	$(NH_4)_2HPO_4$	18	46	0
Basic slag	Ca, Mg, Al silicates high in phosphates	0	8	0
Rock phosphate	$3Ca_3(PO_4)_2 \cdot CaF_2$ mostly	0	5	0
20 percent superphosphate	$CaH_4(PO_4)_2$ and $Ca_2H_2(PO_4)_2$	0	20	0
Concentrated superphosphate	$CaH_4(PO_4)_2$	0	45	0
Superphosphoric acid, polyphosphate	H_3PO_4 and $H_4P_2O_7$	0	76	0
Green sand (Glauconite)	$KFeSi_2O_6 \cdot nH_2O$	0	1	6
Muriate of potash	KCL	0	0	60
Potassium sulfate	K_2SO_4	0	0	50
Potassium magnesium sulfate	$K_2SO_4 \cdot 2MgSO_4$	0	0	21
Potassium nitrate	KNO_3	13	0	44

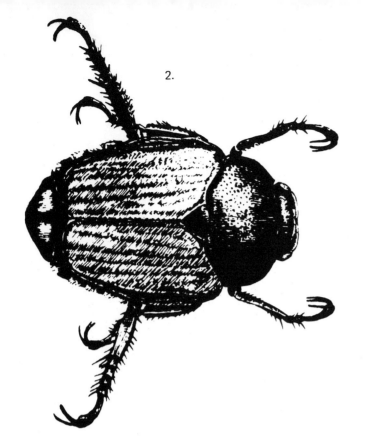

HERBICIDES

It is not a good practice to use herbicides in small ornamental and vegetable gardens containing several crop species because different flowers, vegetables, and weeds vary in their tolerance to herbicides. Some herbicides may remain in the soil longer than one growing season, and may kill or injure some species the following year (especially if excessive rates are used). Ideally, a specific herbicide should be used for each crop species, but most people have small areas of several species in their gardens, and it would often be impractical and expensive to buy the several herbicides that would be needed.

Application methods must be carefully controlled when a herbicide is used on small areas. The tendency is to apply additional amounts if the quantity measured out "looks" as if it is not enough. Check rates of material to use and application techniques on the container label very carefully. Applications must be accurate and uniform. Excessive amounts may cause injury to the present or subsequent crops.

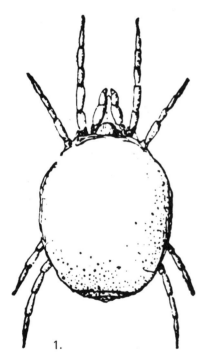

SOME GARDEN INSECT PESTS
1. Spider Mite, 2. Japanese Beetle,
3. Cabbage Looper, 4. Aphids on underside of leaf.

Lawn Weeds Controlled By — 2,4-D

Buckhorn plantain	*Plantago lanceolata*
Carpetweed	*Mollugo verticillata*
Cinquefoils	*Potentilla* species
Daisies	*Chrysanthemum* species
Dandelion	*Taraxacum officinale*
Dichondra	*Dichondra repens*
Docks	*Rumex* species
Hawkweed	*Hieracium* species
Healall	*Prunella vulgaris*
Lambsquarters	*Chenopodium album*
Mayweed	*Anthemis cotula*
Moneywort	*Lysimachia numularia*
Mustards	*Brassica* species
Pennycress	*Thlaspi arvense*
Pepperweed	*Lepidium* species
Plantains	*Plantago* species
Puncture vine	*Tribulus terrestris*
Shepherdspurse	*Capsella Bursa-pastoris*
Speedwell	*Veronica* species
Velvetleaf	*Abutilon theophrasti*
Vervains	*Verbena* species
Wild carrot	*Daucus carota*
Wild garlic	*Allium vineale*
Wild onion	*Allium canadense*
Yarrow	*Achillea millefolium*
Yellow rocket	*Barbarea vulgaris*

Silvex

Black medic (yellow trefoil)	*Medicago lupulina*
Buttercups	*Ranunculus* species
Catsear	*Hypochaeris radicata*
Chickweed (common)	*Stellaria media*
Chickweed (mouse-ear)	*Cerastium vulgatum*
Ground ivy	*Glechoma hederacea*
Knotweed	*Polygonum* species
Lespedeza	*Lespedeza* species
Pearlwort	*Sagina procumbens*
Pennywort	*Hydrocotyle sibthorpioides*
Purslane	*Portulaca oleracea*
Sorrels	*Rumex* species
Spurges	*Euphorbia* species
White clover	*Trifolium repens*

3.

4.

DISPOSAL OF PESTICIDE CONTAINERS AND SURPLUS PESTICIDES CONTROL

Use pesticides safely—read the label. If pesticides are handled or applied improperly, or if unused parts are disposed of improperly, they may be injurious to humans, domestic animals, desirable plants, pollinating insects, and fish or other wildlife, and they may contaminate water supplies. Use pesticides only when needed and handle them with care. Follow the directions and heed all precautions on the container labels.

Store all pesticides in a cool, dry, locked storage area so that they are not accessible to children, irresponsible persons, and animals. Do not dispose of pesticides through sewage systems. Haul them or have them hauled to a sanitary land-fill for burial.

Never place pressure cans on a stove or heater or near any source of heat that might exceed 120 degrees F. Store in a cool place—not in the hot sun. Have empty pressure cans hauled away and buried by experienced disposal crews. Do not incinerate.

Insect Control in the Home Vegetable Garden

SPRAY PREPARATION

To prepare a spray use the following amount of the insecticide selected to each gallon of water.

carbaryl (Sevin) 50%WP	2 tablespoons
diazinon (Spectracide) 50%WP	2 tablespoons
diazinon (Spectracide) 25% LC	2 teaspoons
endosulfan (Thiodan) 50%WP	2 tablespoons
malathion 25%WP	4 tablespoons
malathion 50-57%LC	2 teaspoons
methoxychlor (Marlate) 50%WP	2 tablespoons
rotenone 5%WP	4 tablespoons

WP — Wettable Powder
LC — Liquid Concentrate

The following insecticides are available in small packages as dusts. Apply a light coating of dust at the rate of 1 ounce per 50 feet of row:

carbaryl (Sevin) 4% dust
diazinon 2% dust
malathion 4% dust
rotenone 0.75% dust

The following insecticide is available as a granule for pre-plant and in-furrow application to garden soils at the rate of 11.5 lbs. of granules per 1,000 square feet of garden area:

diazinon (Spectracide) 2% granules

A combination spray of carbaryl (Sevin) plus diazinon (Spectracide) could be used to 14 days of harvest on all crops listed other than potatoes (35 days) or carbaryl (Sevin) plus malathion to 7 days prior to harvest on all crops listed as a general insect control combination applied at weekly intervals.

USE PESTICIDES SAFELY

1. Read the label instructions carefully and follow them exactly when preparing and applying insecticides.

2. Thoroughly wash out sprayer after each insecticide application.

3. Store insecticides in a locked cabinet out of the reach of children.

4. Wash your hands thoroughly before eating or smoking after using insecticides.

5. Insecticides that are relatively safe to use when properly handled will bear a <u>CAUTION</u> statement on the label, while moderately toxic materials bear a <u>WARNING</u> and highly toxic materials bear the word <u>DANGER</u> and the <u>SKULL AND CROSS-BONES</u> poison sign. Use relatively safe insecticides in the home garden.

Crop	Insect	Insecticide	Days-last application to harvest	Remarks
Asparagus	asparagus beetles	carbaryl (Sevin)	1	These beetles eat holes in the spears, lay eggs on them or defoliate later fern growth.
		malathion	1	
		rotenone	1	
		methoxychlor	3	
Green and wax Beans	leafhoppers and lygus bugs	carbaryl (Sevin)	no limitation	These insects feed on blossoms resulting in poor pod set.
	black bean aphid	malathion	1	Occasional pests.
		diazinon (Spectracide)	7	
		endosulfan (Thiodan)	3	
	seed corn maggot	Obtain insecticide treated seed		
Beets and Spinach	leaf miner	diazinon (Spectracide)	14 beets 10 spinach	Insect larvae work in leaves making trails. Treat when white elongate eggs are seen on the undersides of leaves.
	green peach aphid	malathion	7	Control aphids early, as large populations can build up rapidly.
		diazinon (Spectracide)	14 beets 10 spinach	

Crop	Insect	Insecticide	Days-last application to harvest	Remarks
Carrots, Celery, Head lettuce	leafhopper	carbaryl (Sevin) (double indicated rate) malathion (double indicated rate)	no limitation 7	Apply weekly from seedling stage until three weeks prior to harvest.
Corn	borer and earworm	carbaryl (Sevin) (double indicated rate)	no limitation	First generation borers show up in June-July while second generation borers appear in August.
	aphids	diazinon (Spectracide) malathion	7 5	Spray as populations appear.
Crucifers Broccoli Brussells sprouts Cabbage Cauliflower	maggot	diazinon (Spectracide)		Apply in transplant water at rate of 1 cupful of water per plant or as granules in the seed furrow at rate indicated.
	loopers, worms	B.T. Products (Dipel, Biotrol, Thuricide) endosulfan (Thiodan) (double indicated rate)	0 14	Apply at weekly intervals for looper and worm control.
	aphids	diazinon (Spectracide) malathion	7 7	

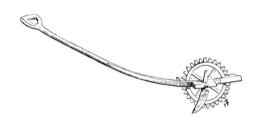

Cucurbits Cucumbers, Melons, Pumpkins, Squash	striped and spotted cucumber beetles	carbaryl (Sevin) endosulfan (Thiodan) methoxychlor	no limitation no limitation 1	Most severe injury to seedling plants.
	melon aphid	malathion diazinon (Spectracide) endosulfan (Thiodan)	3 7 no limitation	Apply as aphids appear.
	squash bug	carbaryl (Sevin) endosulfan (Thiodan)	no limitation no limitation	
	vine borer	carbaryl (Sevin) endosulfan (Thiodan) methoxychlor	no limitation no limitation 1	Make 4 applications at weekly intervals when plants start to vine out.
Onions	maggot	diazinon (Spectracide)		Apply granules in seed furrow, or use foliar spray for flies.
	thrips	diazinon (Spectracide) malathion	10 3	
Peas	aphids	diazinon (Spectracide) malathion	no limitation 3	Spray as populations appear.

Crop	Insect	Insecticide	Days-last application to harvest	Remarks
Peppers	corn borer	carbaryl (Sevin) (double indicated rate)	no limitation	Second generation corn borers can be a mid-to-late August problem on peppers.
	flea beetles	carbaryl (Sevin)	no limitation	Tiny black beetles that eat numerous small holes in leaves.
		diazinon (Spectracide)	5	
		endosulfan (Thiodan)	1	
		methoxychlor	1	
	aphids	diazinon (Spectracide)	5	Spray when these soft-bodied piercing and sucking insects appear.
		malathion	3	
		endosulfan (Thiodan)	1	
Potatoes	leafhoppers	carbaryl (Sevin)	no limitation	Piercing and sucking insects.
	flea beetles	carbaryl (Sevin)	no limitation	Tiny black beetles that eat numerous small holes in leaves.
		endosulfan (Thiodan)	no limitation	
		methoxychlor	no limitation	
	aphids	diazinon (Spectracide)	35	Soft-bodied sucking insects.
		malathion	no limitation	
		endosulfan (Thiodan)	no limitation	
Radishes, Rutabagas, and Turnips	maggots	diazinon (Spectracide)		Apply granules to seed furrow at planting or pre-plant broadcast application.
	flea beetles	carbaryl (Sevin)	3	
		methoxychlor	7	
Tomatoes	flea beetles	carbaryl (Sevin)	no limitation	Tiny black beetles that eat numerous small holes in leaves.
		endosulfan (Thiodan)	1	
		methoxychlor	1	
	aphids	diazinon (Spectracide)	1	Soft-bodied sucking insects.
		malathion	1	
		endosulfan (Thiodan)	1	
	fruitworm	carbaryl (Sevin) (double indicated rate)	no limitation	Larvae eat into fruits.
	hornworm	carbaryl (Sevin) (double indicated rate) or hand picking and destroying the hornworms.	no limitation	Large caterpillars that feed on foliage.

General Feeding Vegetable Insects

	garden slugs	metaldehyde baits		Apply as directed on label.
		beer bait		Place small cans in the ground with lip of can at soil surface at 3 foot intervals and fill 1/2 full of beer. Change twice each week.
	grasshoppers	carbaryl (Sevin)		Apply as needed.

Soil Insects

	white grubs, wireworms	chlordane diazinon (Spectracide) granules, spray, or dust		Apply as a broadcast treatment to the soil surface, just prior to planting. Thoroughly mix the chemical into the top 6 inches of soil.

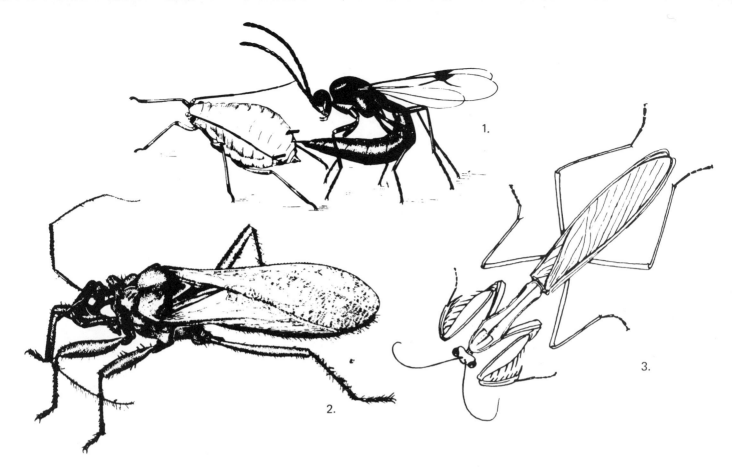

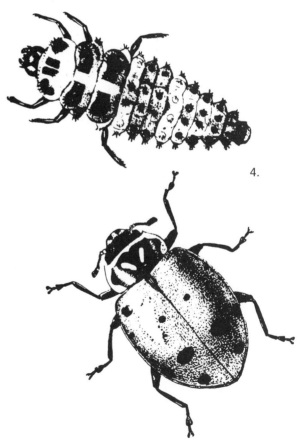

PRECAUTIONS

Pesticides used improperly can be injurious to man, animals, and plants. Follow the directions and heed all precautions on the labels.

Store pesticides in original containers—out of reach of children and pets—and away from food-stuff.

Apply pesticides selectively and carefully. Do not apply a pesticide when there is danger of drift to other areas. Avoid prolonged inhalation of a pesticide spray or dust. When applying a pesticide it is advisable that you be fully clothed.

After handling a pesticide, do not eat, drink, or smoke until you have washed. In case a pesticide is swallowed or gets in the eyes, follow the first aid treatment given on the label, and get prompt medical attention. If a pesticide is spilled on your skin or clothing, remove clothing immediately and wash skin thoroughly.

Dispose of empty pesticide containers by wrapping them in several layers of newspaper and placing them in your trash can.

It is difficult to remove all traces of a herbicide (weed killer) from equipment. Therefore, to prevent injury to desirable plants do not use the same equipment for insecticides and fungicides that you use for a herbicide.

Note: Some States have restrictions on the use of certain pesticides. Check your State and local regulations.

SOME BENEFICIAL GARDEN INSECTS
1. Tiny wasp depositing egg in aphid. 2. Assassin Bug.
3. Praying mantis. 4. Larva and adult of Lady beetle.

61

BOOK TWO...THE PLANTS

SEEDS, GERMINATION & TRANSPLANTING

Ornamental annual plants can be started readily from seed in the spring and will give bloom or satisfactory foliage effects the same season. Nearly all of these can be started in the open ground over at least a part of the United States, and will give the desired results before they are cut off by frost. In order to get a longer season of effect from the plants many of them are usually started under glass, or early plantings are started that way. In the more northern sections of the country some kinds must be started in this way in order to have a season long enough to mature; others so that they may become established before the coming of dry or hot weather, which would be injurious to the young plants but would not affect established ones.

Seed sowing and germination.—Most of the plants mentioned in this book can be propagated from seed. In some cases, however, the seeds require special care in order to insure a good stand of plants, and it is for that reason that the particular methods necessary for that purpose are described.

A few of these plants must be sown where they are to mature, as they will not stand being moved. Many may be sown where they are to grow, though most of them are helped by one or two transplantings. Because better plants are obtained by transplanting most annuals are sown in seed beds and moved to their permanent places. Such seed beds should be in well-prepared mellow soil, preferably somewhat protected from drying winds. If the soil is not mellow, the seedings, especially from the smaller seeds, will have trouble breaking through any crust that may form, especially if moisture conditions are not exactly right. Protection from winds also helps to maintain uniform moisture conditions. The timely use of a watering can is often a great help in promoting germination, but care should be taken not to use it too much. Seed beds require frequent light waterings rather than the infrequent drenchings best suited to more mature plants.

Seeds may be sown either broadcast or in rows. The inexperienced gardner should plant seeds in

rows, especially slow-germinating seeds, as quick-starting weeds may be more readily recognized and removed with less danger of disturbing the germinating seeds. Weeds starting near the seed row may be removed at once with great care or may be left until the seedlings are well sprouted. The dates of sowing the different kinds of seeds will be mentioned under the respective headings in connection with the discussion of other special cultural requirements.

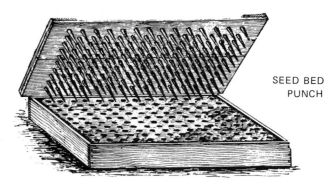

SEED BED PUNCH

The germination of seeds depends upon a proper degree of heat, moisture, and oxygen from the air. Some seeds germinate best under a high temperature (80 degrees to 90 degrees F.), while others do best at a lower temperature (40 degrees to 60 degrees F.). For most seeds, however, a soil temperature of 65 degrees to 70 degrees F. with an air temperature of 60 degrees F. will prove very satisfactory for germination. Strange as it may seem, nature maintains conditions during the early part of the growing season approximating those above specified. But naturally the high temperatures are much later in the season than the low ones. In order to obtain the higher temperatures early in the season a greenhouse, hotbed, coldframe, or a sunny kitchen window must be used.

Seeds in most cases grow best when the moisture in the soil is slight rather than excessive. A good test for moisture is to take a handful of soil and compact it gently in the palm of the hand by closing the fingers. If when released the soil remains solid and retains the impressions of the hand, it is too wet; but if when released it springs back and slowly crumbles or parts, it is in ideal condition for seed sowing. Such soil is well aerated, while the soil containing an excess of moisture has the air largely replaced by water.

The seed bed should be carefully guarded against extremes of moisture. It should not be allowed to get too wet and remain that condition for any length of time; neither should it be allowed to get too dry. In the open these conditions are not likely

to occur during a normal season. However, there are frequent exceptions. If the seed bed is too wet, little can be done to overcome the bad results, but if drought occurs irrigation will remedy the evil. Under artificial conditions, such as are obtained in a greenhouse, hotbed, or coldframe, the moisture content of the soil of the seed bed can be very carefully controlled. The continued atmosphere of such a structure prevents rapid or excessive evaporation, while any loss of moisture from the soil can be made good by watering. On a small scale the same results can be approached by placing a pane of glass over the receptacle in which the seeds are sown.

Slight variations in the temperature of the soil in which seeds are sown are usually a benefit rather than a hindrance to germination. With the grasses and covers and probably with practically all other plants, germination is more rapid and more complete in seeds subjected to alternations of temperature than in those kept under constant temperatures. Under normal conditions the warming of the soil during the day and the cooling at night furnish sufficiently wide variations. While these variations are less easily controlled than the variations in moisture, yet in structures such as hotbeds and coldframes the change from day to night temperatures will be perceptible.

Seeds in order to germinate promptly must be placed under conditions that will enable them to take up moisture readily, and at the same time they must have a temperature that will be congenial to the young plant when it appears. The soil is the medium by which heat and moisture, under normal conditions, are transferred to the seed. In order to insure a quick exchange of moisture from the soil to the seed, the soil should be carefully firmed or compacted about the seed. By compacting the soil about the seed the capillary power of the soil is increased and the soil moisture is more quickly brought to the seed. In outdoor operations large seeds may have the soil compacted about them by tramping the row with the feet, while fine seeds may be treated by resting a board over the row and walking upon it from end to end. In hotbeds, greenhouses, and coldframes the compacting of the soil is usually accomplished by the use of a float, which consists of a piece of board about 6 inches wide and 9 or 10 inches long, with a handle attached, as shown in the drawing. For all conditions save in the open, seeds may be sown in seed pans or in flats, as shown in the drawing. These boxes can be very conveniently and cheaply made from the pine boxes largely used for packing canned goods, soap, or other merchandise. usually 9 or 10 inches deep, which is sufficient to permit cutting them with a ripsaw into three sections, each about 3 inches high. The top and bottom of the box will each make a complete flat, while the middle section will be a frame which can be provided with a bottom by the destruction of a box for three

sections; i.e., four boxes will furnish nine complete flats or by using other lumber for the bottom of the middle section each box will make three flats. Seeds may also be planted directly in the soil of the hotbed, coldframe, or in that upon the greenhouse bench as well as in the garden. Here, too, they may be sown broadcast, but it is preferable to sow in rows.

In covering seeds the rule under artificial conditions is to bury the seed to the depth of its greatest diameter, while outdoors they are usually covered about three to five times their diameter. With seeds the size of a grain of wheat it is safe generally to plant them one inch deep, and for those the size of beans, 2 inches deep. Small seeds, the size of those of petunia or tobacco, should be scattered over the surface and the soil compacted with a float.

Transplanting.—The young seedling plants should be transplanted as soon as the first true leaves are formed, so that they will stand at some distance from one another. Preliminary to transplanting, the seed bed should be wetted thoroughly an hour or so before digging the plants, so that they can be removed from the soil without breaking the roots. The beds, flats, or pots into which the transplanting is to be done are previously prepared with soil that is moist but not wet; that is, it must spring apart again promptly if squeezed in the hand. Holes for the plants are satisfactorily made with a short stick three-eighths or a half inch in diameter and sharpened at one end. A flat stick sharpened at one end, as for example, a 6-inch pot label, makes an excellent implement for digging the seedlings. The seedlings should be carefully loosened in the

soil so that they may be lifted out with any soil that may possibly adhere to the roots, then be placed in the prepared holes at about the depth they were before, and then the earth should be pressed about the roots firmly but gently.

A frequent practice is to dig the plant with the right hand, lift with the left one, and press the soil about the roots with the right one. Sometimes the pot label is used to open the holes as the planting is being done, one motion of the label opening the hole and another motion pressing the soil about the roots after the plant is placed in position.

The plants should be thoroughly but carefully watered at once and then should be kept somewhat shaded until root contact has become reestablished. Longer shading is required in hot, dry weather than in cool, partially cloudy weather. In dark, cloudly weather shading may often be omitted. Watering must receive especial attention until growth starts.

For small, rather slow growing plants, such as pansies, 1 inch apart each way will afford ample room; with most plants 2 inches each way will be best; but with robust growing plants, like the castorbean, 4 inches will not be too much. With such vigorous growing plants, however, it is best to place the seeds directly in pots or cans in order to prevent disturbing the roots of the young seedlings as well as to afford them ample space. If ordinary pots are not available, paper pots may be obtained cheaply, or old strawberry boxes may be used. Transplanting has a tendency to make the plants stocky and provides opportunity for the development of an extensive root system.

CULTIVATION OF ANNUALS, PERENNIALS & BULBS

Annuals

Annuals are flowering plants that complete their growing and flowering and then completely kill back after the first heavy frost. Annuals are the main color source for the summer garden. Petunias, marigolds, zinnias, asters, sunflowers are examples of annuals and as you can see they come in all sizes, all colors, all shapes. They will probably fill all your locations and color requirements for the summer months. The seasoned gardener uses annuals and will fill all the spots in the garden with a little color. Perennials usually bloom in the early summer months and then return to just foliage but annuals are propagated and grown just for the flowers and a wide variety of color. If used properly the annual will give the foundation, the borders, the backyards, windowboxes, rooftops and on and on. (The photo on the front of the book is of annuals that prefer shade.) Nothing looks as nice as white petunias or yellow marigolds with an evergreen back drop.

Most annuals like a well-drained soil in the full sun. There are some that like the semi-shade, like begonias, but usually sunlight, and lots of it, will produce the best results for this type of plant. Be sure to read the seed package, or if you buy seedlings ask about the mature height and when you can expect full color. This will make a difference in the location and you want to improve the landscape not crowd it or put particular plants in a bad location.

General culture for annuals is a well drained, rich soil that has been prepared in advance of the actual planting time. If the area has not been used to grow annuals before I suggest you work in peat-moss, compost and fertilizer in the fall. If this is the usual bed used to grow your annuals, do the preparation in the spring.

Most garden centers and nurseries have a full selection of seeds or you can buy from one of the well-established mail-order seed companies in the fall. Start the seeds indoors in the early spring and transplant in the garden after the last signs of color weather. Make sure the soil is warm enough. I have listed most of the commonly culti-vated flowers and cultural directions for each. In the Back of the Book you will find easy to read charts and planting insutructions.

Perennials

Perennials are flowering or foliage plants that do not need to be taken from the garden in the cold months. As the tops of the plants die back, the roots live from year to year. Most garden centers usually have a large selection of perennials as they need very little maintenance except for the general cultivation of most flowering plants. They are permanent in the garden and are being used more and more as rock gardens and small-plot gardens with very little sunlight (city back yards) are being planted. Perennials will not develop flowers until they reach a certain height and are exposed to low temperatures for a certain length of time depending on the species. The sunlight that the plant is exposed to also is of importance if you are to have mature plants. The combination of temperature and day-light length are the essential elements for full blooming plants. We all know the popular perennials like delphiniums, candytuft and primroses but there is a long list of sizes, colors, growing habits and perfumes that you should utilize.

Aconite, Winter. Plant the bulbs about two inches deep in any garden soil in mid-autumn and do not disturb unless they are desired in new quarters. Then, after the foliage has turned yellow, dig, dry in the shade, clean, and store in a dry, airy room until planting time.

Ageratyn. Sow seeds indoors or hotbed in spring and transplant when two inches high to any garden soil. For later bloom sow in garden when soil becomes warm. For winter bloom, sow in August. Will grow in any good garden soil.

Ajuga. See Bugleweed.

Alyssum, Sweet. Sow seeds indoors or hotbed in spring and transplant when two inches high to any garden soil. For later bloom sow in garden when soil becomes warm. For winter, sow in August. Also readily propagated by cuttings of young shoots placed in sandy shaded soil. Divisions and layers also may be made.

Amaranth. Cultivate like Prince's Feather, which see.

Anemone. Plant tuberous species in the hardy border in mid-autumn and the other species in rockeries, etc., choosing a well-drained, fairly rich sandy loam if possible. The plants may be divided in autumn or spring when the clumps have become weedy or too large for their quarters. For indoor blooming in winter the tubers may be potted from September to October and managed like hyacinths or tulips. By judicious management a succession of blooms may be obtained from January until the outdoor clumps commence to blossom in the spring.

Apios. See Ground-nut.

Aquilegia. See Columbine

Arabis. See Cress, Rock.

Asparagus (A. Sprengeri). Plant seeds in ordinary potting soil at any time during the winter. Transplant the seedlings when large enough to small pots, and keep them growing vigorously in frequently changed larger pots, or while small place in hanging baskets, along the edges of benches, etc. May be propagated by division. Does best in a moderately cool room. Very easily managed. The red berries are beautiful, but they sap the strength of a plant. If the green plant is preferred, pick off the young berries.

Aster China. For earliest bloom sow the seed in a coldframe in autumn, and protect the plants until the ground can be worked in the spring, when they may be transplanted about a foot apart. These should blossom in late spring or early summer. A successional sowing may be made under glass in the winter, and the plant sets in the garden when danger of frost has passed. Usually, however, the seed is sown in a coldframe in early spring and the plants, when about three or four inches tall, transferred to the garden in late spring. These will blossom in late summer. Asters thrive best in rich soil.

Asters, Native. Sow the seeds in a coldframe in early spring, and when the plants are about three inches tall transplant about eighteen inches apart in clumps. Established clumps may be divided in autumn and the pieces reset. Greenwood cuttings root readily.

Aubrietia. Sow seeds where the plants are to remain and thin to about six inches. When once established, further propagation may be made by means of cuttings or layers.

DANEBROG POPPY.

Baby's Breath (Gypsophila). Sow seeds in early spring in a mild hotbed or indoors. Transplant the seedlings when about two inches tall to small pots, and again to any garden soil when the weather becomes settled. For winter bloom, seeds may be sown in late summer, when cuttings or layers of the perennial species may also be made.

Bachelor's Buttons. Sow seeds in mild hotbed in early spring. Transplant the seedlings to small pots when about two inches tall, and when the weather becomes settled transplant to good soil in the garden. After once becoming established, the clumps may be divided in spring. See also Globeflower, Cornflower.

Balloon-Vine. After danger of frost has passed, sow in ordinary garden soil and provide a trellis or wooden fence from seven to ten feet.

Balm, Fragrant. Sow seeds in spring and transplant to permanent bed when the plants become large enough. A moist rich soil is exactly what this plant needs. Plant in masses for better show for singly these flowers lack ornamentation. Divide the plants frequently because the nature of the underground root system spreads the plant rapidly.

Balsam, Impatiens. Sow seed in mild hotbed or window sill in early spring. Transplant the seedlings when about two inches high, the early ones to small pots, the later ones directly into the garden, in good soil in a sunny spot. For winter, cuttings may be made in late summer or early fall and the plants kept in a warm place.

Bean, Hyacinth. Sow like morning glory, but provide a taller and stronger trellis, since the twining vines often grow more than 15 feet.

Beard-tongue. Sow seeds in a mild hotbed or windowbox in early spring then transplant to flats or small pots and when the weather becomes warm enough, plant in the garden. Some species do best in partial shade, but by and large most can stand the sun. Read the seed package for the shady spot variety. All need moist soil and will do well in most garden loams. Many are grown as annuals, but the perennial kinds may be propagated by division.

Bee balm. See Balm, Fragrant.

Begonia (Fibrous rooted). Easily grown from cuttings of firm green stems, which, when rooted, may be planted in ordinary potting soil. Frequent changes of pots and additional fresh soil will help the cultivation. Medium light and good air circulation will also help the growth. Cuttings taken in February and kept growing should become fine plants by the following winter, during the latter part of which they should bloom freely.

Blazing Star. Plant seeds in ordinary soil in the fall of the year. Thin them in the spring or transplant to allow at least 14 inches apart. Where other garden flowers will not grow these hardy plants will thrive in very poor soil.

Bleeding Heart. Plant the roots when the soil can be worked in the spring. The soil should be of a good garden loam, with organic mix. Once established, bleeding heart will do well for years if kept fertilized and the beds weed free.

Bluebells. Sow the seed as soon as ripe. The perfect place is out of the wind but where there is ample sunlight. The foliage will die soon after the flowers drop and they should not be disturbed. Plants do not propagate well by division.

Bugbane. Easily grown and the seeds should be sown in fall or spring where the plants are to remain. I would choose a place well away from the house along a border because of the smell of this rather nice looking foliage plant. Thin the plants so in-

dividual plants are about 15 inches apart. Divide the plants in the fall or spring.

Bugleweed (Ajuga). Used as a ground cover and will tolerate shady places. It is easily propagated by division. Roots easily and fall or spring are the best times to make division. The common ajuga has a purple-green foliage and small redish spike flowers. It spreads very fast so beware.

Bulbocodium. Plant the bulbs in early fall, choosing a light rich soil, planting the bulbs about two inches deep. Allow the foliage to naturally die, do not cut off. It usually blooms a few days or sometimes weeks before the crocuses.

Burning Bush. See Gas-Plant

Butterfly flower. Sow seeds in mild hotbed or windowbox in early spring. The plants can be thinned and transplanted when about two inches high and the weather is completely free of frost. You can wait and sow directly in the beds when the mild end of spring has arrived. The soil can be ordinary garden soil, nothing special. For winter blooms, sow seed in mid-summer and transplant into pots. They should bloom from mid-winter to spring. Keep in well ventilated, open sunlight on the windows or in greenhouses and well watered.

Butterfly-Pea. See Centrosema.

Caladium. See Elephant's Ear.

Calceolaria. The hybrid kind may be grown from seed indoors in the late winter, transferring the seedlings to pots as soon as they are large enough to handle. Place the transplanted seedling in a humid, shady place until the weather becomes somewhat mild. Change the pots as the plant becomes larger if you want specimen plants. Allow the mature plant to become pot bound.

Calliopsis. A popular name for Coreopsis.

Callirhoe. See Poppy-Mallow.

Campion. See Lychnis

Candytuff, Annual (Alyssum). Sow seeds indoors or hotbed and transplant in the garden when the plants are about two inches high or when the season becomes mild. Plant about ten inches apart in good garden soil. The biennial and perennial types are propagated exactly as the annual type. Usually the perennial types are reproduced by stem cuttings in the greenhouse or indoors.

Canna. File holes or punch holes in the seeds and soak in a mild warm water for about 24 hours before sowing in single pots under glass or in a warm spot in late winter. When the plants are about seven inches high transplant in a rich soil anywhere from three to six feet apart. The soil should be light as possible for good drainage is important. In the fall dig up the clumps and dry them out for a few days in a dry open spot. Store in a warm airy cellar. During the winter months divide the clumps allowing at least one eye to each group. Be sure to mark the variety and color for spring planting. Transplant in the garden in the late spring. If you want early flowers transplant in pots indoors then transplant in the garden. This is true of many bulbs and flowers if you have the space and the time.

Cardinal Flower (Lobelia). Sow seeds indoors in late winter then transplant outdoors in the spring in a moist, damp spot. When established they will come year after year. Strong plants may be divided and good green wood may be used for cuttings. When used in borders or as bed plants the plants will reach a height of over eighteen inches.

Cardiospermun. See Balloon-Vine.

Amaryllis

Castor-Oil Bean. Start seed in a mild place indoors or hotbed in early spring and transplant to the garden spacing them about ten inches apart. The soil should be dry, rich and deep.

Catananche. Sow seeds in a mild hotbed or indoors in early spring then transplant when the seedlings are about two inches tall. Plant in the garden after the last frost and when it becomes rather mild. You can sow directly into the beds after the weather has settled. The soil should be light and well drained.

Celosia. See Cockscomb.

Centrosema. Sow seed in early spring using a sandy soil. Provide a trellis or structure for the vine to twine on. It may grow to six feet.

Chamomile. See Marguerite, Golden.

Chionodox. See Glory of the Snow.

Chrysanthemum (C. Coronarium). Sow seeds indoors or in a hotbed in early spring then transplant outdoors about 12 inches apart in ordinary soil. Pinching back mums makes a heavier foliage plant and produces more flowers.

Cimicifuga. See Bugbane.

Clarksia. For early blooms where winters are mild sow seeds in the early fall. In a temperate climate sow in the late spring indoors or in a hotbed and transplant in the garden when the seedlings are about three inches tall. Ordinary garden soil will do.

Clematis. Set the plants (usually nursery grown or mail order in small containers) in a rich light loam. A trellis or construction for the vines should be provided. Clematis grow to huge plants. I have seen them (a single plant) cover the entire front of a New York brownstone. They are rapid growing and can be purchased in a variety of colors.

Canterbury Bells. Sow seed indoors or hotbeds in early spring. Transplant the seedlings about two inches apart in a well drained garden loam. The first year you may be a little disappointed in the blooming ability but after well rooted and established they will bloom profusely in the coming seasons.

Coboea Scandens. Sow the seed in late winter and water sparingly until germination is complete. Transplant the seedlings in the garden and provide a large trellis or wooden structure.

Cockscomb. Sow seed in late spring indoors or in hotbed and when the plants are about two inches tall transplant into pots or flats. When all danger of frost has disappeared, transplant in the garden from 10 to 18 inches according to variety. If the plants drop their leaves during the season, it is for lack of water. Plant in a light, moist rich soil. For winter blooms sow in the late summer.

Coleus. Take cuttings from the garden before the late frost of the season. After a small root system appears on the cutting transplant in two inch pots. They do the best in warm, humid, well lighted rooms. For outdoor use the cuttings are rooted in midwinter and the plants established in pots over two inches. They do well in a rich sandy loam in a semi-bright area. If you want the brilliant colors of some of the new hybrids give the plants as much sun as possible.

Colchicum. Plant bulbs three inches deep in late summer or early fall in light deep sandy loam. Cover the newly planted bulbs with a leaf mulch which should be raked clean in the spring. The fall species

makes the foliage in the spring and blooms without leaves in August and September. They should be left alone until the foliage and the flowers show signs of failing. You can then dig and divide and replant in the ground at the proper time. The spring blooming kinds can be planted like snowdrops in the lawn. Both the spring and fall blooming varieties do well in rock gardens.

Columbine (Aquilegia). The seeds should be sown in the mid-winter and transplanted after the last threat of cold weather. Plant in any good garden soil in the full sunlight. This is a good rock garden plant and likes to grow among rocks out of the wind. You can further propagate by division if you want identical plants to match the existing flowers.

Cone-flower. See Rudbeckia.

Coral Bells. Sow seeds in early spring and transplant to a hotbed or warm window until seedlings reach two inches. Place in garden about two feet apart when the weather becomes warm. If grown as a perennial you can divide the clumps in the spring. Take cuttings for winter use in late summer and for summer use in late winter.

Coreopsis. Sow seeds in late spring or in the garden when the weather has become settled. Your only advantage to growing indoors or in a hotbed or greenhouse is early blooms and sometimes healthier plants. Plant about two feet apart in any good garden loam but make sure you have good drainage. The perennial varieties may be propagated by cuttings in the summer or by division in the spring.

Corn-flower. These flowers are sown in the location they are to grow and thinned to about 15 inches. Any well drained garden soil will do. Many times corn-flower will self sow and surprise you in the spring.

Cosmos. Sow seed in the early spring indoors and transplant in the garden when the soil is warm. Keep out of the wind and plant in a poor soil. Cosmos like the full sun but if planted in a rich humus soil they will grow too fast and produce spindly stems and poor flowers. Many gardeners pinch back the first terminal shoots to produce a fuller plant.

Cotton (Gossypium). Sow seeds in a mild indoor location or greenhouse and transplant in an open location usually as a back drop for smaller plants. Plant about two feet apart.

Cowslip, American. See Shooting Star.

Cowslip, Virginia. See Bluebells.

Crambe. Plant in garden location after weather is warm and thin three or more feet. Flowers do not appear usually until the third year so plant for succession. The foliage is ornamental enough to make a nice border cover.

Cress, Rock (Abrabis). Sow the seeds in the permanent bed in the spring after the last threat of frost. After the seedlings reach about five inches, thin them. Rock cress do well in any poor well-drained soil, but they like lots of sunlight. You can root cress very easily.

Crocus. The common and first bulb of spring is planted in the fall of the year about three to four inches in a sunny place. (See bulb chart in Back of the Book.) After a few years in the ground crocus should be separated and cleaned after the foliage has turned a yellowish color in the late spring. Replant in the fall after storing them in

a cool place for the hot summer months. Many of the bulb catalogues have colors and varieties to suit almost any combination. You can force crocus for winter blooming as well as other types of spring flowering bulbs.

Crown Imperial (See Fritillaria).

Cyclamen. This is a special plant for those that have time and the place to propagate and take care of. The seeds should be sown in the late winter in the house or greenhouse and transplanted from the flats to small pots as soon as the plants are large enough to handle. The soil should be light but rich. After the weather is above 50 degrees place the single potted plants in a shaded area in the garden. By the end of summer the plants should be in a five-inch pot and should bloom about 15 months after the seed has been sown.

Cypress Vine. The seeds should be sown in the early spring in the beds they are to remain in. The soil should be rich and the location sunny. A trellis or wire should be placed above the plants for they twine upwards and reach a height of 12 feet.

Daffodil. These varied spring blooming bulbs should be planted in the fall of the year. Bulbs should be planted eight inches apart in about six inches of light soil and five inches in a heavy soil. See bulb chart in the Back of the

Book for directions for all spring blooming bulbs. Each bulb should produce a clump of bulbs in about three or four years. At this time the clump should be dug and separated, and replanted. If you follow this simple practice you will get large flowers year after year. Daffodils like a partly shaded area.

Dahlia. You can plant the tubers of the dahlia in the early spring in a rich soil but you can get faster flowers if you start in a cold frame or hot bed. In the fall after the tops have been killed back, the tubers should be dug, cleaned and stored in a dry place. The storage room should be dark with good ventilation.

Daisy, English (Bellis). Sow the seeds in the spring and when the seedlings are about three inches, thin and plant about eight inches apart. The soil should be rich and moist, and the location a shaded one. The usual method of propagation is division.

Daisy, Swan river. Sow seeds in a rich good soil in the early spring. The condition during this period should be warm with all possibility of cold over. Transplant about seven inches apart when the plants are several inches tall.

Day lily. See Funkia.

Delphinium. See Larkspur.

Dianthus. Sow seeds in the spring under glass in the

frame or indoors and transplant to the garden when the plants can be handled. They should be planted about a foot apart or more depending on the variety. The perennial variety can be propagated by division in the spring. Dianthus will do well in most garden soils.

Dicentra.. See Bleeding Heart.

Dictamnus. See Gas-Plant.

Dodecatheon. See Shooting-Star.

Doronicum. See Leopard's Bane.

Elecampane. The seeds should be sown in the spring in most garden soils and the location should be bright sunlight. You can divide the clumps in the spring.

Elephant's Ear (Colocasia). Plant the tubers in a frame or hotbed in the early spring or late winter and transplant into the garden keeping the plants at least three feet apart. The location should be very moist and the soil rich in humus. In the fall before the first heavy frost dig up tubers and store in a well ventilated, dry, above-freezing room until the next year.

Flameflower. Plant the roots in a well-drained soil, out of the wind, after the last sign of cold weather in the late spring. Allow at least two-and-a-half feet between plants. Dig the roots in the fall and store in a dry airy room. The plants are left outside in the southern states if they are covered by a mulch for the winter months.

Flax, flowering. Sow the seeds in the late spring in any garden soil. The plants should be thinned to about six inches apart.

Flowering Maple. The common method of propagating maple is cuttings. They can be grown from seed but this is not necessary for the cuttings reproduce in the best manner. These plants are the same in character as geraniums and can be treated in the same way.

Forget-me-not (Myosotis). Plant in the spring in a shady spot in the garden where the location is somewhat moist. The plants should be thinned to about four inches and if the plants get too large during the early summer thin out a little more. Forget-me-not will reseed easily.

Foxglove. The cultivation of foxglove is almost identical as Canterbury bell. The soil should be light and somewhat rich, and will do fine in the shade or sun.

Fritillaria. In the fall plant the bulbs about four inches in a rich, moist, well-drained sandy soil about a foot apart. The location should be out of the direct sunlight. A shaded area under large shrubs or trees is perfect, or a direct northern exposure. Dig the bulbs every two or three years and separate.

Fuchsia. You can grow fuchsia from seed and expect flowers in about a year. I suggest you get some cuttings and propagate this way. It is so much easier and cuts down the time before you see color. The hanging baskets you buy from your local nursery do have a tendency to suffer from white fly infections so be careful. If you bring the plants inside for the winter keep humid and in indirect sunlight. Today there are many new varieties of fuchsia and each one is more remarkable than the next. This is a showpiece and the flowers are very beautiful. I always have been a sucker for the plant, white fly and all. A well drained soil with a little peatmoss is perfect.

Funkia. The root should be planted in the late spring, in a rich, deep moist soil. The ones with the larger leaves need a shady spot and lots of moisture. This is a very hardy perennial and can be left in beds until you really are tired of them. Some varieties produce a lot of seed and they should be sown as soon as ripe in the fall.

Gaillardia. Sow the seeds indoors or under glass in the middle winter months, and transplant in the garden in the late spring. The plants should be planted about a foot apart in a well-drained rich soil. If you have ever germinated these seeds you have found them longer than most but the results are well worth the effort.

Gas-Plant (Dictamnus). Sow the seeds in the fall or as soon as ripe from the mother plant in a deep rich soil. These plants do not transplant well so put them in a place where you will not disturb them for a long time.

Geranium. The mainstay of the window box and the front porch boxes and planters. I guess everyone has grown geraniums or seen them grown but if you haven't, these plants are usually propagated by cuttings and will root very easily. The cuttings should be grown in a loose mix of sand and peat or vermiculite or perilite. After danger of frost in the spring is past you can transplant to a sunny place in the garden and pitch back the first few nodes for a full plant. If you want a full blooming geranium and are window gardening or have them in pots, if a geranium is pot bound, that is if the pot is too small for the size of the plant, the plant will produce more flowers. I tend to tightly plant in boxes for I am interested in the flowers not the foliage. Take off the dead under-leaves and keep clean during the growing season. Do not water the foliage in the hot sun.

Gilia. This is another plant that does not transplant well, so sow the seeds in the fall in the beds they are going to remain in. Cover the new beds with a mulch-like salt hay or leaves and uncover in the spring. A light soil is fine and the plant should be thinned five to eight inches.

Gladiolus. This of course is the mainstay of the commercial flower or cut-flower industry and a great deal of information is available for the hundreds of varieties that are available. The Gladiolus Society will also provide information on new varieties but for the gardener that wants to pick up a couple of corms and grow some glads here are the simple cultural instructions. Plant the corms about two inches deep in a heavy soil and about four inches in a lighter soil. Plant about ten to twelve inches apart, starting with the smaller corms put in the ground as soon as the soil can be worked, and ending up with the larger corms in the early summer. This will give you blooms all summer until frost. In the late fall dig and store the corms until spring. The storage rooms should be cool, dark and well ventilated. There are books devoted to this very popular flower and I suggest if you really want to get into growing glads you pick up a book recommended by the Glad Society.

Globeflower (Trollius). Sow indoors in the early spring and transplant to a permanent place in the garden after the weather is warm. Any good garden soil will do but sunlight most of the day is essential. Plants should have at least ten inches between for proper growth.

Glory of the Snow (Chionodoxa). Bulbs should be planted in about three inches of moist, light soil. Good sunlight is very important for full flowering. Divide the plants every two or three years.

Gloxinia. Propagation of gloxinias is usually accomplished by stem or leaf cuttings. Sow the seed in mid-winter in a warm window or hotbed in a soil that is rich in humus but light in texture. The blooming period is early fall and when the foliage begins to drop it is an indication of the resting period. Do not water during this period and the temperature of the room should be around 50 degrees F. You can place gloxinias outdoors during the summer months and return them to a nice warm window well before any sign of cold weather. At this time the plants should be ready to bloom for the fall months and the blooming period lasts about three weeks.

Godetia. Sow indoors in the early spring in a warm window or hotbed and transplant to the garden when the seedlings are about five inches. They should be spaced every 12 inches in the garden in a poor well-drained soil. These plants do not like a humus base soil but sunlight is important.

Groundnut, Hog. Tubers should be planted about three inches deep in a light soil in the bright sunlight. Usually these flowers are planted in clumps of four or five. A trellis or something for the vines to climb on should be provided.

Gyposphila. See Baby's Breath.

Helichrysum. Sow the seeds in the garden in the early spring when the soil becomes slightly warm. Plants should be about 15 inches apart.

Heliotrope. Propagation of heliotrope is usually done by cuttings of the terminal shoots in sand or other propagation material. The propagation bed should be kept moist. The rooted cuttings are then transplanted in a rich potting soil until planted in the garden. The soil should be well drained but water is important for full growth. Do not let the pot or the bed become dry. A sunny location is important. Plant about three feet apart.

Helipterum. Start indoors in early spring and transplant outdoors in good soil about a foot apart. If you plant directly in the garden the weather has to be completely frost free and the soil warm.

Hollyhock. Sow the seed in later winter indoors in a cool place and transplant to the garden when the seedlings are big enough to handle. The location should be sunny and the soil light and deep. Plant about three feet apart. If you give the plants a head start indoors you can expect flowers the first year, but if started directly in the garden you will have to wait until the second year for any color. Many times hollyhock do not produce well in the third year so every few years plant a different crop on the border or bed you want to show these very tall plants.

Hop (Humulus). Not common but still a good vine for ornamentation. Sow the seed in a warm deep rich soil. The vine does grow fast and reaches a height of over ten feet. Provide a trellis. The perennial hop may be divided in the spring.

Hyacinth. Plant the bulbs in the fall. (See bulb chart in the Back of the Book.) Plant in most soils but a well-drained area is best. Protect in the fall with a mulch. One important thing to remember for bulbs is that the texture of soil determines how deep you plant. Always plant deeper in light soil. When the foliage has turned yellow dig up the bulbs and store in a cool place until fall planting.

Hyacinth, Grape (Muscari). Plant bulbs in fall in a good humus soil. They should be planted about two inches in the ground. Always let the foliage turn brown and die naturally for this is essential for the next season's flowering. You can plant in the lawn like snowdrops.

Hyacinth, Summer. Plant in the spring in a rich deep soil. Most bulbs need a well-drained soil and this bulb is no exception. You can dig bulbs in the fall and store but mulching them does work. To be on the safe side in the colder parts of the country I would dig and store.

Ice-Plant (Mesembryanthemum). You can sow the seeds in a sunny place as soon as the soil becomes very warm. Thin plants to about five inches. Transplant indoors before any sign of frost. These plants withstand long periods without water. A good plant for terraces and hot rooftops.

Iris. Another favorite garden perennial with a huge following. The many varieties and colors make this a most welcome addition to any garden. There are many good books on the iris, and if you really want to grow prize-winning flowers join the Iris Society or look into your bookstore for a good volume. But if you want a few in your garden, plant the tubers or rootstocks in the spring or fall in a moist rich soil. Good cultivation helps develop a healthy clump of irises.

Jonquil. Cultivate and propagate like daffodils.

Kudzu Vine. Many stories about this vine that seems to be swinging around the south have been written in the past few years. A vine that grows fast and covers a lot of territory. Propagation seems to be little trouble. This vine needs a large trellis or porch to climb on. You can root the cuttings or separate the tuberous root sections. It usually kiils back in the northern states.

Larkspur. Start indoors and transplant gradually to larger pots until you can transplant to the garden in a well-drained, good soil in a sunny place. The annual and perennial flowers are propagated the same way except you can divide the perennial kinds in the spring. Many times you can cut the tops after the first flowering and get a second flowering in the late summer or early fall. Divide the clumps of the perennial kind every two to three years for best results.

Leopard's Bane (Doronicum). You can sow the seeds in the garden in a permanent bed in the spring and divide tubers as you need to expand the bed. A well-drained light soil is best.

Leucojum. See Snowflake

Liatris. See Blazing-Star.

Lightning, Scarlet. See Lychnis

Lily. Plant the bulbs in a well-drained deep soil about five inches deep. Different kinds of lilies need to be planted at different depths. When you buy the bulbs from a bulb grower or your local nursery inquire as to the proper planting procedure for each kind. Lilies do well in a shaded area except for L. Candidum. For over-wintering you should mulch the beds well with a straw or leaf mulch. To divide in the spring cut the plants just after new growth has started and transplant in a prepared bed. This should be done as soon as possible. Do not let the divided plants stand out of the soil.

Lily, Day. See Funkia.

Lily-of-the-Valley. The pips should be planted in the late fall in a shaded area in the garden. Give the plants plenty of room to spread in a light well-drained garden loam. You can divide in the spring or late fall.

Linum. See Flax, flowering.

Lobelia. Start the seeds indoors in a warm window and transplant to the garden when the weather is warm. Plant about five inches apart in a rich deep soil in the bright sunlight. You can fertilize heavily with a good organic manure.

Lychnis. Any garden soil will do but the plants must be planted about a foot apart for good flowering results. Divide the perennial species in the spring.

Marguerite, Golden, Chamomile. Plant in a sunny location about two feet apart in the spring after the frost is out of the soil. Most soils will do but a well-drained soil is the best.

Marigold. Plant in the garden in the spring. The taller varieties about eighteen inches apart, the French varieties about a foot and the dwarf varieties six inches.

Maurandia. A trellis should be provided that reaches at least ten feet. Plant in the garden in good soil after the frost is out of the ground. You can propagate by cuttings from the first-year wood.

Mignonette (Reseda). Any good well-drained garden soil is fine. Start seeds indoors and transplant to the garden after the threat of cold weather is past. For flowers in the winter indoors, start the seeds in the midsummer and take cuttings for potting inside.

Miscanthus. Plant five feet apart in a sunny location in any garden soil. You can get a jump on the season by starting the seeds indoors but they can be sown directly in the bed and thinned out. After the plants have been established you can divide the clumps as shown on page 186 in the Back of the Book.

Monarda, See Balm, Fragrant.

Monkey-Flower. Plant in a shady location in the garden as soon as the weather becomes mild. Propagate by cuttings or divide the clumps. The soil can be regular garden loam but must be in a shaded region.

Montbretia. Plant the corms in the spring in any garden soil about four or five inches deep. If you want bloom all summer, plant every ten days or so in different parts of the garden or the same bed. Dig and store in the fall. The old-fashioned way of storing montbretia is in moist but not wet soil. In the southern parts of the country you can mulch and leave in the ground.

Moonflower. The best way to germinate the moonflowers seed is to cut off the points or cut grooves in the seed to hasten the germination process. Sow indoors in late winter and when some foliage appears transplant to a trellis bed for this vine will reach over 20 feet in one season. A deep rich soil is best with lots of sunlight.

Morning Glory. Another full blooming vine for summer color that sort of grows by itself. This plant also needs a trellis string ladder and may reach ten feet. Many garden centers now sell the potted morning glory and the moonflower plants. They self-sow and will germinate in early spring in the beds.

Moss, Pink (Phlox subulata). A rock-garden, low-growing flower that needs little care. The soil can be thin as most alpine gardens tend to be. This plant will produce a mat-like color pattern and is very common in most established rock gardens and wall gardens.

Mourning-Bride (Scabiosa). Scabiosa will grow in most garden soils with little or no care. The smaller varieties should be planted about five inches apart while the larger kinds about 15 inches. The perennial kinds can be divided in the spring or fall. A well-drained soil will help, and plenty of sunlight.

Muscari. See Hyacinth, Grape.

Nasturtium (Tropaeolum). Try and sow the seeds in small pots indoors or in the hotbed in the early spring and transplant to the garden as soon as possible. Plant in a poor soil, the smaller varieties about ten inches apart and the larger kinds three feet. You can propagate by cuttings and over winter indoors.

Nemophila. Sow the seeds in a cold frame or cold part of the house and transplant outdoors in the very early spring. Plant about six inches apart in a well-drained soil of light texture.

Nicotiana. Transplant to the garden after the seedlings are about two inches tall. Plant about 15 inches apart in a good garden soil. In the southern parts of the country it usually over winters with very little trouble.

Pampas Grass. A very tender plant in the north and should be protected in the winter. Pampas grass needs a light, rich soil somewhat moist. Two years is given before they will flower, and propagation is usually division in the spring.

Pansy. Many gardeners sow the seed in the fall for early flowering pansies. The best method is to transplant the seedlings in the fall into a coldframe or cold window in the house in northern light or indirect sunlight. Seeds sown in the spring do not produce flowers the quality of fall planting.

Pea, sweet. For the best results sow the seeds in the fall in about five inches of deep rich loam and a very dry location. A trellis or string ladder is perfect for this is a vine-like plant and needs to climb to

produce the best results. If you want a long flowering period I would cut the flowers as soon as they mature and encourage new growth and flowers. The short varieties do not need trellises and can be planted ten inches apart.

Peony. This plant seems to last forever. I personally know of a clump of peonies that have been producing blooms year after year as long as I can remember and that is well over thirty years. Once established you can forget them except for good feeding but they do not need the best of soils. The perfect maintenance-free perennial.

Pentstemon. See Beard-Tongue.

Petunia. The perfect bedding plant and the biggest money makers for the grower in recent years. Every year there are new colors and new patterns. Petunias provide a splash of color for any border or bed. A bright spot is preferred with a well-drained soil. Pinch back the first couple of nodes in the late spring and you will have color all season. The seed is very small but you can get good results if you are careful. Buy the plants and save yourself some time.

Phlox, Annual. Start the seeds indoors and transplant in the garden when the seedlings are about three inches tall. The soil should be well drained with a little peatmoss. It is becoming more and more common to buy the flats of annuals at the garden centers and I suggest you buy this one.

Phlox, Perennial. Buy from a good perennial grower in your area. Plant in a moist, rich garden loam and divide every four or five years. This is a very common perennial and if you keep weeds and grasses out from around them you will have no trouble.

Poker-Plant. See Flame Flower.

Polyanthus. Plant in a semi-shaded area where the soil is rich and somewhat moist. If the situation gets warm and dry they will fail. You can propagate species you like by division and the divided roots can be kept in a cold frame over winter. After they have flowered you can move them to a shady place in the garden to make room for the all-summer flowering annuals.

Poppy (Papaver). Sow the seeds in the beds where they are going to remain for the poppy is difficult to transplant. This is another plant I suggest you try and buy from your nursery. The perennial varieties can be propagated by division or cuttings in the fall and grown indoors or under glass during the winter months. The perennial kinds of poppy require twice as much room as the annual.

Poppy, California (Eschscholzia). Plant the seeds in the fall in the beds where the plants are to remain. Protect them by mulching during the colder months and fully uncover in the spring. A good soil, rich and deep, is the best and a lot of sunlight.

Poppy, Mexican (Mentzilia). Sow seeds indoors in the early spring and transplant to the garden when about two inches tall. A moist, good soil is best. Allow about a square foot for each plant and they look the best planted in masses.

Poppy, Plume (Bocconia cordata). You can propagate from roots or sow indoors in spring and transplant to a well-drained soil of any kind when the seedlings are three inches tall.

Portulacca. A common annual sold in most garden centers, this is a colorful low-growing plant sometimes called moss-rose. They need a lot of sunlight in a well-drained rich soil. You can transplant when in full bloom.

Primrose. A very large family of hardy perennials that should be planted in every garden. Most varieties need to be shaded in the hot summer

months and grow well in a well-drained, rich soil, slightly moist. One could devote the entire book to this family of plants and some have, so if you want to really grow primroses, pick up a special book dealing with the cultivation of herbaceous perennials.

Rose, Christmas. Plant the root stocks in any light sandy soil but keep out of the sun and keep moist. This is a very hardy perennial and needs little care.

Rudbeckia. A hardy perennial that will grow in most quarters of the garden. Sow the seeds in the spring or fall and can be propagated by division in the spring.

Sacaline. Propagates itself by underground fiberous roots and may become a pest in the garden. Likes a moist rich, deep soil and should be planted where the plants will remain and where you want to fill space.

Salpiglossis. Sow seeds in early spring and transplant when the seedlings are about three inches tall. Plant in the garden in a deep, moist rich soil. Space about two feet apart for maximum growth. A beautiful herb used as a cut flower.

Sage, Scarlet (Salvia splendens). A common nursery annual that is bright red and blue and does well in shady backyards or in the sun. Sow seeds in late winter and transplant in the garden after the threat of frost or any cold weather has past. Any soil will do.

Scilla. Plant the bulbs in late fall in any good garden soil, either in the lawn or in flower beds. Remove the yellow foliage after flowering and leave in the ground. If you want to remove them, dig after the foliage has turned brown and store in a cool, dry place until fall.

Sedum. A large family of flowering rock garden or wall garden plants that need little care once established. Popagation is usually done by off-shoots or division. Sedum root like magic and I have never heard of anyone having trouble with this fast-growing, hard-to-get-rid-of plant. If you can not grow sedum you really have a purple thumb.

Shell-flower (Moluccella). Sow the seeds in the bed where the plants are to remain. The soil can be any good garden soil. Give plants plenty of room for they reseed and may take over a bed. Keep thinned out.

Shooting-Star (Dodecatheon). Propagate by division for germination is very slow. This plant likes the shade in a rich, well-drained soil. A good rock garden plant..

Silk oak (Grevillea robusta). This is basically an indoor plant but it can be grown outdoors in the deep south. It likes any good loam, but with a well-drained nature. Indoors, if you want winter flowers you must sow the seed about ten months before Christmas. Transplant into larger pots as the plant grows and by Christmas they should be in four or five inch pots. They can take a lot of abuse like geraniums.

Snapdragon. Sow indoors in early spring and transplant to cold frame or garden when the weather has become settled. If you plant in the garden the soil has to be warm and the plants have to be thinned about 15 inches. Snaps do well in any garden soil but do require a lot of sun. Plant out in the open like glads.

Snowdrop. Plant about three inches in the lawn or in any permanent bed. You do not have to touch the bulbs for years. When you do finally dig and separate, clean well and place in a cool place until planting time which is fall.

Snowflake. Plant bulbs in five or six inches of good garden loam well out in the sun. This should be done in the fall. Dig and divide every few years.

Squill, See Scilla.

Stock, Ten Weeks. Sow seeds indoors in early spring and transplant to the garden in ordinary soil when the seedlings are about three inches tall and when the weather is warm. Thin to 15 inches apart. Stock like the sun.

Sunflower. A light loam soil in the sun will suit all of the sunflower family. The plants should be spaced about five feet apart depending on variety. Once the plant gets top heavy with some of the new hybrids I suggest you stake next to a trellis or fence and tie them. This is a perfect plant for a summer screen and the birds like the seeds.

Sun-rose (Helianthemum). Sow seeds in place in a light sandy soil. Mulch in the winter in the northern parts of the country. A lot of sunlight in a well-drained soil.

Tigridia. Plant the corms in any well-drained garden soil. Plant about five to ten inches apart depending on your space and treat like glads in the fall. They have to be stored in a cool dry well-ventilated place.

Tuberose. Plant the bulbs in the spring about one inch deep in good garden soil. Space about six inches. Dig before frost in the fall and store in any root cellar. Any shoots should be cut off at the

new planting in the spring and planted separately but it usually takes a few years to flower. Trim off any old root at the time of planting.

Tulip. Here is another large group of flowering plants that has a great color and structure range. Most of the Dutch and American grown bulbs are of good quality. Plant in a sunny location in well-drained garden loam about six inches deep. (See bulb planting chart in Back of the Book.)

Verbena. Sow seed indoors in late winter or very early spring and transplant to garden when the weather is warm. The plants should be at least three inches before transplanting. Space about a foot apart in poor soil, a little further in a humus type soil. You can propagate by cutting for winter use, and soaking seeds in warm water will help germination.

Yucca. Propagate by cuttings of offsets, seed or stem. Propagation can also be accomplished by rhizome cuttings. Plant in a sandy loam about four feet apart. A rocky area in the sun is perfect or a backdrop edge in a rocky border. The spike flower of the yucca has to be surrounded by smaller plants before it has a perfect landscape quality.

Zinnia. Sow the seeds indoors in early spring or sow in place after the season becomes warm. The larger varieties need space to grow, usually about two feet, but the smaller types can be planted as close as four to six inches.

—JAPANESE ROSE (*Rosa rugosa*).

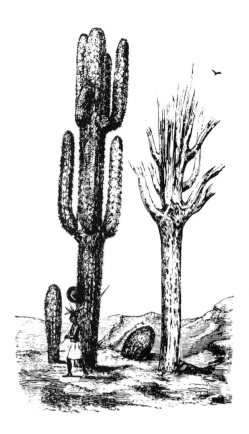

DESERT LANDSCAPE—CACTUS, AGAVE, YUCCA AND OCOTILLO

Native cactus should be used for the dry harsh desert climates of our southwest. It is only natural to use the plant material of this region for the landscape, but other types of trees and shrubs can be used as well.

CACTUS
Cactus is a perennial herb, with a thick waxy coat that makes for resistance to moisture evaporation and offers a plant with drought tolerance. Cacti are leafless and the shapes are too numerous to list. They have spines and when planting you must take into consideration the possibility of children playing nearby. The flowers of most cacti are spectacular in color and the color range goes from deep reds to bright yellows.

TRANSPLANTING CACTUS
Cactus can be planted year round in the lower elevations but the ideal time is between March and October. Warmer temperatures favor fast growth, and thus the plant will transplant easier.

The most important part of transplanting cactus is to plant the desired species in the original directional orientation. The south and southwest parts of these plants become tough and will resist sunburn. The tender parts if transplanted in the opposite direction will sunburn and rot. If you are digging cactus mark the side with white chalk or something that can be washed off to insure

proper direction. The way to remove cactus from the soil is as follows:

1. Cut around the base of the plant about a foot from the base. Lift the plant out of the ground by placing a shovel under the stem or base. Let any loose dirt fall from the root section.
2. Prune off any damaged roots.
3. Prune back the lateral root stubs to about eight inches.
4. Dust the pruned ends with sulfur to prevent infection and hasten callusing.
5. Place newly dug plants in a shaded area for about ten days to allow roots to heal.
6. Replant cactus in dry soil and do not water until new growth appears on the tips of the plant.
7. Larger saguaros should be planted a few inches deeper than the original location and even mounded up around the base of the plant to help support them.

SOIL FOR CACTUS
A sandy, gravel, well-drained soil is the best for cactus. Organic material can be used in moderation but is not necessary. The lighter the soil the better, but support is also important. An open location is the best place for new cacti plants, away from areas where water is likely to collect. Do not plant

against a west wall or a south wall. Reflected heat or sunlight may burn the plant. The soil should slope away from the plants so that water will not collect at the base. Do not plant cactus too closely; they need ventilation and good air circulation. If a smaller plant is found naturally in a shaded area, transplant according to what is natural.

CARE OF THE CACTUS

Cactus should not be cultivated for several feet around the plant. This would disturb the shallow lateral root systems. You can rake very lightly for ornamental reasons. A bed of crushed stone or granite for decoration is fine but do not use any material that will reflect the sun's bright rays.

Watering cactus is not necessary except for periods of long dry spells. If water is allowed to collect around the base of the plants rot will occur. Do not spray water on to cactus. What I am saying is that after the plant has been transplanted successfully, leave it alone.

Cactus usually do not need to be fertilized but a little fertilizer early in the growing season may help new growth. Do not fertilize or water in the fall for this makes the plants more susceptible to winter injury.

AGAVE, YUCCA, OCOTILLO

One of the best succulents families for the southwest landscape is the agave. This high-moisture plant comes in various sizes and shapes, one of the most common being the century plant. The colors that you can choose from vary enough to make this family of plants an important part of any desert landscape.

The yucca is a common desert plant that has a hanging effect and is taller than the agave family. Yucca grow at the very tips and flowers are spike-like and will add beauty to your design.

The last family of plants to consider is the ocotillo. This plant has another unique geometric that neither the cactus nor the agave has for it has low-branching, leafy, whip-like canes that produce bright red flowers. At the end of a high moisture period there are produced a large number of foliage canes. The odd shape and the bright flowers make it a must in any desert landscape.

The transplanting procedure is about the same as cactus but the best time to transplant is during the warmer seasons. One of the most difficult desert plants to transplant is the Joshua Tree. It is not recommended that you prune the tops of any agaves, yucca cacti, or ocotillo plants. You can use a rooting stimulating to help the recovery of the newly transplanted plant but sometimes it takes up to a year to recover their natural and perfectly healthy place in the landscape.

There are a few insects that harm native desert plants but by and large these plants are vigorous when treated with care. Spider mites on yuccas, mealy bugs on the stems and tender roots of some cacti, Cochineal scale on prickly pear cactus, and of course the mammals of the desert—all these do damage as they do in any locale around the country. I happen to love animals so I am probably too tolerant. For example the native woodpecker of the desert does a great deal of damage to the giant saguaro cactus. You will have to decide for yourself, but remember plants and animals do live and depend on each other for survival.

One final word on the removal and transplanting of cactus, agaves, yuccas and ocotillos. These plants are protected by state laws like many wild native orchids and ferns of the northeast. Buy from an established source and if you have any doubt of the origin of your plants contact the nearest Extension Service Agent.

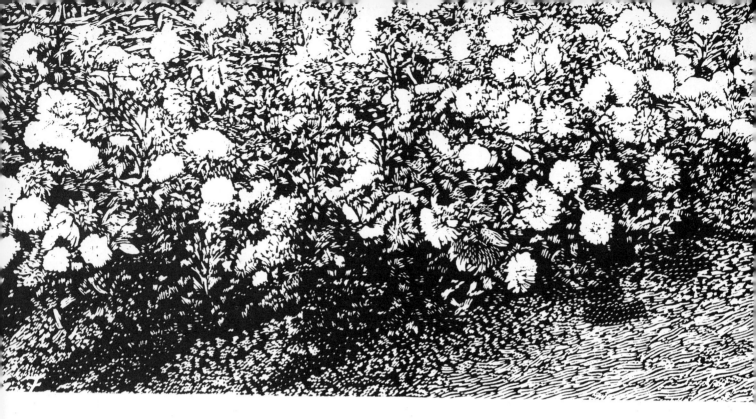

PLANTING LARGE CANNED SHRUBS IN THE GROUND

PLACE THE PLANT
IN THE PLANTING HOLE
AND PUT SOIL AROUND IT
AS DESCRIBED IN THE TEXT.

WATER AREA THOROUGHLY
AND THEN DO NOT DISTURB
PLANT OR SOIL.

MAKE A DEPRESSION
AROUND THE PLANT
TO HOLD WATER.
LEVEL SOIL AROUND
PLANT AFTER 6 TO
8 WEEKS.

FERTILIZER SHOULD
NOT BE MIXED INTO
THE PLANTING HOLE.
IT SHOULD BE MIXED
IN THE SOIL AROUND
THE HOLE TO AVOID
DAMAGE TO THE
PLANT.

PROVIDE A DRAINAGE
AREA OF GRAVEL OR
CINDERS IF SOIL TENDS
TO HOLD WATER.

84

PLANTING LARGE BALLED AND BURLAPPED TREES IN THE GROUND

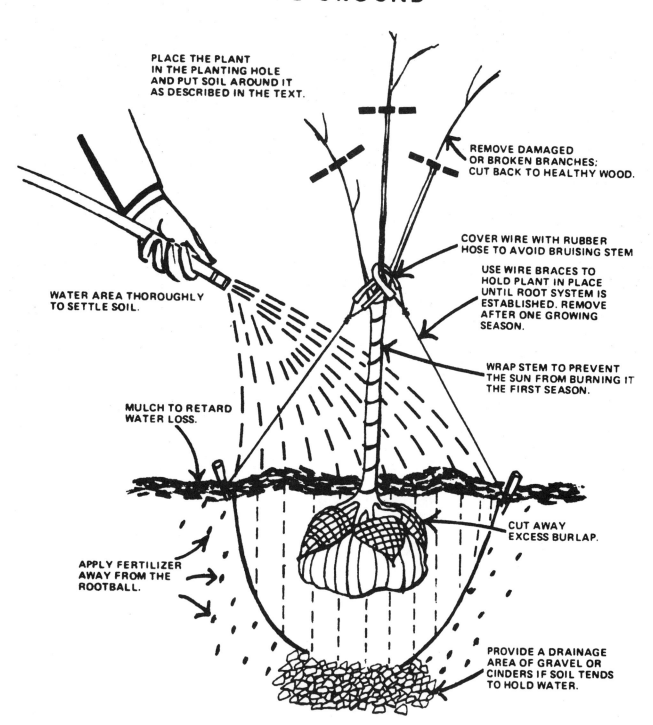

PLACE THE PLANT IN THE PLANTING HOLE AND PUT SOIL AROUND IT AS DESCRIBED IN THE TEXT.

REMOVE DAMAGED OR BROKEN BRANCHES; CUT BACK TO HEALTHY WOOD.

COVER WIRE WITH RUBBER HOSE TO AVOID BRUISING STEM

USE WIRE BRACES TO HOLD PLANT IN PLACE UNTIL ROOT SYSTEM IS ESTABLISHED. REMOVE AFTER ONE GROWING SEASON.

WATER AREA THOROUGHLY TO SETTLE SOIL.

WRAP STEM TO PREVENT THE SUN FROM BURNING IT THE FIRST SEASON.

MULCH TO RETARD WATER LOSS.

CUT AWAY EXCESS BURLAP.

APPLY FERTILIZER AWAY FROM THE ROOTBALL.

PROVIDE A DRAINAGE AREA OF GRAVEL OR CINDERS IF SOIL TENDS TO HOLD WATER.

Place the potted bulbs in a cool, bright room. Keep them at a temperature of 55 degrees F. until they bloom. Water the bulbs daily.

1.

2.

FORCING BULBS

3.

1. Clean the pot and cover the drainage hole with a clay plug.

2. Cover the bottom of the pot with a mixture of equal parts garden soil, sand, and sphagnum moss. Set the bulbs firmly in the soil mix with the flat side of each bulb facing toward the outside of the pot.

3. Cover the bulbs with the soil mix. Press it firmly around and over the bulbs.

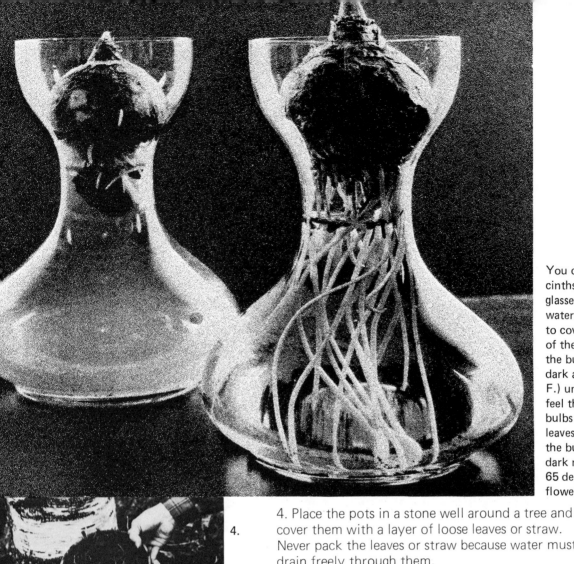

You can force hyacinths in hyacinth glasses. Put enough water in each glass to cover the bottom of the bulb. Keep the bulbs in a cool, dark area (40 degrees F.) until you can feel the flower bulbs beneath the leaves. Then move the bulbs to a cool, dark room (55 to 65 degrees F.) for flowering.

4.

4. Place the pots in a stone well around a tree and cover them with a layer of loose leaves or straw. Never pack the leaves or straw because water must drain freely through them.

5. If you do not have a stone tree-well, you can bury the potted bulbs in a pit. Set the pots close together and cover them completely with soil. Put a wire screen over the pots to protect the bulbs from rodents, moles, and other animals.

6. You also can force bulbs in vermiculite. Follow the same steps that you would if you were using a soil mix.

7. Inspect your bulbs occasionally. When the shoots are well out of the soil, bring the bulbs into a cool room for flowering. The shoots will be pale green to almost colorless.

5,6,7.

TREES AND SHRUBS FOR SUMMER COLOR

The greatest amount of color in the summer garden is usually found in the borders and flower beds. Annuals and some perennials provide the bulk of the color in most summer gardens. If you do not plant these flowers you have a few shades of green only, an all-green garden. There is a group of small flowering trees and shrubs and a few vines that will break up the monotonous patches of green texture and offer some color. If you choose the correct plants for the right place, the amount of maintenance for the vast amount of color is well worth the effort. I have tried to provide a cross section of the country with a variety of plants that grow in certain regions. Refer to the zone map with the zone numbers in the back of the book and match the number after each shrub with the numbers that correspond with your locale. After you determine the geographic suitability, next consider the design potential and the other requirements that the plant may have—soil preference, shade, protection from the wind and pollution. If you meet all of these requirements, seriously consider the plant, for it will provide color year after year. I will list the most common of these useful plants in alphabetical order by using their common names. Many of the mail-order nurseries and many of the retail garden centers only have the plants tagged with their botanical names. I have included a list of both at the end of this section.

FLOWERING SHRUBS

Beautyberry Zones 5-9

This is a medium sized shrub that grows about six feet tall. It is not hardy for colder climates and will die back in the winter, but will produce new shoots each spring. The shrub blooms in the late summer sometime between July twentieth and August fifteenth, and produces small clusters of pink flowers. Purple or white berries follow the flowers and last into the fall. This shrub likes to be planted in a sheltered place out of the wind and likes the sun. It will grow in some shade. This is a perfect shrub for city gardens that have enough sunlight, for most backyards in the city are sheltered enough for protection.

Bluebeard Zones 5-10

This is a small growing plant perfect for borders or back-drops in the perennial garden. It grows about four feet and has a very delicate violet blue to light blue (sometimes white) lasting until frost. Place Bluebeard in the sun in a well-drained sandy loam. Protect in the winter and prune back to the ground in the spring. Nothing is quite as beautiful as a back-drop of Bluebeard with a bed of white petunias mixed with some pink petunias.

Bottlebush Buckeye Zones 5-10

This shrub is sometimes used as a deciduous hedge or screen. It grows well over 15 feet and sometimes under the right conditions will spread 25 feet wide. It propagates itself by suckers. The flowers are spikes of white that appear on the very ends of the branches. These usually appear in the months of July and August. All flowering shrubs need some sunlight and this is no exception.

Butterflybush Zones 5-9

This is a most hardy plant and produces large flowers of various colors from July until frost. It grows about eight feet tall and the flowers sometimes stand well over ten inches and are very fragrant.

As the name implies, it really does attract butterflies and bees. It is a perfect plant to place near a vegetable patch, for the bees and butterflies will help pollinate the tomatoes and eggplant. Butterflybush likes the sun and will grow in most garden soils. I had one in a backyard in New York City that did beautifully year after year. If it does happen to "kill back" during a rather harsh winter, do not fear. It will grow back. Keep it clean of dead wood.

Buttonbush Zones 4-10

This is a tough native plant that grows upwards of ten feet. It has white flowers that begin in the middle of summer and continue until frost in some places. This plant is perfect for the wet spot on your property or backyard. It prefers some shade and a lot of humidity. A perfect backyard city plant.

Carolina-Allspice Zones 5-10

Sweetshrub, as it is called in some parts of the country, grows about five feet and it blooms from May until mid-July. The flowers are an earthy red and the scent is spicy. I have seen flowers over two-and-a-half feet wide. The soil should be well drained but type of soil is not that important. It is maintenance-free after it has become established. A perfect hedge back-drop or screen.

Chaste-tree Zones 5-9

In the southern parts of the country it is a large shrub sometimes reaching a height of over 30 feet. The flowers are varied and are borne in terminal clusters over six inches long. The foliage of the plant is silver-gray and has a pleasant smell. The colors of the flowers are white, purple and light violet.

In the northern regions this is a smaller plant and usually dies back to the ground in the winter. This plant prefers a light sandy soil and plenty of sunlight. In the north, prune it back in the spring for a better growth pattern. Protect it from harsh winters by mulching it with leaves or straw.

Cornish Heath Zones 6-10

This is not a native flowering shrub but has adapted well to this country. It is a native of southern Europe. It is a very small shrub and perfect for the rock garden or border planting. It very seldom grows higher than 15 inches but makes up for height in beautiful, bright pink-violet flowers that bloom all summer. The heath should be placed in a poor soil but in the sunlight. Do not fertilize but keep wet in the hot months until the plant is well established. Many gardeners cut the plant back to the ground just after the flowering period. This seems to stimulate the growing habits of the plant.

Crapemyrtle Zones 7-10

This is another combination tree-shrub, depending on the region grown. It sometimes reaches a height of 20 feet in the deep south. It starts to bloom in July and sometimes continues until late September. The flowers are long and come in various colors. Usually the crapemyrtle bloom in a rush of color then have periods of sporadic blooming during the rest of the season. A well-drained soil and full sun are best for this plant.

Devil's Walkingstick Zones 7-9

Another common name for this large shrub is hercules-club. I would suggest a spot in the open for this large plant that sometimes will reach over 20 feet. The flowers are white and appear in late summer. The blossoms are small but are clustered. This plant grows best in a moist rich soil in full sunlight.

Flowering Raspberry Zones 3-4

This fragrant purple flowered shrub grows about five feet and blooms from June until September. A semi-shady location is the best and a moist condition will benefit the growth.

Germander Zones 6-10

Use this small plant for a hedge or border. It grows about 12 inches high and has red-purple flowers that begin in July. This flowering shrub has been used as a formal bedding plant for years and the flowers are often used as cut flowers. A well drained soil and a sunny location are perfect.

Glory Bower Zones 6-9

This is a very tall-growing shrub. I have seen it upwards of twenty feet. The flowers are white and appear at the ends of the branches towards the end of July and last for about three weeks in August. Berries follow the blooms and are reddish to blue. Glory bower does best out of the sun but can stand indirect sunlight. The soil requirements are just a common garden loam.

Glossy Abelia Zones 5-10

Grow this semi-evergreen in a well-drained soil, preferably in a sunny location. The branching habit of the abelia is dense and spreading and bears clusters of pink flowers in July and August. The fall color is particularly beautiful, being a bright bronze color.

Heather Zones 6-10

This small rock-garden plant comes in various colors and prefers a poor soil. It grows about a foot tall and bears flowers in the summer months. The flowers are upright spikes of various colors. Full sunlight is perfect and in the colder parts of the country I would protect the plant in the winter with a straw or evergreen branch mulch. Cut back in the spring for a full summer plant.

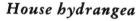

House hydrangea

Hydrangea

There are four members of the hydrangea family that are readily available in nurseries that do well in most areas of the country. They are hydrangea peegee, snowhill or hills of snow, house hydrangea, and oakleaf hydrangea. All have large colorful flowers and once established are easy to care for and maintain.

Hydrangea Peegee Zones 4-10

This hydrangea is probably the most common and the most colorful of the hydrangea group. It flowers from middle August and lasts until heavy frost. The blooms are white and it can be trimmed and pruned to tree shape. Plant in the spring in a well-drained soil and in the sun if possible. It will tolerate some shade but prefers the sun.

Hills of Snow Zones 4-10

This is much smaller than the peegee, growing only about four feet. The flowers are round with a white globe-like structure. The blooms begin in July and usually last until the first frost. A well-drained soil out of the wind is best.

House hydrangea

The great ornamental value of the house hydrangea is your ability to change the color of the flower by changing the Ph of the soil. If you add lime the flowers will become pink. You can make the flowers a light blue by adding iron. Most of the chemicals used to change colors are found in garden centers and are not harmful to the soil. House hydrangea usually grow about eight feet in the middle and deep southern states but will freeze back to about three feet in the far northern states. Soil conditions are important and house hydrangea needs a moist, well-drained soil in the sun.

Oakleaf hydrangea Zones 5-10

This is not as common as the other three forms of hydrangeas but is hardy and rather beautiful. In comparison it is rather slow growing and has flowers from pink to a purple appearing in June. This type of hydrangea needs a rich humus soil and prefers the shade.

Kashmir-False Spirea Zones 6-10

This is a big shrub usually growing eight to ten feet tall and flowers in July and August. The blossoms are white and clustered about ten inches long. I would leave a lot of room for this plant for it spreads and is used for back-drops and corner plantings. Any well-drained soil will do and full sun is preferred.

Leatherwood Zones 5-10

This is a very large shrub sometimes growing well over 20 feet. It is used as a screen or back-drop. The flowers are white and look like lily of the valley. It flowers in July and August, needs a sandy soil and will tolerate some shade but prefers the sun.

Nandina Zones 7-10

This is commonly called Chinese bamboo. It reaches a height of about ten feet and bears large white flowers in clusters. Either sun or shade in the south, but full sun in the northern regions.

New Jersey-Tea Zones 4-10

A small shrub with fragrant white flowers. It will grow in any soil and will do well in most kinds of indirect or direct sunlight. This is a hard plant to transplant and must be set out in the spring. An interesting historical note on this plant is that it was used as a tea substitute during the American Revolution.

Ocean-Spray Zones 4-10

This is a rather large shrub that produces clusters of drooping white flowers in July and August. It is used as a back-drop in a perennial bed or bulb border. The soil conditions are general and it does well in either full sun or partial shade.

Potentilla Zones 1-10

This is a small shrub usually growing only a few feet tall. The flowers are yellow and white and look like tiny roses. This shrub flowers all summer until frost. A lime soil is preferred, and place in the sun.

SWEET-SCENTED SHRUB.
(CALYCANTHUS FLORIDUS.)

Rose of Sharon Zones 5-10

An old fashioned backyard shrub that grows fast and is tolerant of most conditions. It reaches a height of ten feet and has flowers of various colors. You can prune this shrub to a tree shape or let the bottom branches grow out to form a large shrub.

Shrubby Bushclover Zones 4-10

This is a tall shrub reaching a height of eight to ten feet. It has small flowers of red-purple. It likes a well-drained sandy soil in a sunny place. You can prune heavily in the fall without hurting the possibility of next season's flowering periods.

Spirea Zones 4-10
Japanese White Spirea

A small shrub growing about three feet tall and generally used as a mix plant in general landscape work. The flowers appear in July and August and require very little care. Plant in the full sun for best color results.

Froebel Spirea

Same culture as the Japanese white but has red flowers and will bloom throughout the summer if you prune the first show of flowers in the early summer.

Stewartia Zones 5-10

There are four common varieties of Stewartia that are sold throughout the country. All the varieties need a rich soil, slightly moist and a little acid. All of the varieties need a shaded area and indirect sunlight. Cold winds in the winter months do some damage to all of the varieties so plant accordingly.

Japanese Stewartia

Blooms in July and the flowers and white and cup shaped. Grows about 30 feet.

Mountain Camellia

A rather large shrub usually reaching a height of ten to 15 feet. Flowers in late June and July and the blooms are white with a touch of orange.

Showy Stewartia

A large shrub about 15 feet with white flowers appearing in June and July.

Silky Camellia

About 12 feet is the maximum growth on this June flowering shrub. The flowers are white with traces of red and purple at the bottom of the petals.

St. John's-wort

All of the commercially available varieties are listed below and all bear yellow flowers. They flower most of the summer months and are used as foundation or border plants.

Aaron's Bear Zones 6-10

Sometimes used as a ground cover for it only grows a little over a foot. It likes indirect sunlight and produces a bright yellow flower in late July and early August. Grow in a sandy well-drained soil.

Golden St. John's-wort Zones 6-8

A landscaper's delight for it grows in the shade and reaches only three feet tall. It blooms from late June until frost. A perfect filler plant for color in the backyard where other plants will not produce color. The size of the flower is almost two inches across and is a show all summer.

Goldflower St. John's-wort Zones 7-10

A combination of a waxy fragrant leaf and yellow flower make this a most attractive plant for small-plot gardening. It does well in the shade thus making it a perfect plant for shady city gardens. If the winter is very cold it may die back but will grow back in the spring and produce full effect. Only transplant in the spring.

Kalm St. John's-wort Zones 5-8

A small shrub used for rock gardens and small planting. It grows only two feet tall and flowers in late July and August.

Shrubby St. John's-wort Zones 4-8

A taller variety than other members of the family usually reaching a height of five to six feet. It flowers from late summer until frost.

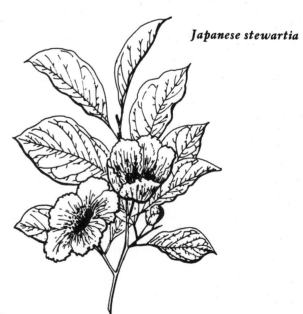

Japanese stewartia

Summersweet Zones 3-9

A plant found in many seaside plantings for it is resistant to salt spray. It is called a peppertree in parts of the country. It reaches a height of five to six feet and the flowers are white and sweet. The flowering period is from mid-summer until late September. This is another plant for moist, shady backyards in the city. Sometimes it is hard to transplant, depending on the local conditions, for it needs a moist acid soil. If your local conditions do not meet these requirements I would mix leafmold or peatmoss with your soil and firmly pack the base of the plant.

Swamp Azalea Zones 4-8

This plant sometimes called swamp honeysuckle does well in a moist acid soil and produces light purple and white flowers that are sticky in the mid-summer months. It usually reaches a height of six feet and should be transplanted in the spring in the north and in the south transplant in the winter months.

Tamarix Zones 2-9

A tall-growing shrub that will reach a height of 15 feet and has a light texture. It flowers in July and the blooms are pink. The soil conditions are lime and dry and full sun. A good shrub for an informal garden or mixed screen. This is a fast grower so keep pruned.

VINES

Bittersweet Zones 4-10

Bittersweet, both American and Oriental, reach heights of well over 30 feet and climb on walls and wooden structures. The plants bear yellow flowers in the summer months and berries in the fall of an orange color. This plant has a male and female plant and you must have both to bear fruit. The male pollinates and the female bears the fruit. Any good garden soil will do for cultivation. Plant in the spring with peatmoss.

Clematis

This is a large family of plants and the commercially available are discussed here. Clematis has to grow in a limestone type soil and some may find it rather hard to cultivate. Ask the advice of the local grower or landscape gardeners for more specific cultural instructions for your area. This family produces a wide range of colors and shapes so you can choose a color and shape to suit your fancy. The flowers range from one inch to ten inches. The growing habits of the plants vary from ten feet to 50 feet. Be sure you put the right plant in the right place. Some of the clematis vines flower on last year's wood and

some bloom on this year's wood. Before you prune ask your nurseryman the proper procedure for each type of clematis.

Sweet Autumn Zones 5-10

The most common is this clematis that bears white flowers in late summer. The flowers appear on this year's wood and the foliage is dark green. The average growing height is about 30 feet.

Anemone Flowered Clematis Zones 6-10

A hybrid with pink, red and white flowers that bloom in mid-summer. It bears flowers on last year's wood.

Scarlet Clematis Zones 4-9

This clematis grows well in the southwest but does fairly well in some northern regions. It is smaller than the other members of the family, growing only about six to eight feet. The flowering period runs from mid-summer until frost. Because of its tender nature it sometimes kills back to the ground in the cold but will develop fully the next year. It bears on this year's wood.

Jackman Clematis Zones 6-10

Another very common clematis is the Jackman. This plant blooms on this year's wood and it can be pruned in the spring to the size you desire. The color of the flower is a soft purple about six inches across. The growing habits are achieved by twisting about wires or poles. It grows fast and should be in sun for the full effect of color.

CLEMATIS JACKMANII, HENRYII, AND PANICULATA.

The general culture of clematis is the same for all of the family. The soil should be alkaline and well drained. Place the plants close to the support structure and keep in mind that the base of the plant should be cool and shaded. Try and separate the new vines in the early stages of growth in different directions for I have seen a tangle of vines that only bass fishermen see on the hottest day of the year.

Honeysuckle Zones 5-9

Of the many varieties of honeysuckle only two have a quality worthy of summer color. Both these plants will grow well over ten feet and like the bright sun. Plant about three feet apart for a screen on a wooden structure. A common well-drained garden loam is suitable.

Halls Honeysuckle

This plant sometimes reaches a height of over 20 feet and is very hardy. The flowers are yellow and white and bloom from mid-summer until a heavy frost.

Sweet Honeysuckle

This honeysuckle has a very fragrant odor and blooms in June. The colors are white to a light yellow. The flowers are shaped like a trumpet and are about two inches long.

Silver Fleece Vine Zones 5-10

I have heard this plant called the silverlace and sometimes it is packaged as silverlace. It blooms in August and the flowers are pink, white and a light green. This vine grows, depending on the conditions, from ten to 30 feet.

Trumpet Vine Zones 4-10

This vine will cling to walls by root endings. It flowers in mid-summer and the blooms are red to orange. This plant needs a lot of room and may reach well over 30 feet in a nice warm place.

TREES

Most of the trees, large and small, that are sold in the commercial market place for color are the spring flowering varieties like the crabs. If you shop around and have space let me suggest some summer flowering plants with a different texture and different color. Because of the limited number of trees that do flower in the summer months try and fit at least one of those mentioned below into the landscape and place it in a vista-like place for show.

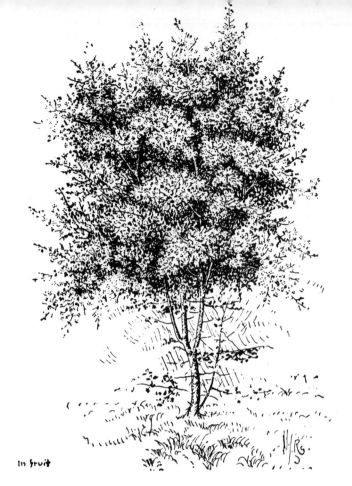

In fruit

Franklin Tree Zones 6-9

This is a small flowering tree that seldom reaches over twenty feet. It prefers a shady location thus making it a good plant for a shady backyard or under a grouping of larger shade trees in a suburban setting. The white flowers appear in mid-summer and have a blooming period of about three weeks. Franklin tree prefers an acid soil in a moist location.

Goldenraintree Zones 6-9

This is a small umbrella-type tree that bears yellow flowers in July. The maximum growth is around 18 feet. After the flowers fall a fruit of yellow-green takes over and stays around for about four weeks. The plant does well in most soils but likes the sun.

Japanese Pagodatree Zones 4-10

Many people know this as the Chinese scholar tree and it is a large tree reaching over 50 feet. The flowers appear in August and are pale yellow followed by a light green pod that sometimes stays with the plant all winter. Plant in a well-drained ordinary soil in the sun.

Maackia Zones 5-10

Maackia amurensis grows about 40 feet while the M. chinensis has been known to reach over 60 feet. Both plants bloom in mid-summer and bear white flowers about five inches long. Any soil will do but a sunny location is best.

The bridal wreath, most beautiful of all spiraeas (S. Van Houttei). Don't let anyone cut off all these beautiful, long, arching sprays. Don't prune any shrub before flowering, or you will sacrifice flower buds.

MOCK-ORANGE, LARGE-FLOWERED (*Philadelphus grandiflorus*).

SWEET-SCENTED CLEMATIS.
(CLEMATIS FLAMMULA.)

GORDON'S MOCK ORANGE.
(PHILADELPHUS GORDONIANUS.)

Mimosa Zines 7-10

Mimosa, also known as silk tree bears clusters of pink flowers in mid-summer and the flowers are born on this year's wood. You can prune heavy in the spring or dormant season. In the cooler regions of the country protect the plant until it has a chance to establish. Any garden soil will do for cultivation. The foliage is also very attractive. The long compound fine-textured foliage is equally as attractive as the flowers and has ornamental value as a different landscape plant.

Sorreltree Zones 5-8

Called sourwood in parts of the country this plant bears white flowers in July in the form of drooping clusters. The fall foliage is an added attraction, turning a bright red. The seed clusters remain on the tree well after the leaves have dropped and make an attractive winter geometric. A moist acid soil is best, out in the sun if possible.

Sorreltree

Mimosa

COMMON AND BOTANICAL NAMES OF SHRUBS FOR SUMMER COLOR

Azalea, Swamp—Rhododendron viscosum (L)
    Torrey
Beautyberry-Purple—Callicarpa japonica Thunb.
Beautyberry-White—Callicarpa japonica
    leucocarpa Sieb.
Bluebeard—Caryopteris incana (Houtt.) Miq.
Buckeye, Bottlebrush—Aesculus parviflora Walter
Bushclover, Shrubby—Lespedeza bicolor Turez.
Butterflybush—Buddleia davidii Franch.
Buttonbush—Cephalanthus occidentalis L.
Carolina-Allspice—Calycanthus floridus L.
Chaste-tree—Vitex agnus-castur f. latifolia
    (Mill.) Rehd.
Cinquefoil, Bush—Potentilla fruticosa L.
Crapemyrtle—Lagerstroemia indica L.
Devils-Walkingstick—Aralia spinosa L.
Germander—Teucrium chamaedrys L.
Glory Bower—Abelia grandiflora Rehd.
Glossy Abelia—Clerodendrum tichotomum Thunb.
Golddrop—Potentilla fruticosa var. farreri Besant
Heath, Cornish—Erica vagans L.
Heather—Calluna vulgaris (L.) Salisb.
Hydrangea:
House—Hydrangea macrophylla (Thunb.) Seringe
Peegee—Hydrangea paniculata f. grandiflora
    (Sieb.) Schelle
Snowhill—Hydrangea arborescens f. grandiflora
    Rehd.

Oakleaf—Hydrangea quercifolia Bartr.
Kashmir False-Spirea—Sorharia aitchisoni Hemsl.
Leatherwood—Cyrilla racemiflora L.
Nandina—Nandina domestica Thunb.
New Jersey-Tea—Ceanothus americanus L.
Ocean-Spray—Holodiscus discolor var. aria-
    efolius (Sm.) Ascherson and Graebner.
Raspberry, Flowering—Rubus odoratus L.
Rose-of-Sharon—Hibiscus Syriacus L.
Spirea:
Froebel—Spiraea bumalda f. froebelii (Froeb.) Rehd.
Japanese white—Spiraea albiflora (Miq.) Zabel
Stewartia:
Japanese—Stewartia pseudo-camellia Maxim.
Mountain Camellia—Stewartia Pentagyna L'Her
Showy—Stewartia ovata var. grandiflora (Bean)
    Weatherby
Silky Camellia—Stewartia malachodendron L.
St. Johns-wort:
Aarons-Beard—Hypericum calycinum L.
Golden—Hypericum frondosum Michx.
Goldflower—Hypericum moserianum Andre
Kalm—Hypericum kalmianum L.
Shrubby—Hypericum prolificum L.
Summersweet—Clethra alnifolia L.
Tamarix—Tamarix pentandra Pall.

VINES

Bittersweet—Cealstrus articulatus Thunb.
Clematis:
Anemone Flowered—Clematis montana Buch.-Ham.
    ex DC.
Scarlet—Clematis texensis Buckl.
Jackman Clematis—Clematis jackmanii Moore
Sweet Autumn—Clematis paniculata Thunb.
Honeysuckle:
Halls—Lonicera japonica var. halliana (Dipp)
    Nicholson
Sweet—Lonicera caprifolium L.
Silver Fleece Vine—Polygonum auberti L. Henry
Trumpet vine—Campsis radicans (L.) Seem.

TREES

Franklin Tree—Franklinia alatamaha Bar tr. ex.
    Marsh
Goldenraintree—Koelreuteria paniculata Laxm.
Japanese Pagodatree—Sophora japonica L.
Maackia—Maackia amurensis Rupr.
Mimosa—Oxydendrum arboreum (L) DC.
Sorreltree—Albizia julisbrissin Durazz.

A VERY SHADY BACKYARD IN NEW YORK CITY

A good listing of annuals for backyards includes: Begonias, Impatiens, Salvia, Basil (to keep away mosquitos).
Annuals potted and spread around the patio area lend a quality of garden to the world of brick.

ROSES

ROSES FOR THE HOME LANDSCAPE

Of all the garden flowering plants roses are still the most popular and the most widely grown in all parts of the country. With the wide selection of colors, varieties and various growing habits, roses can be utilized for many parts of the garden. Everybody has seen the classic rose garden with the tea roses, the hanging roses falling gracefully from the arbors and trellises, the hedge plants with the deep thorny foliage and the small flowers. Roses are still the most valuable of all garden plants and should be used for the color, decoration and hardiness.

If you follow these few tips you will grow successful roses.

1. Buy number one plants from known growers, not culls.

2. Grow in the sunlight (at least eight hours a day during the growing season).

3. Cultivate the beds and keep weed free.

4. Water the fertilizer regularly.

5. Prune the plants every year and protect them in the winter months.

6. Keep the plants clean either by commercial sprays or organic methods. Roses are susceptible to black spot, aphids and other insects.

Roses fall into two main categories, bush roses and climbing roses. Climbing roses must be supported either by trellises or arbors or just tied to a fence, and bush roses usually stand free except for some of the grandifloras that sometimes have to be staked.

Bush roses are classified into these categories:

1. Hybrid teas. These are the everblooming widely grown plants. A single rose is produced on a stem and these are the most common for cut flowers.

2. Floribundas. These are small bush roses that bear many flowers on a single stem. The foliage resembles that of the hybrid tea but will tolerate more neglect.

3. Grandifloras. These too resemble the tea rose but the flowers are somewhat smaller than the tea and the plants usually grow taller.

4. Polyanthas. These are smaller than the grandifloras and bear flowers in clusters like the floribunda. This plant is usually used as mass border plantings and hedge rows. The polyanthas are very hardy and do well in colder climates.

5. Hybrid Perpetuals. These are the old fashioned roses of yesteryear. The blossoms are larger than the tea rose. Before the development of the hybrid tea rose these were the roses that were the common garden rose. They do not bloom as long as the newer tea rose but are very hardy and can stand cold climates without too much winter protection.

6. Multi-flora or shrub rose. This is a dense grower

1

2

3

with small flowers usually used for hedges and general landscape work. They also serve as a useful screen plant and bear attractive seed pods in the fall.

7. The Old Fashioned Rose. This is an older and more fragrant rose that you will still find in many New England gardens. Thought of as a colonial rose the old fashioned rose is very hardy and requires little care. They bloom in the middle of summer and include the ever-popular moss rose.

8. Tree Rose. This is a grafted rose. The plant is usually formed by grafting a tea or floribunda on upright stems. Most of the more common tea and floribunda roses now can be brought as tree roses. The plant blooms all summer like a tea rose and has a spectacular head on top of the stem.

9. Miniature Roses. The smallest of the roses, the miniature does not grow more than six inches. This is a good rock garden plant or a border plant mixed with other smaller perennials.

10. Climbers and Ramblers. Every year more and more varieties of climbers and ramblers are being developed due to the popularity of habits these plants have. They have to be trained on trellises or arbors but they can and do produce canes up to 20 feet in one season. In a few years you will get more than your money's worth. They are perfect to cover up "ugly spots" on buildings or pipelines.

Basic Cultivation and Care of Roses

Roses grow in the open sunlight and must have at least seven hours of sunlight during the growing season if they are to produce the maximum number of roses. Plants that are planted in shady areas will not produce proper flowers but will develop many diseases due to the moisture on the foliage.

The best time to plant roses is when they are dormant. I prefer to plant in the spring. That gives the root section a complete growing season

to develop, thus securing a hardy plant for the colder months. I usually space roses about three feet apart in the garden but I give climbers and ramblers much more room, about ten feet.

The soil should be a good organic mix with plenty of peatmoss and good drainage. If you can grow flowers or small shrubs in your garden, roses should do fine. Remember roses like to be cultivated and cared for. If you do not have the time or energy to cultivate, feed, water and prune, then grow ground cover.

SIX WAYS TO GROW ROSES

1. Rose trees are very popular in California where they can be out of the ground all year. In the northern parts of the country they must be buried as you cover up the budding section on a regular tea rose.

2. A door trellis front or back yard. Most of the new climbing teas or floribundias will give a great color show in such a place.

3. Many of the old-fashioned roses are still capable of covering huge areas. I have seen climbers well over thirty feet.

4. A "rose bed" usually of the shrub type or floribundas.

5. A tea rose of the formal rose garden. This is the cut rose that comes by the doz. in most of your better florists.

6. The classic look of the arbor still has a lot of charm and is perfect for showing off climbing roses.

4   5   6

Planting the Rose

If you are planting bare-root plants, make the hole deep enough so you can spread the roots. Mound up some soil in the middle of the hole (as indicated in the drawing) so the root section slopes down and forms a cone. Press the soil around the roots, filling in all of the spaces. Start at the bottom of the root section and work your way to the top. When you finish the plant should be firm and ready to prune. I add water right away to help settle the soil firmly around

the roots. I have found that mulching the rose bed is the best way to reduce cultivation and prevent weed growth. I use only peatmoss. Many of the other types of mulches like hulls or coco mulch produce a fungus and this could cause trouble with the plant. As the watering goes on during the season peatmoss will work its way into the soil, stimulating growth and keeping the soil loose. It is the perfect soil conditioner.

Roses need a lot of water. During the growing season a tea or floribunda will put on all its growth, sometimes up to six feet. This takes a vast amount of water and fertilizer.

Roses do best in a slightly acid soil (Ph 6.0). You can test your soil by using an inexpensive soil testing kit. It is easy and helps you further understand the chemistry of the garden. There are many rose fertilizers on the market but most garden fertilizers will do. I would apply about three pounds per every 100 square feet. I usually just sprinkle a large tablespoonful around the base of the rose and water it in. I suggest not using any fertilizer after August first in colder climates for this may stimulate growth when you want the plant to go dormant. In many parts of the country there may be various mineral deficiencies. You must check your local soil and determine what the plant requires. For example, a lack of iron in the plant may cause it to turn yellow. If this is not a problem in your region—good, but check it out.

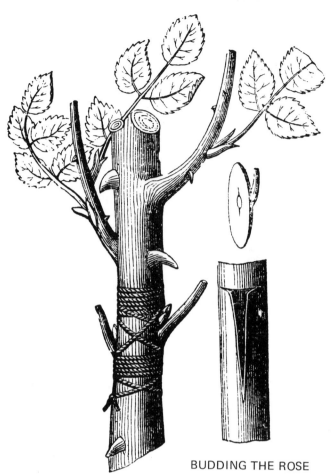

BUDDING THE ROSE

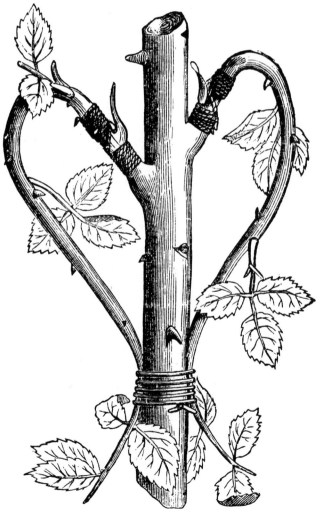

BUDDING IN THE BRANCHES

106

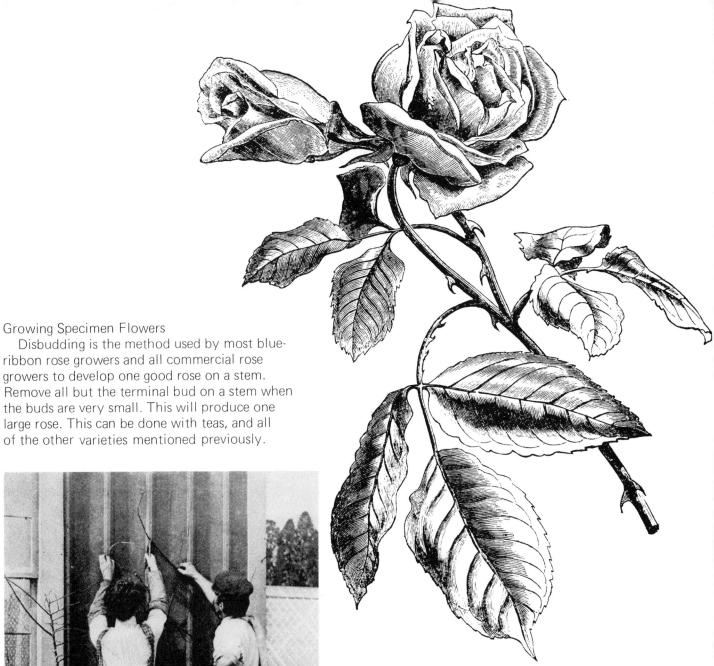

Growing Specimen Flowers

Disbudding is the method used by most blue-ribbon rose growers and all commercial rose growers to develop one good rose on a stem. Remove all but the terminal bud on a stem when the buds are very small. This will produce one large rose. This can be done with teas, and all of the other varieties mentioned previously.

Pruning Roses Step by Step

1. In the spring loosen soil around the budded rose and remove mulch or soil back to the union or joint.

2. Prune off dead wood and diseased canes.

3. Prune off canes that criss-cross.

4. Shorten canes down to 12 to 14 inches.

5. Cut at 45 degree angle, about one-quarter inch above a strong bud.

6. Cover the cut with a pruning paint or compound.

7. Spray with a dormant spray to kill any insect that may have over-wintered on the plant.

8. Add some new soil around the base and some new peatmoss.

TRAINING A CLIMBING ROSE

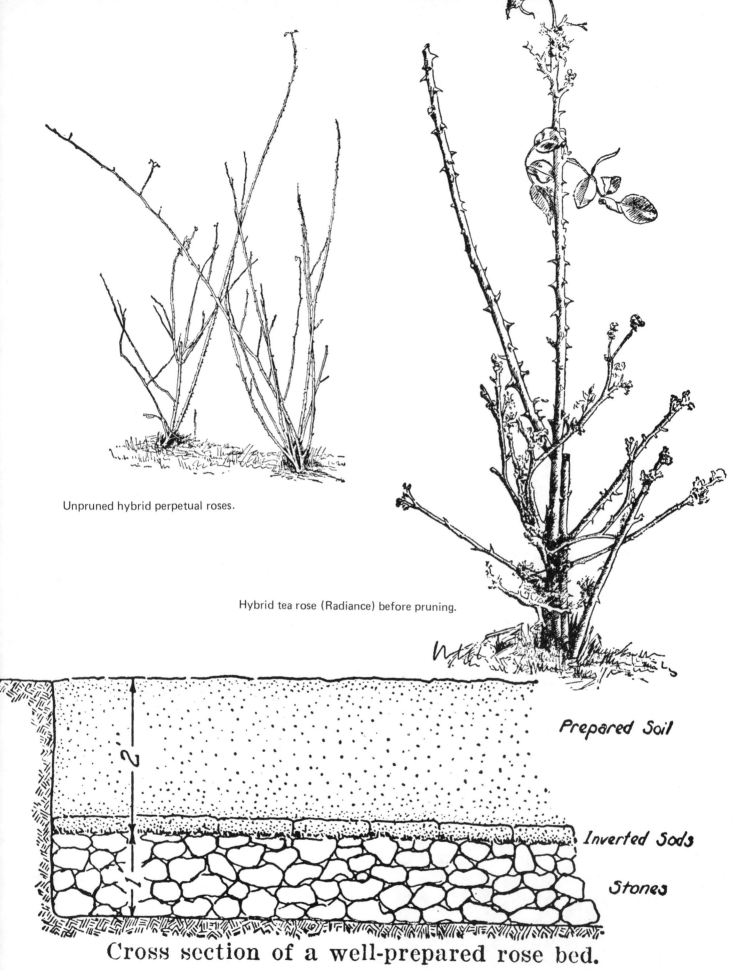

Unpruned hybrid perpetual roses.

Hybrid tea rose (Radiance) before pruning.

Prepared Soil

Inverted Sods

Stones

Cross section of a well-prepared rose bed.

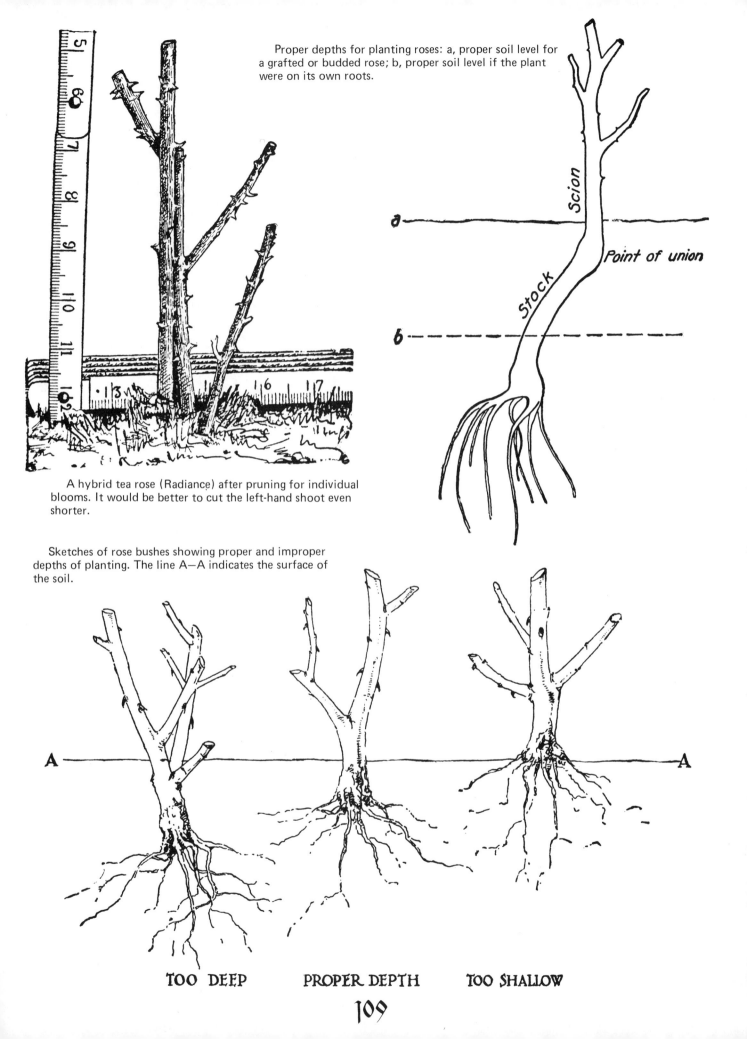

Proper depths for planting roses: a, proper soil level for a grafted or budded rose; b, proper soil level if the plant were on its own roots.

Scion

Point of union

Stock

A hybrid tea rose (Radiance) after pruning for individual blooms. It would be better to cut the left-hand shoot even shorter.

Sketches of rose bushes showing proper and improper depths of planting. The line A—A indicates the surface of the soil.

A — A

TOO DEEP   PROPER DEPTH   TOO SHALLOW

109

GRASSES AND GROUNDCOVERS

Following are descriptions of common lawn grasses and ground cover plants, including statements on how they grow, where they grow best, their requirements, and how to establish them.

GRASSES

ANNUAL BLUEGRASS

Annual bluegrass (Poa annua) has little value as permanent turf because it dies suddenly when high temperatures occur in June, July, or August. It is used chiefly to overseed warm-season turf grasses during the winter months. Only small amounts of seed are availble. It normally begins growth in late summer or early fall from seed produced earlier in the same year. It will often grow throughout the winter.

Annual bluegrass requires a cool, moist soil and good fertility. It will survive under close mowing and shade. It produces large quantities of seed heads even when mowing as low as ¼ inch. It is a pest in many highly specialized turf areas, particularly golf courses.

BAHIAGRASS

Bahiagrass (Paspalum notatum) is a low-growing perennial that spreads by short, heavy runners. It grows best in the southern Coastal Plains region. It is established by seeding.

Common bahia, which has extremely coarse-textured leaves, is recommended for forage only.

Paraguay and Pensacola, strains having finer-textured leaves than common bahia, are useful on large areas such as airfields, where good cover is more important than turf quality. These strains produce a dense rather coarse and uneven turf, and are difficult to mow with an ordinary reel-type mower.

BERMUDAGRASS

Many varieties or strains of bermudagrass (Cynodon dactylon) are sold. Each variety generally has a specialized use. Common bermuda, a coarse-textured grass, is the only variety for which seed is available. Other varieties are established vegetatively.

Bermudagrass is commonly grown in the southern part of the United States. Common seeded bermudagrass is not suited to the northern part of the United States, but vegetative plantings of cold-tolerant sections have survived as far north as Chicago and New York.

Varieties of bermudagrass used in lawns in the southern part of the United States include Tiflawn, Everglades No. 1, Ormond, Sunturf, Texturf 10, and Texturf 1F. Tiflawn is finer in texture than common bermudagrass, and it is deep green. It has outstanding disease-resistant qualities. Tiflawn is a vigorous grower and will form a heavy mat unless it is mowed closely and often. The texture of Everglades No. 1 is finer than that of Tiflawn, and the green is darker. This grass tends to grow prostrate. Ormond is coarser in texture and grows more upright than Everglades No. 1. Of the three varieties, Everglades No. 1 requires the least maintenance.

Varieties of bermudagrass that are used in high-quality lawns receiving maximum maintenance, and in golf course putting greens and fairways, include Tifgreen, Tiffine, Tifway, Bayshore, and Tifdwarf. These varieties are medium green. They are fine in texture.

A variety of bermudagrass called U-3 has been grown successfully in the vicinity of Philadelphia, Pa., Norfolk, Nebr., Cleveland, Ohio, and St. Louis, Mo. It is most widely used in the socalled "crabgrass belt," a roughly triangular region cornered on Philadelphia, St. Louis, and Richmond, Va. U-3 has finer blades than common bermudagrass. It resists disease and insect damage, and holds its color late into the fall when properly fertilized. It grows well in hot, humid weather. Tufcote is also grown in this area.

Bermudagrass grows vigorously, spreading by aboveground runners and underground rootstalks. It often becomes a serious pest in flower beds and other cultivated areas. Once established in those places it is difficult to eradicate.

Bermudagrass will not thrive under conditions of shade, poor drainage, high acidity, or low fertility. It requires frequent heavy applications of nitrogen in amounts of water during the dry periods. It must be clipped closely in order to form a dense turf.

BLUE GRAMAGRASS

Blue gramagrass (Bouteloua gracilis) is a low-growing, perennial grass that is adapted to a wide range of soil conditions throughout the Great Plains region. It is highly drought resistant. Its use as a turf grass is limited to cool, dry places where little or no irrigation water is available.

Blue gramagrass is a bunch-type grass that can be established easily from seed. Unless watered, it becomes semidormant and turns brown during severe drought periods. Seed produced in a given area should be used for plantings in that area only.

BUFFALOGRASS

Buffalograss (buchloe dactyloides) is a stoloniferous perennial grass that is used commonly in sunny lawns of prairie homes in the Great Plains region. It is highly drought resistant. The grass is fine leaved and dense during the growing season. It turns from grayish green to the color of straw when growth stops in the fall. It grows best in well-drained, fairly heavy soils. Buffalograss can be established by sodding or seeding.

CANADA BLUEGRASS

Canada bluegrass (Poa compressa) forms a thin, poor-quality, open turf. It can be used in seed mixtures on playgrounds, athletic fields, or similar areas.

Canada bluegrass will grow in sandy or gravelly

soils of low fertility. It will not grow well in soils having high acidity or poor drainage. It will not withstand clipping below 1½ inches. It is extremely tough and resists wear.

CARPETGRASS

Carpetgrass (Axonopus compressus) is a rapidly spreading stoloniferous perennial grass that produces a dense, compact turf under mowing, but is quite coarse textured. It can be established quickly by seeding or by sprigging or sodding. Seeding is the cheapest method.

Carpetgrass grows best in moist, sandy-loam soils or those that have a relatively high-moisture content throughout the year. It does not grow well in dry soils or in regions that remain dry during part of the growing season. It will thrive under limited fertilization in poor soils, but is extremely sensitive to lack of iron. It resists disease and insect damage, but does not tolerate water spray. It will withstand trampling and heavy wear.

Carpetgrass produces tall seed heads that are difficult to mow and make the lawn look rough or rugged. Mowing frequently with a rotary mower to a height of 1 inch is recommended.

CENTIPEDEGRASS

Centipedegrass (Eremochloa ephiruroides) spreads rapidly by short creeping stems that form new plants at each node. It forms a dense, vigorous turf that is highly resistant to weed invasion. It is usually established vegetatively; some seed is available.

Centipedegrass is considered the best low-maintenance lawn grass in the southern part of the United States. It requires less mowing, less watering, and less fertilizing than other southern lawn grasses. It is seldom damaged by disease or insects, but may be severely damaged by salt water spray. It is sensitive to the lack or iron. An annual application of a complete fertilizer will improve the quality of centipedegrass lawns. Although it is drought resistant, centipedegrass should be watered during dry periods.

Centipedegrass should not be planted in farm lawns; it may escape into pastures and destroy their grazing value.

COLONIAL BENTGRASS

Colonial bentgrass (Agrostis tenuis) is a fine-textured, turfed-type grass with few creeping stems and rhizomes. It forms a dense turf when heavily seeded and closely mowed.

Colonial bentgrass is used chiefly in high-quality lawns and putting greens. It is more expensive to maintain than ordinary lawn grasses. It is popular in the New England States, Washington, and Oregon.

Colonial bentgrass requires fertile soil and frequent fertilizer applications. It must be watered during dry periods. It is susceptible to a wide variety of diseases. It must be mowed closely; when cut about 3/4 inch it becomes fluffy and forms an undesirable spongy mat.

Several strains of colonial bentgrass are sold. Highland is the hardiest variety. It is bluish green. It is not as drought resistant or as aggressive as Highland. Although Astoria requires more care than Highland, it produces a better-quality lawn if properly managed. Other colonial bentgrass suitable for lawns include New Zealand browntop and some strains of German bentgrass.

CREEPING BENTGRASS

Creeping bentgrass (Agrostis palustris) is not often used in home lawns, but it is used extensively in golf course putting greens throughout the United States. It has profuse creeping stems that produce roots and stems at every node, and it develops a dense sod. It must be mowed closely (3/16 to 3/8 inch), brushed regularly, and top-dressed periodically to prevent formation of an undesirable mat or thatch.

Creeping bentgrass requires soils having high fertility, low acidity, good drainage, and high water-holding capacity. A regular program of fertilization, watering, and disease control must be followed to maintain good-quality turf.

Varieties available include Seaside, which is established by seeding and is used in golf greens along the west coast; Penncross, a seeded type that is available for specialized turf areas; and several strains that have been selected from established greens and are established vegetatively—Arlington, Collins, Cohansey, Washington, Congressional, Pennpar, Pennlu, and Old Orchard.

CRESTED WHEATGRASS

Crested wheatgrass (Agropyron cristatum) is a perennial bunchgrass. It thrives in most soils in the central and northern Great Plains and Intermountain regions. It is recommended in dry, cool areas of those regions where irrigation water is not available. It is established by seeding.

Crested wheatgrass will withstand long, dry periods and heavy wear if not cut too closely. It makes most of its growth in the spring and fall; it becomes semi-dormant and turns brown in the hot summer months.

JAPANESE LAWNGRASS

Japanese lawngrass (Zoysia japonica) is a low-growing perennial that spreads by above-ground runners and shallow rootstocks. It forms a dense turf that resists weed invasion and disease and insect damage.

Japanese lawngrass grows best in the region south of a line drawn from Philadelphia, Pa., westward to San Francisco, Calif. It will survive in the region north of that line but its use there, except in some localities, is impracticable because of the short summer growing season. The grass turns the color of straw when the first killing frost occurs in the fall and it remains off-color until warm spring weather.

Common Japanese lawngrass is coarse in texture. It is somewhat undesirable for home lawn use but is excellent for large areas such as airfields and playgrounds. Meyer zoysia, a selection of common Japanese lawngrass, is more desirable than Japanese lawngrass for home lawns. It is more vigorous, retains its color later in the fall, and regains it earlier in the spring. Meyer zoysia sod is available from a number of nurseries. There is no seed.

Although Japanese lawngrass will survive in soils of low fertility, it makes best growth when given liberal applications of complete fertilizers having a high nitrogen content. It is relatively drought tolerant in the humid regions. It is highly resistant to wear and will withstand close clipping.

Japanese lawngrass may be established by sprig planting the stems, by spot sodding, or by seeding. Three to four growing seasons are generally required to get complete coverage.

Emerald zoysia is a hybrid between Japanese lawngrass and mascarene grass that has proven superior to Meyer zoysia in the southern part of the United States. The grass is fine leafed, dense growing and dark green in color.

KENTUCKY BLUEGRASS

Kentucky bluegrass (Poa pratensis) is a hardy, long-lived, sod-forming grass that spreads by underground rootstocks. It is one of the most widely used lawn grasses in the United States. It is the basic lawn grass in cool, humid regions and in cool, dry regions where adequate irrigation water is available.

Common Kentucky bluegrass will not withstand poor drainage or high acidity. It grows best in heavy, well-drained soils of good fertility that are neutral or nearly neutral in reaction. In soils of low fertility, liberal applications of nitrogen, phosphorus, and potash are needed. Bluegrass is highly drought resistant; it has the ability to go into a semi-dormant condition during hot summer months.

Common Kentucky bluegrass may be injured if mowed shorter than 1½ inches. It will not tolerate heavy shade. Because it becomes established slowly, common Kentucky bluegrass is often planted with faster-growing grasses that provide cover and prevent weed invasion while the bluegrass is becoming established.

MERION

Merion Kentucky bluegrass has proved superior to common Kentucky bluegrass in many regions of the United States. It can be clipped more closely, and is less susceptible to leafspot disease than common Kentucky bluegrass, although it is susceptible to rust and stripe smut. Merion Kentucky bluegrass also appears to be more heat and drought tolerant, more vigorous, and more resistant to weed invasion than common Kentucky bluegrass. For best growth, it requires greater fertility and more maintenance than common Kentucky bluegrass. It responds well to high applications of nitrogen.

Among other varieties of Kentucky bluegrass found commercially are: Newport, Park, Nugget, Pennstar, Windsor, Baron, and Fylking.

KIKUYUGRASS

Kikuyugrass (Pennisetum clandestinum) is a perennial grass that spreads by coarse underground rootstocks. It produces a coarse-textured spongy or matted turf that is 3 to 5 inches thick and difficult to mow at lawn height. Its use has been confined to locations in coastal California, where it is now considered a pest and is being eradicated. It is not recommended for lawn use.

MANILAGRASS

Manilagrass (Zoysia matrella) is closely related to Japanese lawngrass and has many similar characteristics. It is stoloniferous, and forms a dense carpet-like turf that resists weeds, wear, disease, and insect damage. Manilagrass is adapted to the southern part of the United States.

Manilagrass is sensitive to highly acid soils. It responds well to liberal applications of nitrogenous fertilizer. It turns brown when the first killing frost occurs and remains dormant until spring. It is established by sprigging or spot sodding.

113

MASCARENEGRASS

Mascarenegrass (Zoysia tenuifolia) is a low-growing stoloniferous grass that is adapted to very few locations in the United States. Its growth requirements with respect to moisture, nutrients, and soil are about the same as those for manilagrass, but it is not as winter hardy as manilagrass or Japanese lawngrass. It becomes sodbound and humps up as it grows older, which encourages weed invasion. Limited amounts of mascarenegrass sod are available in Florida and California.

MEADOW FESCUE

Meadow fescue (Festuca elatior) is a hardy, short-lived perennial that is used primarily for pasture and hay. It does not form a solid sod. It grows best in heavy, moist soils, and will withstand extremely wet soils. An excellent seed producer, it is often found in poor-quality lawn seed mixtures.

ORCHARDGRASS

Orchardgrass (Dactylis glomerata) is a tell-growing, perennial bunchgrass that forms coarse-textured tufts but never a solid turf. It does not grow well in soils having high acidity or poor drainage, but it resists drought and tolerates shade. It can withstand low fertility.

Seed is abundant, and it is sometimes used in poor-quality lawn seed mixtures.

RED FESCUE AND CHEWINGS FESCUE

Red fescue (Festuca rubra) and Chewings fescue (F. rubra var. commutata) rate next to Kentucky bluegrass as the most popular lawn grasses in the cool humid regions of the United States. Red fescue spreads slowly by underground rootstocks. Chewings fescue is a bunch-type grower. Both are established by seeding.

Both fescues are used extensively in lawn seed mixtures. The grow well in shaded areas, and they tolerate high acidity. They require good drainage but will grow in poor, droughty soils.

Red fescue and Chewings fescue are fine textured. They have bristlelike leaves that stand upright. When seeded heavily they form a dense sod that resists wear. They heal slowly when injured by insects, disease, or other means. Mowing consistently below 1½ inches can cause severe damage. The grasses grow slowly.

Improved strains of red fescue on the market include Pennlawn, Illahee, and Rainier. No improved strains of Chewings fescue are on the market.

REDTOP

Under lawn conditions, redtop (Agrostis alba) is a short-lived perennial. It seldom lives more than two seasons when closely mowed. It is commonly used in lawn seed mixtures in the northern temperate regions of the United States to provide quick cover while more permanent grasses are developing. It is often seeded alone in temporary lawns. In the southern part of the United States it is used for winter overseeding of bermudagrass to provide year-round green color.

Heavy seeding helps overcome redtop's tendency to develop a coarse open-type turf. Redtop tolerates a wide range of soil and climatic conditions, including temperature extremes. It grows in soils that are highly acid and poorly drained. It resists drought and has a low fertility requirement.

RESCUEGRASS

Rescuegrass (Bromus catharticus) is a short-lived perennial bunch grass that grows best in fertile soils in humid regions where the winters are mild. It is sometimes used in the southern part of the United States as a winter grass in large bermudgass plantings, such as golf course fairways.

ROUGH BLUEGRASS

Rough bluegrass (Poa trivialis), also known as roughstalk bluegrass, is a shade-tolerant perennial that is useful in lawns only in the extreme northern part of the United States. It is established by seeding. It is seriously injured by hot, dry weather. It has leaves of the same texture as Kentucky bluegrass. The stems and leaves lie flat, giving the turf a glassy appearance. Roughstalk meadowgrass is lighter green than Kentucky bluegrass. It spreads by short above-ground runners.

Roughstalk meadowgrass has a shallow root system, and will not withstand heavy wear. It should be used in shady areas where the traffic is not heavy.

RYEGRASS

Italian or annual ryegrass (Lolium multiflorum) and perennial ryegrass (Lolium perenne) are propagated entirely by seed that is produced in the Pacific Northwest, or imported. Much of the ryegrass used for lawns in the United States is a mixture of annual, perennial, and intermediate types.

Many commercial lawn seed mixtures contain too much ryegrass; the ryegrass competes with the permanent grass seedlings for moisture and nutrients. On sloping areas, it is sometimes advisable to include a small amount of ryegrass in the lawn seed mixture to help prevent soil erosion. The use of perennial ryegrass in lawn seed mixtures often results in ragged-appearing lawns that are difficult to mow. Coarse clumps of ryegrass may persist in the lawn for several years.

In the southern part of the United States annual or common ryegrass is used for winter overseeding of bermudagrass in lawns, and on golf greens and tees. Among fine-textured ryegrass varieties are Pennfine, Manhattan, Norlea, Pelo, and NK101.

ST. AUGUSTINEGRASS

St. Augustinegrass (stenotaphrum secundatum) is the No. 1 shade grass of the southernmost States. It is a creeping perennial; it spreads by long runners that produce short, leafy branches. It can be grown successfully south of Augusta, Ga., and Birmingham, Ala., and westward to the coastal regions of Texas. It is established vegetatively. Seed is not available.

St. Augustinegrass will withstand salt water spray. It grows best in moist soils of good fertility. It produces good turf in the muck soils of Florida. Liberal applications of high-nitrogen fertilizers are necessary, especially in sandy soils.

St. Augustinegrass can be seriously damaged by chinch bugs, and it is susceptible to army worm damage and several turf diseases.

TALL FESCUE

Tall fescue (Festuca arundinacea) is a tall-growing perennial bunch grass that has coarse, dense basal leaves and a strong, fibrous root system. It is also used for pasture. It is established by seeding.

Because of their wear-resistant qualities, two improved strains of tall fescue, Kentucky 31 fescue and Alta fescue, are used often on play areas, athletic fields, airfields, service yards, and other areas where a heavy, tough turf is needed rather than a fine-textured turf.

Tall fescue will grow in wet or dry, acid or alkaline soils, but it grows best in well-drained, fertile soils. It will withstand a moderate amount of shade.

TIMOTHY

Timothy (Phleum pratense) is a coarse perennial bunch grass that grows best in the northern humid regions of the United States where its main use is hay for livestock. It has no use as a lawn grass, but is often found in poor-quality lawn seed mixtures. It is sometimes suitable in nonuse areas to provide cover.

WEEPING LOVEGRASS

Weeping lovegrass (Eragrostis curvula) is a vigorous perennial bunch grass that grows best in the southern Great Plains region. It is an excellent erosion-control plant on nonuse areas but is not good for home lawns because it will not withstand frequent close mowing. It grows in any type of soil but grows best in sandy loams.

VELVET BENTGRASS

Velvet bentgrass (Agrostis canina), the finest textured of the bentgrasses, is used mainly in high-quality lawns and putting greens in the New England States and the Pacific Northwest. It forms an extremely dense turf from creeping stems. It can be established by seeding or by vegetative planting.

Velvet bentgrass is adapted to a wide range of soil conditions but makes its best growth on well-drained, fertile soils having low acidity. It is not as aggressive as creeping bentgrass and is slow to recover from all types of injury. It requires close mowing, regular brushing, and periodic topdressing. A regular program of fertilizing, watering, and disease control is necessary to maintain high-quality turf. Only one variety of velvet bentgrass is available in the United States: the Kingstown variety.

GROUND COVER PLANTS

Vines and other low-growing plants can often be planted on areas where it is difficult to establish or maintain satisfactory grass cover. Such areas include heavily shaded places, steep banks, rough and rocky areas, terraces, and drainage ditches.

DICHONDRA

Dichondra (Dichondra repens, D. Carolinensis) is a perennial that forms a low, dense mat under favorable conditions. It can be establishing by seeding or by vegetative planting. Dichondra is native to the Coastal Plain States from Virginia to Texas, but it is not considered a desirable lawn plant except in central and southern California.

Dichondra is closely related to the milkweed and the morning-glory. Its leaves are pale green, and kidney shaped. It grows best in heavy soils. The plant does not require a high fertility level, but it requires large amounts of water. It will grow in partial shade, but is stemmy and undesirable and will crowd out all other vegetation, including bermudagrass.

ENGLISH IVY

English ivy (Hedera lelix) is a hardy trailing evergreen vine that thrives in shaded areas but will grow in direct sunlight. It develops a very dense mat that should be pruned occasionally. English ivy is particularly useful on steep banks or around the base of trees.

JAPANESE SNAKEBEARD (MONDO)

Japanese snakebeard (Ophiopogon japonica), or Lilyturf, is a bunch-growing member of the

English ivy as a groundcover under trees in California. In the northern United States the English ivy is not reliably hardy, and the best plant for covering the ground in the shade of trees and shrubs is running myrtle (*Vinca minor*), an evergreen trailer with thick, waxy leaves and blue, five-lobed flowers.

lily family. It grows 8 to 12 inches high, and bears purple to white flowers. It is used in the southern part of the United States under trees in poor soils. It is propagated vegetatively, and should be set close together because it spreads slowly.

JAPANESE SPURGE

Japanese spurge (Pachysandra terminalis), or Pachysandra, is a low-growing evergreen plant that spreads by suckers. The plants are about 8 inches high. They have dense wedge-shaped leaves and bear inconspicuous greenish-white flowers. They are established by division or by cuttings. Plants should be set 1 foot apart.

Japanese spurge is used in the Eastern United States from New England to Georgia. It is particularly recommended in Virginia, North Carolina, South Carolina, Kentucky, and Tennessee.

LIPPIA

Lippia (Lippia canescens) is used as a substitute for grass throughout the Southwest, particularly in Arizona. Lippia leaves are dark green. They are oblong, and seldom more than 1 inch long. Lippia will not survive temperatures below freezing, and may be injured by temperatures somewhat higher than freezing. It is also susceptible to nematode damage. Lippia has been known to crowd out bermudagrass when mowed regularly. It is established by vegetative planting.

PARTRIDGE BERRY

Partridge berry (Mitchella repens) is a low-growing creeping evergreen that is native to the Southeastern United States. It grows well in shaded areas having moist, fertile soils. Its leaves are small, glossy and round. It produces pinkish-white flowers in the spring; these are followed by scarlet fruit in the fall and winter.

Partridge berry is established by cuttings from vegetative material that can be found along streambanks and in wooded areas in the southeastern part of the country.

PERIWINKLE COMMON

Common periwinkle (Vinca minor) or myrtle, is a hardy low-growing evergreen that spreads by creeping stems. It has small, dark-green, glossy leaves. It develops violet blue flowers.

Common periwinkle will form a dense mat that shades out weeds and grasses. It grows best in moist soils that are high in organic matter. It is partial to dense shade, but it will grow satisfactorily under dry conditions in direct sunlight. Periwinkle is established by cuttings and can be planted any time when the soil is not frozen.

WHITE CLOVER

White clover (Trifolium repens) is regarded by some as a desirable ground cover plant in lawns. It is regarded by others as a pest.

Grass growing in proximity to white clover may be benefited by the nitrogen-fixing ability of the nodules on the clover roots. The plant often grows in patches of varying size, giving the lawn an uneven appearance. Some persons object to the white flower the plants form, and to the fact that it attracts bees. Another disadvantage is that white clover disappears during hot, dry weather. Contrary to claims made, white clover will not compete successfully with crabgrass.

FOOD
GARDENS

THE VEGETABLE GARDEN

The Site

A sandy well-drained garden soil with a southern slope is perfect. The sun will warm up a spot like that sooner and the soil will be nice and loose. Never garden in a low spot or on a steep slope. If all you have is a low spot or steep slope, take up something else, like ship-building in bottles.

Plant as close to the tools or tool shed as possible and to the water source. Plant out in the sun away from larger plants like shade trees or large shrubs. Vegetables need a lot of sunlight, good drainage and plenty of food. Keep the weeds away and the plants green.

A Garden Plan

As in any garden planning, a plan to scale on paper is a must. Plan the garden as to time available, and size of required harvest. If you plan to can or freeze vegetables, take that into consideration. Here are some basic steps to help you limit the work, and the time in the garden, to actually making the plants grow. Any small garden should be pleasureful, but unnecessary work may turn you off and limit your fun in the dirt.

1. If you are growing certain perennial crops like asparagus or herbs try and locate them in a special place away from the annual vegetables. Do not work around a bed of strawberries to plant corn.

2. Plant tall plants on the north side of the garden so as not to shade the smaller plants.

3. Try and plant all the early crops together so you can get two crops in a single season in the north and maybe three or four in the deep south.

4. If you are in an area that only has a short season try and space the leaf lettuce and other fast-growing greens so you can get at least three separate pickings for the salad. Just time them every two weeks.

5. Buy good seed from established seed dealers.

6. Follow directions on the seed packages for each variety. The growers and propagators of the seed know more than anyone else the habits and the time required to harvest in different parts of the country. I suggest you pick up a copy of FOOD GARDENS (A Gardener's Catalogue Book) for it covers all the parts of the country and fully explains how to grow almost every kind of vegetable.

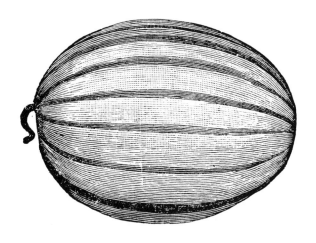

7. Common sense says not to grow melons in a five by five plot. Grow the vegetables you have room for.

8. Your tools may decide the spacing in the garden. Hand tools and hand working the row takes less spacing than machine cultivators.

9. If you plant the same thing year after year give the soil some life or rotate the kinds of vegetables grown. We all like tomatoes and corn, some peas and green beans, a couple kinds of herbs and a melon or two. Feed the ground.

Following is a list of drawings to help you fully understand various gardening procedures.

Suggestions for Container-Gardening Success—Use Proper Containers. There are many different types of pots or containers on the market or around your home suitable for growing plants. Containers should have drainage holes in the bottom. If this is impossible, put one inch layer of pebbles, gravel or other coarse material in the bottom before planting. Wooden containers should have one inch "feet" for elevation off the patio floor. Container size is important; it's better to plant in something a little too large rather than too small.

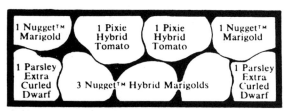

Tomato—Marigold—Parsley
Window or Patio Box
3 ft. long, 1 ft. wide, at least 8 in. deep.
2 Pixie Hybrid Tomato Plants, 2 Extra Curled Dwarf Parsley Plants, and about 5 Nugget™ Hybrid Marigold Plants make an attractive, productive combination.

Box Gardens
Larger planting boxes are excellent to supplement gardening in individual containers. Window boxes about 2 to 3 feet long, 8 to 12 in. wide and 6 in. or more deep are handy and attractive to use for house decoration when planted with flowers such as Begonias, Coleus and Impatiens (in semi-shade), Alyssum, Geraniums, Dwarf Fresh Marigolds, Nugget Marigolds, and Petunias in the sun; or a pretty, edible vegetable-flower combination such as Pixie Hybrid Tomatoes, Nugget Marigolds and Dwarf Curled Parsley.

Similar size boxes are just as useful on patio, balcony or roof-top and can be planted entirely in vegetables if you prefer. Bush Snap Beans, Swiss Chard, Herbs, Loosehead Lettuce, Parsley, Radishes and Pixie Hybrid Tomatoes are especially good for such boxes.

You can grow vegetables "in the air" for easy picking and to give vertical accents to the patio garden design or provide screens. Plant three or four cucumbers in a box about 3 ft. long and 11 in. wide and deep. Furnish support such as Trellis Netting about 6 ft. high for the vines to climb. Pole Beans and Tomatoes (except dwarf plant types) can be handled in a similar way. So can Morning Glories, Moonflower, Climbing Nasturtiums and other flowering vines for a colorful curtain or background.

Still larger box gardens can substitute for a vegetable or flower plot where there is no suitable ground area. An amazing amount of tasty produce can be grown easily and conveniently in boxes about 3 to 4 ft. and at least 6 in. deep. Each box needs several holes in the bottom for drainage and should be raised off the earth or floor slightly, or even higher for ease in care.

Spring, after danger of heavy frost, starts the planting season in each box garden. A good choice of varieties includes one row each (6 in. apart) of Green Ice Lettuce, Ruby Lettuce, Cherry Belle Radish, Bloomsdale Long Standing Spinach and Burpee's Rhubarb Swiss Chard. Put three Pixie Hybrid Tomato seedlings in the end of the box. Fill the corners with a couple of Dwarf Curled Parsley plants.

Planter Box Vegetable "Garden" 3 by 4 ft., at least 6 in. deep.

An amazing amount of tasty vegetables can be grown in this box garden by replanting Radish, Lettuce and Spinach rows (after harvest) with Beets, Bush Beans, baby Carrots, dwarf Kale, Lettuce for fall crop, etc.

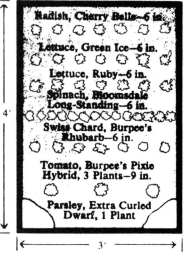

Lettuce, Radishes and Spinach mature fast. Following harvest, replant the area immediately with Bush Snap Beans, Beets, Carrots, Dwarf Kale, or whatever compact varieties you prefer. These suggestions are a starter in helping you develop your box garden for maximum production from spring to late fall. While vegetables are attractive, you can make box gardens even prettier by including a few plants of Dwarf French or Nugget Marigolds or other compact, colorful annuals.

Redwood is the most permanent for making containers. Pine and other types of lumber, including plywood, are satisfactory, but containers should be painted or treated with a greenhouse-type wood preservative (not creosote) before use. Set containers in their permanent "garden" location before filling with planting mix. They are heavy, awkward and almost impossible to move afterward.

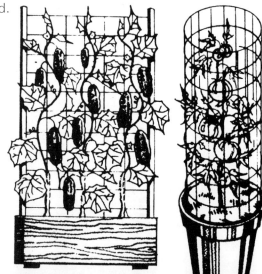

Recommended Varieties and Container Size

VEGETABLES

Minimum Container Size—Width and Depth
(1 plant each unless noted)

Bean, Bush Snap, Burpee's Greensleeves ℗	6 in. (2 each), 12 in. (4 each)
Bean, Pole Snap, Kentucky Wonder	12 in. (2-4 each on poles or trellis)
Bean, Pole Lima, King of the Garden	12 in. (2-4 each on poles or trellis)
Swiss Chard, Burpee's Fordhook Giant	6 in.
Swiss Chard, Burpee's Rhubarb	6 in.
Cucumber, Burpee Hybrid	12 in. (3 each on trellis)
Cucumber, Burpless Hybrid	12 in. (3 each on trellis)
Burpee's Curlycress™	6 in. (broadcast seed)
Eggplant, Burpee's Black Beauty	12 in.
Eggplant, Early Beauty Hybrid	12 in.
Herbs, Chives	6 in.
Oregano	6 in.
Sweet Basil	6 in.
Sweet Marjoram	6 in.
Lettuce, Burpee Bibb	6 in.
Lettuce, Burpee's Green Ice ℗	6 in.
Lettuce, Oak Leaf	6 in.
Parsley, Extra Curled Dwarf	6 in.
Pepper, California Wonder	12 in.
Pepper, Sweet Banana	12 in.
Spinach, Malabar	8 in. (2-3 each trailing or on trellis)
Squash, Burpee Golden Zucchini ℗	12 in.
Squash, Burpee Hybrid Zucchini	12 in.
Strawberry, Baron Solemacher	6 in.
Tomatoes, Burpee's Pixie Hybrid	8 in. (staked)
Burpee's Big Girl™ Hybrid VF	12 in. (on support)
Burpee's VF Hybrid	12 in. (on support)
Basket Pak	12 in. (on support)
Red Cherry	12 in. (on support)
Yellow Plum	12 in. (on support)

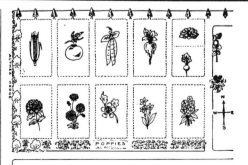

Two crops on the same ground. The vegetables at the ends of the rows suggest the first planting; those in the middle indicate the succession crops

showing vegetables in the northern tier of beds and flowers in the southern tier.

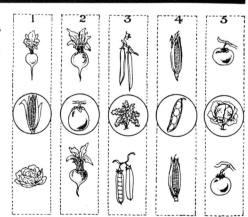

VEGETABLES FOR DIFFERENT PURPOSES

Very Easy to Grow: Bush Bean, Beet, Carrot, Collards, Corn, Cucumber, Curlycress, Dill, Kale, Leaf Lettuce, Pumpkin Radish, Rutabaga, Squash, Swiss Chard, Turnip.

For Winter Use: These vegetables may be left in the garden during winter and dug whenever you can get into the soil. Garden should be mulched to prevent alternate freezing and thawing of the ground. Parsnips, Root Parsley, Salsify, Horse Radish, Kale (Frost improves the flavor; leaves to be picked during the winter).

May be Stored in a Frost-Free Place: Beets, Cabbage, Carrots, Celery, Onions, Parsnips, Pumpkins, Rutabaga, Winter Radish, Winter Squash, Turnips. Store beets, carrots, parsnips and winter radishes in a galvanized trash can sunk into the ground to within one inch of the rim. Put on lid, cover with straw to insure easy opening. Or pack roots in slightly damp sand, peatmoss or newspapers and put in dark basement, shed or pit just above freezing.

Keep cabbage, pumpkins, rutabagas, winter squash and turnips in the same place on slatted boards or a mesh frame off the floor. Dig celery before a hard frost, leave roots on, pack stalks upright in boxes with a layer of moist sand in the bottom.

Hang onions in mesh bags in an airy place, or spread out in slatted trays off the floor.

Early Maturing: Specific varieties within the following classes will reach maturity in the number of days indicated and, therefore, are especially valuable for gardeners living in the far north.

Cress—10 days, Radish—22 days, Mustard—35 days, Scallions—40 days, Loosehead Lettuce—40 days, Spinach—42 days, Turnip—45 days, Bush Snap Bean—48 days, Summer Squash—50 days, Cucumber—53 days, Early Peas—55 days, Kale—55 days, Kohlrabi—55 days, Swiss Chard—60 days.

TROUBLE SHOOTING

If you follow the simple principles of efficient growing, your garden should be healthy and fruitful. Occasionally, though, something is bound to go wrong. Here are a few tips to help prevent or diagnose the difficulties.

Corn: If the ears are blank or poorly filled out, the plants were probably left too close together. Single plants should be a foot apart. If you plant in groups or hills or two or three plants, groups should be three feet apart. Plant corn in blocks of short rows to insure effective pollination.

Cucumbers and Squash: Lots of flowers but no fruits developing, or only a few misshapen ones? Both of these varieties have two types of flowers—male with powdery pollen, and female with a baby fruit at the base of the petals. Sometimes only one type occurs for awhile, but this condition usually corrects itself before long. Both types are necessary for pollination and fruit development. Even then plenty of bees need to transfer pollen to the sticky stigmas in the female flowers—or you may have to do it yourself. Incomplete pollination may cause bent or misshapen fruit.

Flowers: If plants get tall and scraggly, they're too crowded, short of sun—or both. Most annuals need all-day sun to do well.

Head Lettuce: Plants that shoot up stalks, instead of heading, are "bolting" or going to seed. Lettuce needs cool weather and enough room to head nicely. Start seeds early in the spring, or grow as a fall crop. Thin or space plants at least 12 in. apart. Leaf lettuce is easier to grow.

Lima Beans: Blossoms may drop before any beans set if weather is very hot, or cold and wet at blooming time. An overdose of fertilizer excessively high in nitrogen, like manure, may do the same thing.

Melons: Bad, bitter flavor is not caused by crossing with cucumbers—this is impossible. Instead, cold, wet weather during the ripening period, or diseased vines, cause poor taste. Melons need fertile, well-drained soil, a long growing season, and warm sunny weather while ripening to be sweet and tasty.

CATERPILLAR OF LARGE CABBAGE BUTTERFLY.

Oddities: What causes a marigold, or some other flower variety, to develop a thick, flat stem topped with a cluster of blooms? Fasciation! Something happened—possibly an injury—to the growing tip of the plant, so that all the side branches grew fused with the main stem. Likewise all the lateral flower buds are joined with the terminal, making one big cluster of blossoms. Fasciation, always a conversation piece in your garden, usually isn't hereditary.

The "odd ball" zinnia with green buds that grow bigger and bigger but never open into flowers is a "freak" that turns up once in a great while. Enjoy it for its unusual looks—it is sterile and can't produce seed. Apparently a number of previously hidden hereditary traits come out into the open in the "freak" to cause the strange appearance.

Harris Seed Co.   Harris Seed Co.

N
W ─┼─ E
S

SUGGESTED PLAN FOR A VEGETABLE GARDEN
SPRING and SUMMER
20 x 55 Feet

NORTH ─────────────────────────────────────

	EARLY SWEET CORN	MID-SEASON SWEET CORN	LATE SWEET CORN
		BLOCK PLANTING	

16½' TOMATOES 8 STAKED PLANTS
3'   BROCCOLI
1½'   TOMATOES 8 STAKED PLANTS
1½'   LEAF LETTUCE   HEAD LETTUCE
1½'   CUCUMBERS 5 HILLS
1½'   RADISHES
1½'   SQUASH, 4 ACORN BUSH, 4 SUMMER BUSH
1½'   EARLY CABBAGE PLANTS
1½'   6 PEPPER PLANTS   4 EGGPLANT
2'   BUSH LIMA BEANS
2'   BUSH LIMA BEANS
1½'   SNAP BEANS   FOLLOW WITH SPINACH
1½'   SNAP BEANS   FOLLOW WITH KALE AND LETTUCE
1½'   SNAP BEANS   FOLLOW WITH CABBAGE AND CAULIFLOWER
1½'   BUSH PEAS
1½'   BUSH PEAS   FOLLOW WITH SNAP BEANS
1½'   SPINACH
1½'   BEETS   FOLLOW WITH BRUSSEL SPROUTS AND ENDIVE
1½'   BEETS
1½'   CARROTS SECOND SOWING
1½'   CARROTS
1½'   SWISS CHARD   PARSLEY
1½'   ONION SETS
1½'   RADISHES   FOLLOW WITH BEETS

SOUTH ─────────────────────────────────────

Dotted rows indicate varieties which mature quickly, and which will be removed to make room for long season vegetables.

By making succession plantings, the garden space can be utilized to full extent, and with proper care a large quantity of high quality vegetables can be raised. For instance, by referring to the plan, you will see that Peas are followed by Snap Beans, and Snap Beans by Cabbage, Cauliflower, Kale, Lettuce and Spinach.

Also Beans are sown at 2 week intervals to give a continuous supply.

SAME PLAN — LATE SUMMER and FALL
20 x 55 Feet

NORTH ─────────────────────────────────────

	EARLY SWEET CORN	MID-SEASON SWEET CORN	LATE SWEET CORN
		BLOCK PLANTING	

16½' TOMATOES 8 STAKED PLANTS
3'   TOMATOES 8 STAKED PLANTS
1½'   CUCUMBERS 5 HILLS
1½'   SQUASH, 4 ACORN BUSH, 4 SUMMER BUSH
1½'   6 PEPPER PLANTS   4 EGGPLANT
2'   BUSH LIMA BEANS
2'   BUSH LIMA BEANS
1½'   SPINACH
1½'   KALE AND LETTUCE
1½'   CABBAGE AND CAULIFLOWER
1½'   SNAP BEANS
1½'   BRUSSEL SPROUTS AND ENDIVE
1½'   BEETS
1½'   CARROTS
1½'   CARROTS
1½'   SWISS CHARD   PARSLEY
1½'   ONION SETS
1½'   BEETS

SOUTH ─────────────────────────────────────

This is how the garden looks after quick maturing varieties have been harvested, and succession plantings made.

For a plot 20 by 30 feet, omit Corn, Cucumbers, and Squash. For a still smaller plot, omit one row of Lima Beans, one row of Snap Beans, Eggplant, Peppers, and one row of Tomatoes.

FRUIT TREES

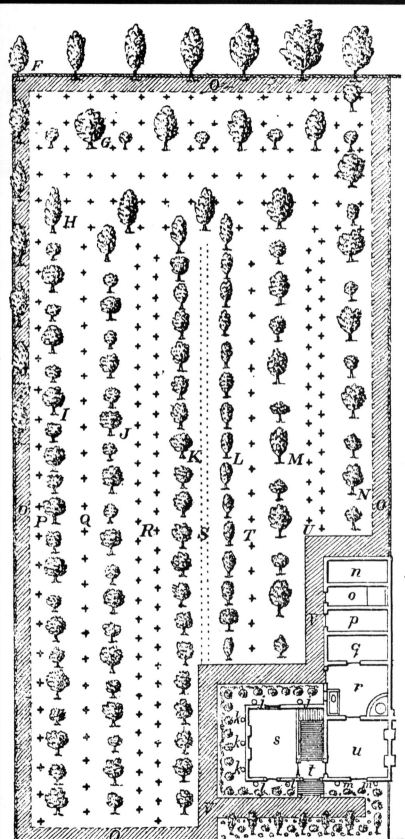

Plan for a Small Fruit Orchard.

References : F, Damsons, **12** ft. apart, planted **1** foot from the hedge ; G, four low standard Apples, **15** ft. apart, with standard Filberts between ; H, four low standard Apples, **15** ft. apart. Space between F, G and H, Red and White Currants, **5** ft. apart, as shown by the crosses ; I, large permanent bush Apples, **12** ft. apart, and between them temporary trees ; J, large permanent bush Apples, **12** ft. apart, with smaller temporary trees between, of small varieties ; K, pyramid or bush Apples, **6** ft. apart, root pruned, or **12** ft. unrestricted ; L, pyramid Pears on Quince, **6** ft. apart, root pruned, or if on Pear stocks and unrestricted, **12** ft. ; M, Plum standards, **15** ft. apart, with dwarfs between ; N, Plum standards, **15** ft. apart, with low standard Nuts between ; O, ash path ; P, Gooseberries, temporary ; Q, Black Currants ; R, Gooseberries ; S, Strawberries ; T, Blackberries or Black Currants ; U, Raspberries ; V, gravel path. Fruit trees against dwelling : *j*, Morello Cherries ; *k*, Pears ; *l*, Apricots ; *m*, Plums, all upright trained. Reference to house ; *n*, ashpit ; *o*, earth closet ; *p*, coal-house ; *q*, pantry, over all store-rooms ; *r*, scullery ; *s*, sitting-room ; *t*, entry and stairs ; *u*, kitchen, three bedrooms over.

FRUIT TREES

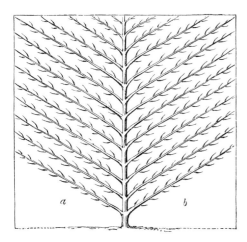

OBLIQUE TRAINING

Production, Tree Life, and Start of Bearing of Various Fruit Trees

Fruit tree	Years from planting to bearing	Useful life in years	Estimated production per tree at		
			3 years	6 years	10 years
Apples					
Dwarf	2 to 4	10 to 15	0 to 2 pecks	1 to 2 bushels	3 to 5 bushels
Semidwarf	3 to 4	15 to 20	0 to 2 pecks	1 to 3 bushels	4 to 10 bushels
Spur type	3 to 4	15 to 20	0 to 2 pecks	1 to 3 bushels	4 to 10 bushels
Standard	4 to 6	15 to 20	none	0 to 2 bushels	5 to 15 bushels
Apricot					
Standard	3 to 5	15 to 20	0 to 1 peck	1 to 2 bushels	2 to 4 bushels
Nectarine					
Standard	2 to 3	10 to 15	1 to 2 pecks	1 to 3 bushels	3 to 5 bushels
Peach					
Dwarf	2 to 3	5 to 10	1 to 2 pecks	1 to 2 bushels	1 to 2 bushels
Standard	2 to 3	10 to 15	1 to 2 pecks	1 to 3 bushels	3 to 5 bushels
Pear					
Dwarf	3 to 4	10 to 15	0 to 2 pecks	1 to 2 bushels	1 to 3 bushels
Plum					
Standard	3 to 5	15 to 20	0 to 2 pecks	1 to 2 bushels	3 to 5 bushels
Sour cherries					
Meteor, North Star, and Suda Hardy	2 to 3	10 to 15	0 to 1 peck	1 to 2 pecks	2 to 3 pecks
Standard	3 to 5	15 to 20	0 to 1 peck	2 to 4 pecks	8 to 12 pecks
Sweet cherry					
Standard	4 to 7	15 to 20	none	0 to 3 pecks	8 to 16 pecks

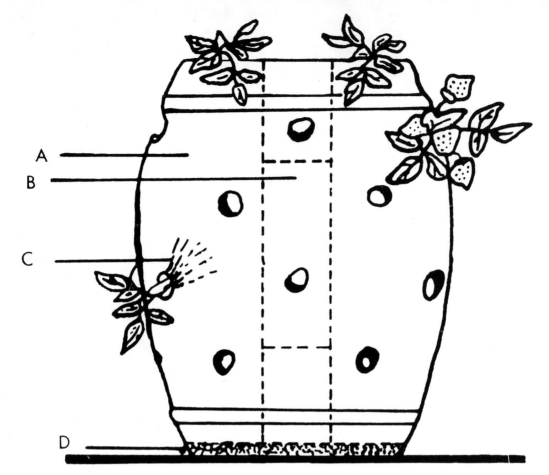

Construction of a strawberry barrel. A. Fertile garden soil. B. A core of sand for even watering, made by using a can as a form. C. Plants set with roots spread out and at a slight upward angle to allow for settling of the soil. D. Layer of gravel or broken crockery for drainage.

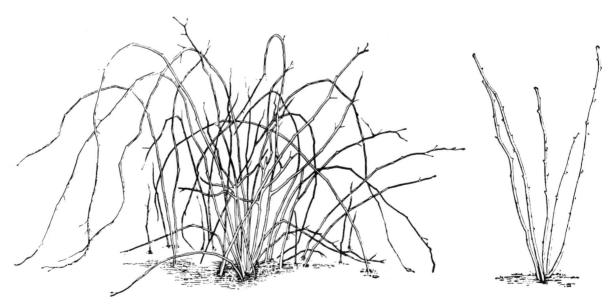

Red raspberry plant before (left) and after (right) dormant pruning.

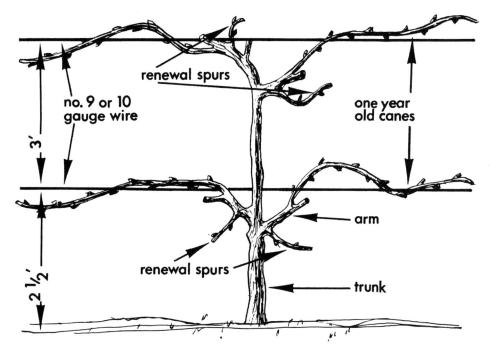

renewal spurs

no. 9 or 10 gauge wire

3'

one year old canes

arm

renewal spurs

trunk

2 ½'

A grapevine after three growing seasons. A maximum of 12 to 15 buds may be left on each lateral cane.

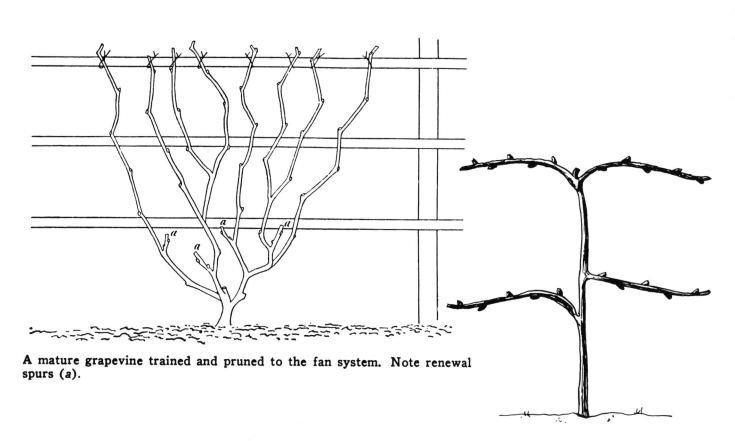

A mature grapevine trained and pruned to the fan system. Note renewal spurs (a).

After two growing seasons, 4 lateral canes may develop on vigorous plants, and 4 to 6 buds may be left on each lateral cane.

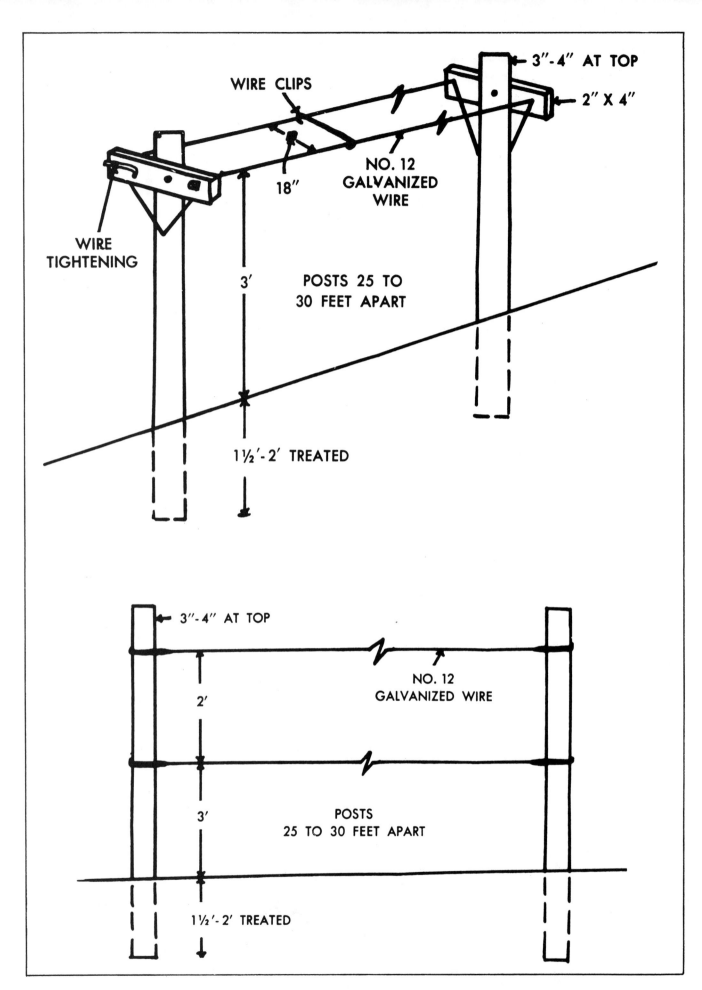

WIRE CLIPS

3"-4" AT TOP

2" X 4"

18"

NO. 12
GALVANIZED
WIRE

WIRE
TIGHTENING

3'

POSTS 25 TO
30 FEET APART

1½'-2' TREATED

3"-4" AT TOP

NO. 12
GALVANIZED WIRE

2'

3'

POSTS
25 TO 30 FEET APART

1½'-2' TREATED

Trellises. Horizontal trellis suitable for red raspberries, and which requires minimum tying of canes (top). Two-wire vertical trellis to which canes are tied (bottom).

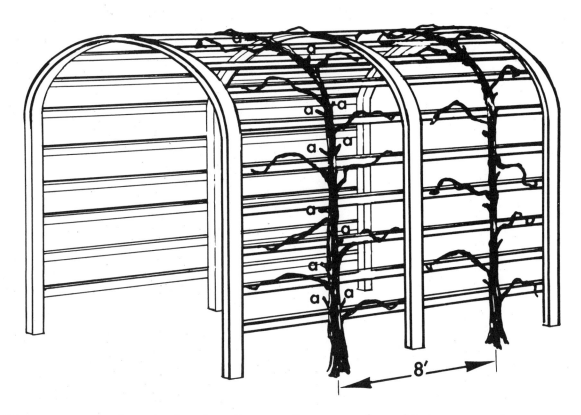

Mature grapevines trained and pruned on an arbor. Note renewal spurs a.

Fruit[a]	Planting distance[b]		Interval from planting to fruiting	Life of plants	Height of mature plant	Estimated annual yield per plant[c]	Suggested number of plants for family of 5
	Between rows	Between plants					
	feet	*feet*	*years*	*years*	*feet*		
Strawberries (matted row)............	4	2	1	3–4	1	½–1 qt. per foot of row	100
Currants.............................	6–8	4	2	12–15	3–4	3–4 quarts	4–6
Gooseberries........................	6–8	4	2	12–15	3–4	4–5 quarts	4–6
Raspberries							
Red...........................	6–8	3–4	1	8–10	4–5	1½ quarts	20–25
Black.........................	6–8	3–4	1	8–10	4–5	1 quart	20–25
Purple........................	6–8	3–4	1	8–10	4–5	1 quart	20–25
Blackberries							
Erect.........................	6–8	4–5	1	10–12	3–5	1 quart	15–20
Trailing or semi-trailing............	6–8	6–10	1	8–10	6–8 (staked or trellis)	4–10 quarts	8–10
Blueberries..........................	8–10	6–8	2	20+	6–10	3–4 quarts	8–10
Grapes..............................	8–10	8–10	3	20+	6 (trellised)	¼–½ bushel	5–10
Everbearing strawberries (hills)........	1–1½	1–1½	½	2–3	1	½ quart	100
Everbearing raspberries...............	8	3	½	8–10	4–5	1 quart—spring ½ quart—fall	15–20 15–20

SPACING, BEARING AGE, AND PRODUCTION OF SMALL FRUITS

[a] Listed in approximate order of ripening from early spring to fall.
[b] Minimum suggested spacings. See discussion of plant spacings in text.
[c] At full bearing age, with good care.

Suggested Planting Instructions

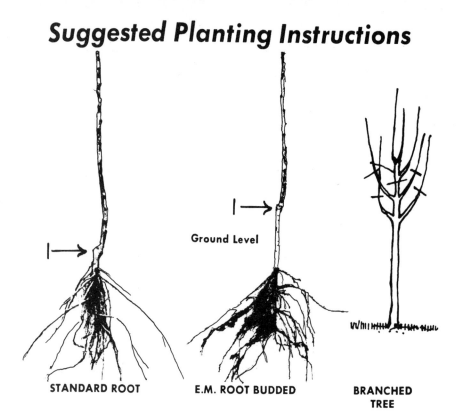

STANDARD ROOT **E.M. ROOT BUDDED** **BRANCHED TREE**

Ground Level

1. Proper Pruning is of first importance. One year "whip" prune back to 30"-36", Branched trees approximately 1/2 - 2/3 on branches, also top in proportion. Exception . . . if central leader training is planned, important to head trees rather severely.

2. Cut off any broken or badly bruised roots, all other roots should be shortened a little.

3. Hole should be large enough to spread out roots and so tree can be planted about depth indicated on above photo. Standard Root-bud union (1) plant about 2" below ground level, depending upon local climatic conditions. Malling Root-bud union (1) plant well above ground level to insure no eventual scion rooting.

4. During planting, use plenty of water and be sure soil is well worked in around roots so no "air pockets."

5. If replanting in old orchard soil, recommend using virgin soil in the hole.

6. Do not use packing material either with the soil or for mulching, and use fertilizer sparingly if at all. Exception . . . since introduction of slow release nitrogen fertilizers, such as Agriform Orchard Starter Tablets, new plantings can be safely fertilized and better results assured.

7. Water often and cultivate well during the first season. Watch for cut worms, insect pests and sun scald.

ORCHARD PLANTING CHART

Space between rows in feet.

	6	7	8	9	10	12	14	16	18	20	22	24	26	28	30	32	34	36	38	40
5	1452	1240	1089	966	871	726	622	544	484	435	396	363	335	311	290	272	256	242	229	208
6	1218	1037	907	806	727	605	518	453	403	363	330	302	279	259	242	226	213	201	191	181
8	907	777	680	605	544	453	388	339	302	272	247	226	209	194	181	169	160	151	143	121
10	726	622	544	484	435	363	311	272	242	218	207	181	167	155	145	136	128	121	114	108
12	605	518	453	403	362	302	259	226	201	181	165	151	139	129	121	113	106	100	95	90
14	518	444	388	345	311	259	222	194	172	155	141	129	119	111	103	97	91	86	81	77
16	453	388	339	302	272	226	194	169	151	136	123	113	104	97	90	85	80	75	71	66
18	403	345	302	268	224	201	172	151	134	121	110	100	93	86	80	75	70	67	63	60
20	363	311	272	242	218	181	155	136	121	108	99	90	83	77	72	66	64	60	57	53
22	330	282	247	220	207	165	141	123	110	99	90	82	76	70	66	61	58	55	52	48
24	302	259	226	201	181	151	129	113	100	90	82	75	69	64	60	56	53	50	47	45
26	279	239	209	196	167	139	119	104	93	83	76	69	64	59	55	52	49	46	44	41
28	259	222	194	172	155	129	111	97	86	77	70	64	59	55	51	48	45	43	40	38
30	242	207	181	161	145	121	103	90	80	72	66	60	55	51	48	45	42	40	38	36
32	226	194	169	151	136	113	97	85	75	66	61	56	52	48	45	42	40	37	35	34
34	213	183	160	145	128	106	91	80	70	64	58	53	49	45	42	40	37	35	33	32
36	210	172	151	134	121	100	86	75	67	60	55	50	46	43	40	37	35	33	31	30
38	191	164	143	127	114	95	81	71	63	53	52	47	44	40	38	35	33	31	30	28
40	181	155	136	121	108	90	77	66	60	54	48	45	41	38	36	34	32	30	28	27

Space between trees in the row in feet.

Number of trees per acre.

ORCHARD RENEWAL SYSTEMS

Any system of interplanting should be considered as an "orchard renewal," rather than "tree replacement" system. Many systems have been used for orchard renewal. The following systems based on a 30 x 30 planting can be used as examples, which give most of the possibilities.

Chart 1 . . . Replanting to the existing planting. In this system trees can be planted within the row between the old tree locations. Also, permanent or semi-permanent trees can be planted between rows. In a 30 x 30 planting the renewal orchard at 15 foot spacing will total 193 trees per acre.

If at some future time it is found desirable to remove a part of the trees, the alternate rows can be eliminated as indicated—with remaining trees or a diamond at 21.2 foot spacing (96 trees per acre). This is the easiest system and if the present planting distance is acceptable, it is a good system.

A variation of this planting is having rows 15 feet apart with trees within the row 10 feet apart, total 290 trees per acre. Advance planning is required as to methods of size control and training since extremely high density plantings are developed. This system does get the orchard back into production rapidly.

Chart 2 . . . Straddle row or offset spacing. With this system the orchard is renewed with 3 rows for each 2 existing rows. If the original spacing was 30 feet between rows, the new spacing becomes 20 feet. Trees are interplanted in every other existing row. In addition, 2 rows are planted straddling the alternate row and 20 feet on either side of it —217 trees per acre. This system allows replanting without tree removal and at such time the old permanent trees are removed, those necessary to fill every other existing row can be replanted.

Chart 3 . . . Other offset row system. Several other offset row systems may be included in renewals. By planting rows 7-1/2 feet on each side of existing rows, adequate work space is maintained, all trees are planted at one time and good planting distances can be established . . . eventually removing the old permanent trees without having to add additional replants. A more dense planting can be established with trees 10 feet apart within the row.

These orchard renewal systems together with complete block removal are but a few of the many systems which should be considered. Where existing trees are retained, they should be removed within 2 to 5 years to allow the new orchard to develop properly. The important thing is to utilize the trees now being planted so that they become productive units as soon as possible. Before beginning a renewal planting, time spent planning the renewal planting will be well rewarded.

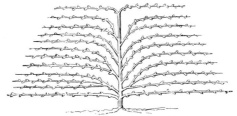

Fan and Horizontal Training combined.

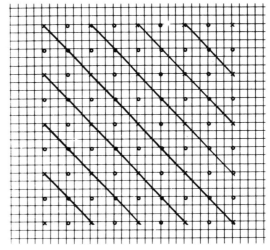

Chart 1

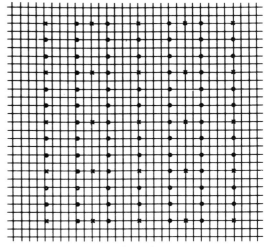

Chart 2

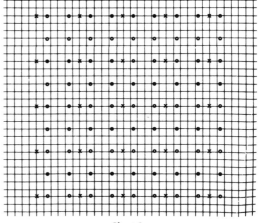

Chart 3

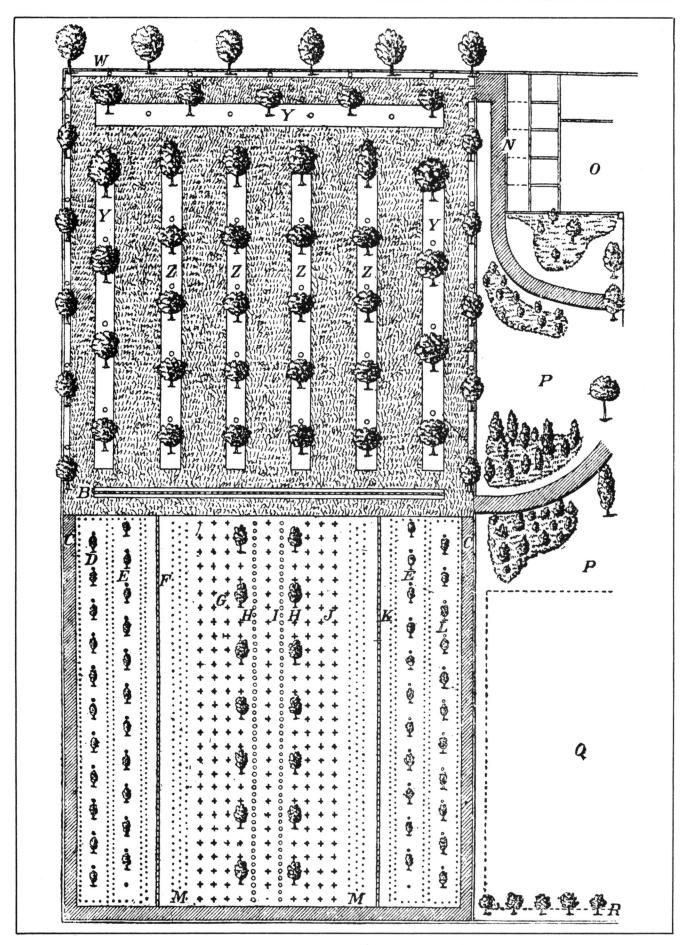

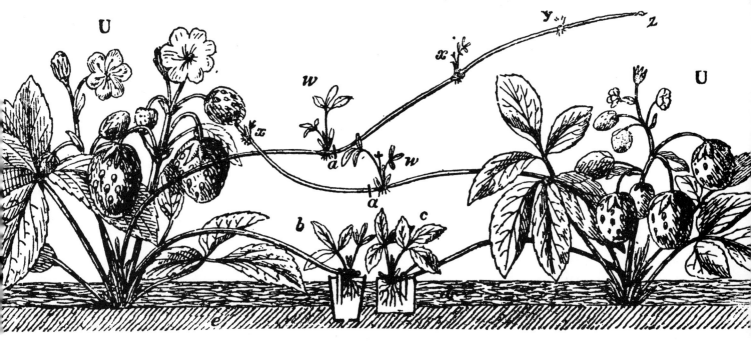

LAYERING STRAWBERRY RUNNERS

References: U, one-year-old plants in fruit:
w, first runners of layering size: x, second
runners, only to be used when runners are
scarce: y, third runners: z, runner wire extending;
a, point of cutting off runner wires; b, runner
layered in 3 in. pot and secured with a wire peg;
c, runner layered in square of turf, pegged and
emitting roots; d, chopped straw to keep
the fruit clean.

Key to plan at left.

A LARGE PRIVATE FRUIT GARDEN AND ORCHARD

References: W, Damsons, 15 ft. apart; X, strong culinary Plums, 15 ft. apart; Y, strong-growing Apples, 15 ft. apart; Z, Apples, with Pear at north end of strip, 12 ft. apart, 24 ft. between the rows; A, moderate-growing Plums, 15 ft. apart. The strips, in all cases, are equal in width to half the distance the trees are apart, but the outside strip is only half the width, including the hedge or fence clear of which the trees are planted. The permanent trees are portrayed; the small circles indicate the sites for temporary trees. The white space is soil kept clear for the trees, and manuring; the shaded part, grass. B, espalier for Cherry trees; C, gravel path; D, bush or pyramid Apples, or culinary Cherries, 6 ft. apart; E, bush or pyramid Pears, 6 ft. apart; F, espalier for large-fruited Apples, diagonal cordons; G, Gooseberry bushes, 5 ft. apart; H, dwarf standard Apples, Pears or Plums, 20 ft. apart, with Currants between; I, Blackberry, crosses; and Raspberry (two rows), small circles; J, Black, Red and White Currants, 5 ft. apart; K, espalier for large-fruited Pears, diagonal cordons; L, choice bush or pyramid Plums, 6 ft. apart. All the permanent trees are shown; the temporary in the same lines are represented by dots. The bush or pyramid Apple, Pear and Plum tree borders are margined by Strawberries; also espaliers for Apple and Pear, shown by the dotted lines. M, Strawberries; N, poultry houses and yard; O, stable yard; P, pleasure ground; Q, tennis ground; R, standard double Thorn, Laburnum and other ornamental trees.

BOOK THREE...THE GARDEN

After the basics, and the general cultivation methods of the plants to be selected for the garden, we go into the area to be planted, built and designed. Every professional walks into this area with a notebook for roughing out the dimensions of the space, and for general information like existing trees or shrubs, existing stone work like walls and walks, available sunlight and its directions, and finally the wind directions if you live on a terrace or roof garden. Of course wind direction is important anywhere, for many plants, such as rhododendrons and other broadleaf evergreens, will not tolerate a strong winter wind.

Before you begin to pick the plants out of picture books or from memory, I suggest you find out what is available in your area by visiting a few garden centers or nurseries. Many times certain plants are available in only certain seasons and if you want to make room for a continual color you must leave room for those plants or bulbs. For example, fall flowering mums are usually available only in the fall. That is when they are the most saleable for they are in color. But you must remember that these are perennials and will be green all summer until the fall flowering season. If you only have a small amount of space, say in a city backyard, and want color all summer, you could put a few mums in a couple of tubs or boxes and leave the beds for annuals that will provide color all summer.

All I am saying is to plan for what you want and do not let the space overcome you. Too many gardens after a few seasons tend to take over due to poor planning and poor maintenance. You should grow what you want in the space that you have, of course taking into consideration light availability and climatical conditions. You can't grow oranges outside in the northeast, but holly does not do so well on the desert, either.

Having been a part of many plant selection committees I will now proceed—in print—into the empty space and talk about weather, soil, maybe a favorite plant like old-fashioned lilac. What you suggest comes up after every lull in the conversation, and finally there is the matter of what all this will cost.

The cost depends on you. You can pick the most expensive plants like very rare alpine plants of an evergreen nature, or your choice can be a bucket of pansies. You can have a formal Japanese garden built, or maybe an old-fashioned English garden with an aquatic pond for water lilies, or you can plant a tree and a couple of roses. The price breakdown is something you must take into consideration before you begin the long process of planning and building a garden. If price is of no concern, and I have had such clientele (they are always called clientele if price is of no concern), then you can stand back and watch the professional design, lay out and plant almost any kind of garden to scale to fit your area. But if you fall into the general realm of reality where money is of importance, before you begin asking questions do a little research into the price, structure of plants, stone work, sodding versus grass seed, and labor costs of all of the above.

Come as an informed consumer and you will get the best answers. If you can tell the difference between a norway spruce (green tipped) and a colorado blue (blue tipped but turns green) and a costa blue spruce (all blue) and the cost of all three, this sort of broad information will make the professional give you good answers to your questions. If you come into a garden center and ask for a Christmas tree in July, the owner will probably let you speak to the kid that works part time. Go to the expert and do not waste his or her time. Most city and small-plot gardeners are totally at the mercy of the garden store operators. This is where they keep the plants, the annuals, the bulbs, the fertilizer and the tools. This is where the information is and where the fun begins.

There are two different kinds of backyards. The first are found in the big cities like New York City and the others are found in cities like Syracuse or Dallas. The New York City type of backyard usually is a shaded, overly humid place that will not get very much sunlight throughout the entire day. Special consideration must be afforded to the selection of plants and the methods of planting.

I have personal experience with both types of space and can relate that they are as different as black and white. I could not grow good roses or high sunlight annuals in my New York City backyard and the yard I had in Syracuse I could not grow those plants that need shade to survive. In the Back of the Book I have a selection of good plants for the shade and good plants for the sun. There is some mixing but if you stick to the well-established shady location flowers and those that really do need a lot of sun you can not make too many mistakes. You can go out and spend a lot of money and buy a lot of flowers that will end up as long green shoots without flowers or you can spend your money and buy the right plant.

The problem of too much moistness in the backyards is due to lack of sunlight and sometimes to poor drainage. You can not correct the light problem but you can correct the soil condition. If most of your plants in the backyard are in the ground I would suggest a sandy loam or mix in some perilite or vermiculite for a loose soil. This not only helps the plants develop but will allow the water to drain through more easily.

If you do have a "fast running soil" you have to supply more fertilizer than normal and I suggest you feed the plants (ornamental) with a foliage feeder. This is liquid fertilizer that is sprayed on the foliage for fast reaction. Many nurseries use this type of feeding to improve the appearance of the green parts of the plants before sale. This also applies to any container-grown plant material. Most containers should be planted with a good loose mix such as mentioned above and the plants should be watered and fed more often. This may take a little more work but the results will be well worth your time. If your backyard is built on fill or hardpan directly under the top soil I would drive holes into the pan or fill to allow for better drainage. This can be done by pounding a steel pipe into the ground every few feet and breaking the impervious layer. It always works. It is simple and solves the problems of water accumulating on the surface. If you have very little topsoil and the root systems are just above the hardpan, root damage could result to all of your plants including evergreens and the trees and shrubs.

On the back jacket of the book you will see a maze of color that flowered in a very shady backyard in New York City. The annuals are begonias (fiberous rooted), impatiens, salvia, coleus, and the ground cover is English and Baltic ivy. I also would recommend for a maintenance-free yard ground cover that has a flower like ajuga or vinca and broadleaf evergreens like rhododendrons.

Your selection for city backyards may be more limited but can be as interesting as any other garden. Many native plants such as ferns prefer the shade, for in the wild state they grow in dense forests. If you want to mix ivy and ferns, begonias and aguga, salvia and rhododendrons, skimma and tuberous begonias, or all of the above you can have a color show and green show that will be as fine as any garden. Grow what you can but grow it right.

The other kind of backyard is just a smaller version of any suburban yard and usually has plenty of sunlight without the problems of big-city yards where you are surrounded by buildings. In this yard you can grow most flowers and vegetables without any real problems. This yard usually has a few containers but most of the planting is directly in the ground or beds. The only problem that one might have is space. Of course this is always the problem with all small-plot gardeners and, depending on what you have in mind, can be overcome by careful planning.

If you really plan the space and understand the growing habits of plants (you do not plant melons that need a great deal of space), then even if you only have a few feet you can grow a couple of vegetables. Grow something with an upright growing habit or that will grow up a trellis. Most of small-plot gardening is common sense and general understanding of the amount of space a mature vegetable or ornamental plant needs to produce fruit or full blossoms. I have put in the Back of the Book good charts that list the growing habits of most of our common vegetables and flowers. This information is generally given in spacing requirements for each row or plant. On the back of seed packages you will also find many cultural and spacing requirements. If you could just keep these packages and paste them on boards, after a few seasons you would probably have as good a book on how to grow as the most expensive gardening books. If you cannot find information in a hurry in a book then the book is worthless. The Back of the Book has such maps and charts to be used as you use tools.

Terraces and Rooftops

A terrace or rooftop is a very special place, high in the air overlooking a large-city skyline. Years have proven that some of the most beautiful gardens in the world are surrounding penthouses hanging, like gardens of old, off the sides of giant buildings. This kind of garden is usually container gardening. I have seen many permanent beds, built right into the roof or terrace, but by and large the secret of successful terrace and rooftop gardening is the proper use of the container. I have included in the section called Basics a special listing of container sizes and proper soil mixes. And I repeat here that proper handling of containers is the key to beautiful gardens where the sun comes in at all directions and the wind is a very important factor. Plants have to be planted and arranged in a certain way on terraces and rooftops to protect them from the city heat, the direct sunlight and the colder winds of winter. When I say that the containers are the key to success, this includes the location of the container as well as the proper soil mixes and correct planting procedure. On the next few pages I will show you pictures of various kinds of containers and the proper way to plant trees, shrubs, bulbs, flowers and so on. Once the plants are in the containers you then have to contend with the elements. First let's discuss the wind.

Terraces and rooftops are windswept and cold in the winter months. Plants must be protected either by covering the containers with burlap or covering with some mulch-like straw or evergreen branches. All of the smaller deciduous trees, especially fruit trees, should have the trunks wrapped with tree wrap (you can buy this product at any garden center) to prevent winter cracking of the bark of the trunk. The cause of this is the hot winter sun on one side of the tree while the other side is extremely cold. The difference of temperatures causes damage to the trunk. If you prune in the fall, cover the wounds with a sealer. All new plants should be wrapped and staked for at least a few years until the root sections have had a chance to develop to the point of not being disturbed by the winds. All evergreens and broadleaf evergreens should be covered with boards built over them. Never wrap burlap around an evergreen for when the burlap has been wet and gets cold and freezes and the freezing may reach the needs or foliage of the plant. This is the same reason—the freezing—you never plant under a drip line of a house where the winter water will hit the plant. This will freeze the foliage as well as wet burlap would. Let the air circulate around the plants but keep the wind off of them.

The Suburban Scene

Where does one begin when considering such a wide diversity as the suburban homes and gardens? I have designed many complete suburban homes from the construction of the lawn to the planning and planting of the garden. Each one was different, each had its own characteristics. There are many books written by landscape architects and garden planners with very complicated plans that only an architect could read and only someone living in a two hundred thousand dollar house could afford. I love these gardens and the houses, but to begin with simple ranch-type suburban houses and expand to very elaborate English tudors would fill as many pages as writing about the causes and effects of history on our civilization. I want to give you something to work with so I have broken the planning down into sections. All property has corners, driveways and walks. Most have backyards and front lawns.

As one pulls up to any suburban home the first thing you see is the total effect and the combinations of plants. The overall design has to be taken into consideration. If you plan the small areas and plant properly you will get the total effect you are looking for.

Let us start with the front of the house and gradually work our way to the backyard and the recreation areas. The front of the house is usually show and not utilized as a play area. All of the touch football, the swimming, and cook-outs are done in the rear of the house. The front is just lawn and a good foundation planting. If you are in a home without older trees on the property I suggest you start by placing shade trees in the right places (see drawings) for shade, wind breaks and design. Larger trees are usually used to frame the house and sort of make the house and the smaller plants a picture. You should use shade trees for all of the above and it can be done.

After you have picked the sites for the shade trees and the larger plants you then begin to fill

and design around the larger plants. This is the place you might need some professional help, but if you want to go it alone you must understand all the sizes and shapes of the plants to be used in the foundation planting. If you buy all deciduous plants, you will have nothing but branches and twigs in the winter. If you mix evergreens (needled and broadleaf) with flowering shrubs and leave room for flowers in season you are on the right track. Travel around your area and look at some attractive plantings. Go up and ask the people what the plants are and inquire where they bought them. Most people love to talk about their gardens and if you pay them a nice compliment they will maybe invite you in for tea. Gardens are very personal and gardeners are always ready to tell all. If you see a nice grouping of plants, go talk to the owners. If they don't mind, take a picture and use it for a planting key. This is how landscape salesmen sell new work—by taking photographs of existing work. After you have collected these mental and photographic pictures, rough out what you like of all the possibilities.

Flowers yellow.
 Opening 11 to 12 A. M.
  Spreading by runners..............N. Mexicana
  Without runners......N. tetragona, var. helvola
 Opening from 7 to 8 A. M.
  Petals broad, concave; flower cup-shaped,
    N. Marliacea, var. chromatella
  Petals narrow, spreading........N. odorata, var.
   sulphurea and N. sulphurea, var. grandiflora
Flowers pure white.
 Leaves ovate, small.................N. tetragona
 Leaves circular.
  Strongly sweet-scented.
   Flowers 2-5 in. across; lvs. 4-8 in......N. odorata
   Flowers 1-3 in. across; lvs. 3-5 in..N. o., var. minor
   Flowers 3-6 in. across; lvs. 8-12 in.....N. o., var.
     gigantea
  Odorless or nearly so.
   Petiole marked with longitudinal brown stripes,
     N. tuberosa
    Flowers very double..N. t., var. Richardsonii
   Petiole uniformly colored.
    Sepals rounded to the receptacle.
     Always sterile.
      Flowers and leaves rising from the water,
        N. Marliacea, var. albida

      Flowers and leaves floating,
        N. alba, var. candidissima
     Fertile.
      Petals spreading in all directions,
        N. Gladstoniana
      Flower more cup-shaped.........N. alba
       Very double......N. a., var. plenissima
       Very large.........N. a., var. maxima
    Sepals joining the receptacle by a sharp angle,
      N. candida
Flowers red or pink.
 Flowers small, pink, opening about 11 A. M.
  Plant a single crown without offshoots,
    N. Laydekeri, var. rosea
  Plant with many side shoots,
    N. Laydekeri, var. prolifera

Flowers 3-7 inches across.
 Petals all alike in color—pink.
  Leaves deep red beneath..N. odorata, var. rosea;
    N. exquisita; N. rosacea
  Leaves pink or green beneath....N. Caroliniana;
    N. odorata, var. Luciana; N. tuberosa,
    var. rosea; N. t., var. superba
 Outer petals whitish, shading to pink or red at centre
   of flower.
  Plants very robust; fls. and lvs. rising above water.
   Flowers soft flesh pink......N. Marliacea, var.
     carnea; N. Wm. Doogue
   Flowers deep rose color.N. Marliacea,var. rosea
  Less robust; fls. floating, deep red at centre.
   Leaves blotched with brown.
    Flowers rosy lilac..N. Laydekeri, var. lilacea
    Flowers deep red.
     Sepals and petals in fives.....N. gloriosa
     Sepals and petals in fours.
      Stamens deep orange.
        N. Marliacea, var. flammea
      Stamens cardinal....N. Marliacea, var.
        ignea
   Leaves dark green.
    Fertile.
     Inner petals bright red..N. alba, var. rubra
     Inner petals deep carmine....N. Froebelii
    Sterile hybrids.
     Flowers opening in early morning..N. Wm.
       Falconer; N. James Gurney; N.
       James Brydon

     Flowers opening after 9 A. M..N. Ellisiana;
       N. sanguinea; N. Marliacea, var.
       rubro punctata; N. Laydekeri, var.
       purpurea
 Outer petals yellowish, shading to red at centre of flower
  Leaf with a notch on border of sinus.N.Robinsoni
  Sinus entire.N. Seignoreti; N. aurora; N. fulva;
   N. Andreana; N. lucida; N. Laydekeri
   fulgens; N. chrysantha; N. Arethusa; N.
   Arc-en-ciel

AQUATIC POOL DESIGN

A listing of plants for aquatic pools is found in the Back of the Book.

Building around natural landscapes such as stone or trees creates additional beauty.

Leave room for outdoor furniture and room to move about.

Informal use of stone creates a natural surrounding. Try and build a pool that looks like it always has been there.

Containers on the deck.

Leaves on the pool.

A FORMAL PERMANENT STONE WALK
THIS IS A JOB FOR AN EXPERIENCED STONE MASON
OR VERY SERIOUS STUDENT OF GARDEN DESIGN.

INFORMAL STONE PATTERNS
THESE SMALL BACKYARD PATTERNS ARE USUALLY CONSTRUCTED
ON A BED OF SAND WITH A PEA GRAVEL BASE. AFTER THE FIRST COLD
SEASON THE STONE WILL SETTLE AND A NICE TOUCH IS TO PLANT GRASS
BETWEEN THE STONE. YOU CAN USUALLY FIND BROKEN STONE PERFECT
FOR SUCH DESIGNS ANYWHERE A CONSTRUCTION CREW IS PUTTING IN A
FORMAL PATIO OR STONE FRONT HOUSE.

TREES

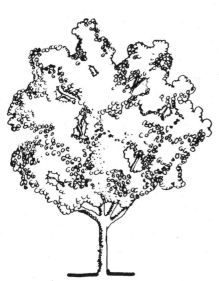

ROUND—GLOBE—SHAPED

Arnold Crabapple • Japanese Maple
Mulberry • Green Ash • Pistachio
Hawthorne Sycamore

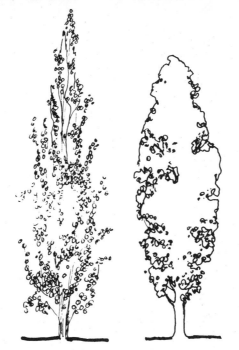

FASTIGIATE TREE OR COLUMNAR TREE

Dawyck Beech • Siberian Crabapple
English Oak • Poplar • Sargent Cherry
Sentry Ginkgo • Lombardy Poplar
Pyramidal European Birch
Linden

BROAD OVAL TREE

Bradford Pear
Sugar Maple • Labarnum
European Mountain Ash

FAN SHAPED—HORIZONTAL BRANCHING

Flowering Dogwood
Silk Tree • Redbud
Amur Maple

SHRUBS

MEDIUM 5'–12'

Snowball • Forsythia • English Privet

TALL 12'–18'

Crapemyrtle • Spindle Tree
Russian Olive • Lilac

LOW 1½'–5'

February Daphne • Bush Cinquefoil
Anthony Waterer Spirea
Japanese Barberry

LOW, GROUND COVER OR VINES

CONICAL TREE OR TRIANGLE

American Sweetgum
Pin Oak

Prostrate Pyracantha

GROUND COVER 6"–18"

Cranberry Cotoneaster
Carpet Bugle • Memorial Rose
Aaronsbeard St. Johnswort

Lantana

VINES

Wisteria • Passionflower • Bittersweet
Virginia Creeper • Clematis • Grapes

144

CONIFERS

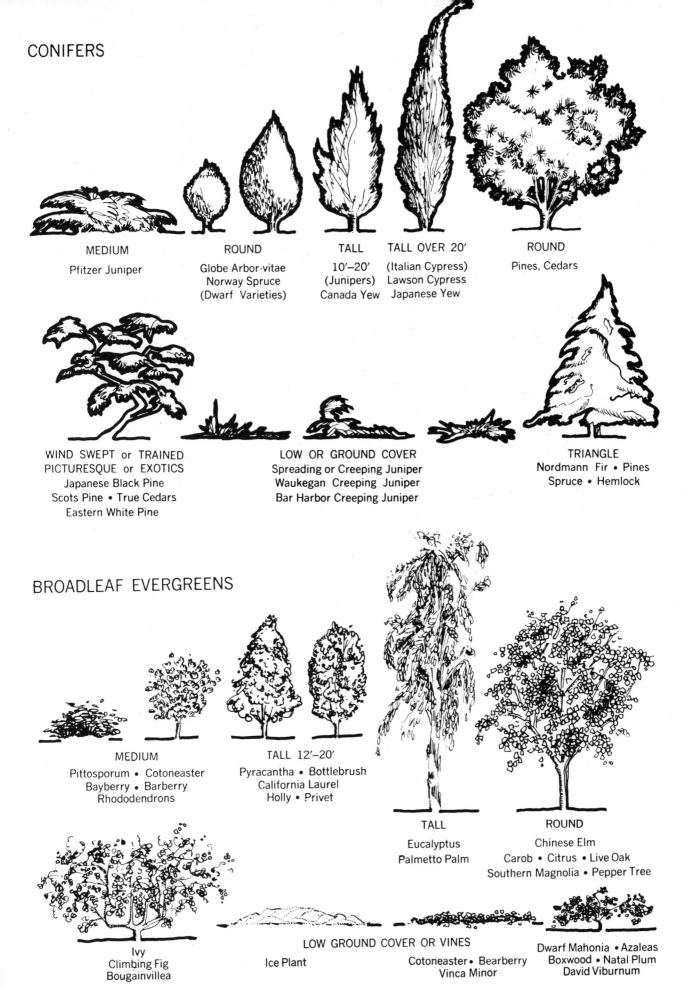

MEDIUM
Pfitzer Juniper

ROUND
Globe Arbor-vitae
Norway Spruce
(Dwarf Varieties)

TALL
10'–20'
(Junipers)
Canada Yew

TALL OVER 20'
(Italian Cypress)
Lawson Cypress
Japanese Yew

ROUND
Pines, Cedars

**WIND SWEPT or TRAINED
PICTURESQUE or EXOTICS**
Japanese Black Pine
Scots Pine • True Cedars
Eastern White Pine

LOW OR GROUND COVER
Spreading or Creeping Juniper
Waukegan Creeping Juniper
Bar Harbor Creeping Juniper

TRIANGLE
Nordmann Fir • Pines
Spruce • Hemlock

BROADLEAF EVERGREENS

MEDIUM
Pittosporum • Cotoneaster
Bayberry • Barberry
Rhododendrons

TALL 12'–20'
Pyracantha • Bottlebrush
California Laurel
Holly • Privet

TALL
Eucalyptus
Palmetto Palm

ROUND
Chinese Elm
Carob • Citrus • Live Oak
Southern Magnolia • Pepper Tree

Ivy
Climbing Fig
Bougainvillea

LOW GROUND COVER OR VINES
Ice Plant

Cotoneaster • Bearberry
Vinca Minor

Dwarf Mahonia • Azaleas
Boxwood • Natal Plum
David Viburnum

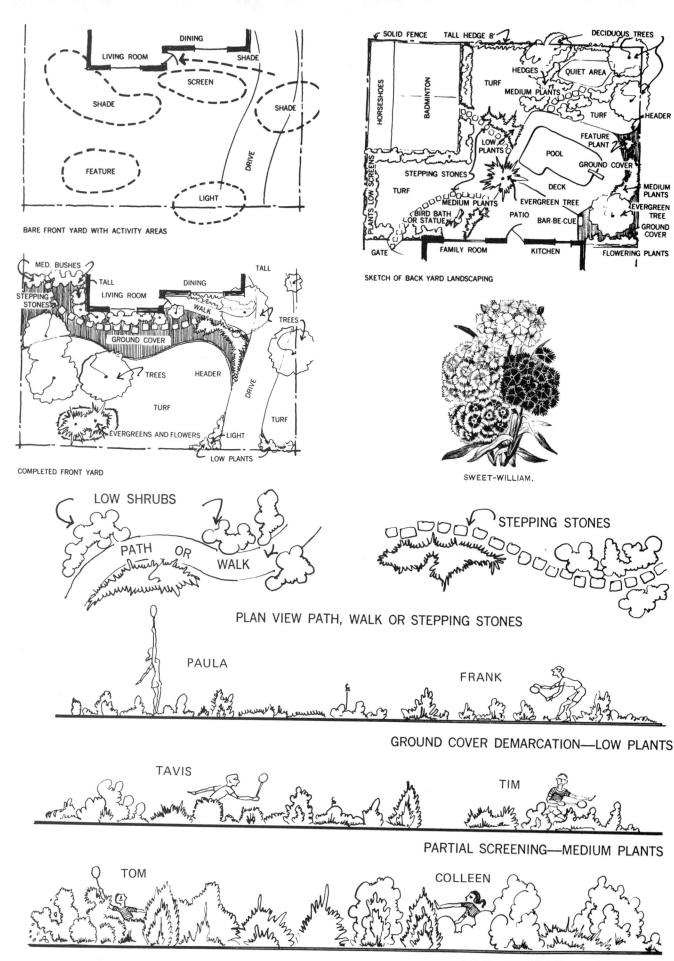

BARE FRONT YARD WITH ACTIVITY AREAS

SKETCH OF BACK YARD LANDSCAPING

COMPLETED FRONT YARD

SWEET-WILLIAM.

PLAN VIEW PATH, WALK OR STEPPING STONES

GROUND COVER DEMARCATION—LOW PLANTS

PARTIAL SCREENING—MEDIUM PLANTS

SOLID SCREENING—TALL PLANTS

146

FRONT DOOR—SUBURBAN

The front entrance should be framed with upright evergreens for summer and winter color. Have space between the major plants for flowers in season as indicated in photo. The hanging basket balances the entrance and door.

PLANT KEY

1. Upright yew
2. Andorra juniper
3. Upright euonymus
4. Mugho pine
5. Pachysandra
6. Mums
7. Fuchsia (hanging)
8. Vinca minor (myrtle)

ROCK GARDENS

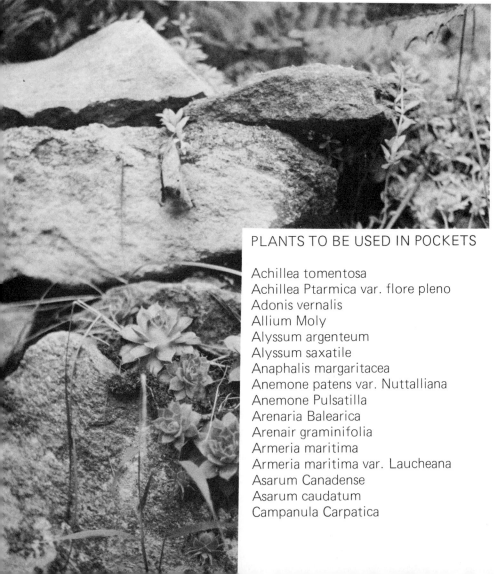

PLANTS TO BE USED IN POCKETS

Achillea tomentosa
Achillea Ptarmica var. flore pleno
Adonis vernalis
Allium Moly
Alyssum argenteum
Alyssum saxatile
Anaphalis margaritacea
Anemone patens var. Nuttalliana
Anemone Pulsatilla
Arenaria Balearica
Arenair graminifolia
Armeria maritima
Armeria maritima var. Laucheana
Asarum Canadense
Asarum caudatum
Campanula Carpatica

Campanula persicifolia
Ceratosigma plumbaginoides
Colchicum autumnale
Coreopsis rosea
Corydalis glauca
Corydalis nobilis
Cotyledon spinosa
Dianthus atrorubens
Dianthus fragrans
Dianthus plumarius
Dicentra Canadensis
Dicentra cucullaria
Dodocatheon Meadia
Doronicum Caucasicum
Draba incana var. arabisans
Dracocephalum nutans
Epigaea repens
Galax aphylla
Gentiana acaulis
Gentiana Andrewsi
Gentiana Saponaria
Gentiana verna
Gerandium Robertianun
Gypsophila repens
Helianthemum lavandulaefolium
Helianthemum vulgare
Hepatica acutiloba
Hepatica triloba
Heuchera sanguinea
Iberis sempervirens
Iberis Tenoriana
Iris pumila
Iris verna
Leucojum aestivum
Linum perenne
Lotus corniculatus

Lychnis Viscaria var. splendens
Mertensia Virginica
Oenothera Missouriensis
Ornithogalum umbellatum
Platycodon grandifolrum var. Mariesii
Polemonium humile
Polemonium reptans
Potentilla Sibbaldia
Potentilla splendens
Primula elatior
Primula farinosa
Primula officinalis
Primula vulgaris
Prunella grandiflora
Pyrola rotundifolia
Rhazya orientalis
Rhexia Virginica
Sabbatia campestris
Sagina procumbens
Saxifraga aizoides
Saxifraga Aizoon
Saxifraga granulata
Saxifraga umbrosa
Scilla Sibirica
Sedum roseum
Sedum spectabile
Sempervivum arachnoideum
Sempervivum fimbriatum
Sempervivum Pomelii
Sempervivum tectorum
Shortia galacifolia
Silene Zawadskii
Statice Gmelini
Stokesia cyanea
Trautvetteria palmata
Trollium Asiaticus
Trollius laxus
Tunica Saxifraga
Veronica gentianoides
Veronica incana
Veronica Ponae
Veronica spuria
Viola cucullata
Waldsteinia fragarioides

PLANTS FOR MOIST PLACES

Calla palustris
Lobelia cardinalis
Lobelia syphilitica
Myosotis palustris
Parnassia Caroliniana
Parnassia palustris
Pinguicula vulgaris
Potentilla palustris
Saxifraga Pennsylvanica
Spigelia Marilandica
Spiranthes cernua
Ranunculus flammula

PLANTS MOST SUITABLE FOR THE DEEPEST RECESSES

Anemone Japanica
Convallaria majalis
Cornus Canadensis
Cypripedium parviflorum
Cypripedium pubescens
Cypripedium spectabile
Dicentra spectabilis
Dictannus albus
Funkia lancifolia
Funkia lancifolia var. albo-marginata
Funkia ovata
Funkia Sieboldiana
Helleborus niger
Lobelia cardinalis
Lobelia syphilitica
Orchis latifolia
Pachysandra terminalis
Polygonatum biflorum
Saxifraga crassifolia
Tiarella cordifolia
Trillium cernuum
Trillium grandiflorum
Trillium sessile
Uvularia grandiflora
Viola Canadensis
Viola striata

PLANTS FOR CONSPICUOUS POSITIONS

Acanthus mollis
Acanthus candelabrum
Aquilegia Canadensis
Aquilegia caerulea
Aquilegia Olympica
Dictamnus Fraxinella
Digitalis purpurea
Eryngium planum
Fritallaria imperialis
Lychnis Chalcedonica
Papaver nudicaule
Papaver orientale
Spiraea Aruncus
Verbascum Chaixii

150

PLANTS FOR OVERHANGING LEDGES

Ajuga Genevensis
Ajuga reptans
Antennaria plantaginea
Anthemis nobilis
Arabis albida
Aubrietia deltoidea
Cerastium Bierbersteinii
Cerastium purpurascens
Cerastium tomentosum
Daphne Cneorum
Linnaea borealis var. Americana
Mitchella repens
Phlox reptans
Phlox subulata alba
Phlox subulata atropurpurea
Sedum acre
Sedum album
Sedum Hispanicum
Sedum purpureum
Sedum Sieboldi
Sedum Sieboldi var. variegatum
Sedum ternatum
Stellaria graminea
Stellaria Holostea
Veronica rupestris
Vinca minor

SOME OF THE BEST OF THE TRUE ALPINES

Androsace alpina
Androsace sarmentosa
Anemone alpina
Antennaria alpina
Aquilegia alpina
America alpina
Cerastium alpinum
Cheiranthus alpinus
Campanula Garganica
Campanula muralis
Campanula pulla
Campanula rotundifolia
Campanula turbinata
Campanula Waldsteinii
Dianthus alpinus
Dianthus glacialis
Gentina verna
Geum montanum
Globularia nana
Leontopodium alpinum (Edelweiss)
Linaria alpina
Lychnis alpina
Potentilla aurea
Primula Mistassinica
Reseda glauca
Saxifraga caesia
Saxifraga Cotyledon
Saxifraga Cotyledon var. pyramidalis
Saxifraga crustata
Saxifraga geranioides
Saxifraga longifolia
Saxifraga oppositifolia
Silene acaulis
Soldanella alpina
Veronica alpina

WILD FLOWERS

MARSH MARIGOLD

WHITE

American bugbane
Bearberry
Bishop's-cap
Black cohosh
Bloodroot
Boneset
Bowman's root
Bunchberry
Canada anemone
Canada mayflower
Canada violet
Common yarrow
Confederate violet
Creeping snowberry
Culver's root
Dutchman's-breeches
Dwarf ginseng
Early white snakeroot
False spikenard
Flat-topped aster
Frostflower aster
Galax
Ginseng
Golden seal
Goldthread
Grass of Parnassus
Hairy alumroot
Hepatica
Large white trillium
Mayapple
Mountain lady's-slipper
Musk mallow
Nodding mandarin
Nodding trillium
Ox-eye daisy
Ozard trillium
Painted trillium
Partridgeberry
Purple loosestrife
Pussytoes
Red baneberry
Rock geranium
Rue anemone
Seneca snakeroot
Shinleaf
Shooting star
Showy lady's-slipper
Small white lady's-slipper
Snow trillium
Spikenard
Spring beauty
Squirrel corn
Starflower
Star-flowered false Solomon's
Star-of-Bethlehem
Sweet white violet
Tall meadow rue
Trailing arbutus
Twinflower
Twinleaf
Two-leaved toothwort
White baneberry
White mertensia
White phlox
White turtlehead
Wild calla
Wintergreen
Wood anemone
Woodland strawberry

PINK TO RED

Bearberry
Blazing Star
Bowman's root
Cardinal flower
Common milkweed
False dragonhead
Fringed polygala
Jessie's red violet
Joe-pye
Kansas gay feather
Mountain phlox
Musk mallow
Nodding wild onion
Oswego tea
Partridgeberry
Pink bleeding heart
Pink lady's-slipper
Pink skullcap
Prairie phlox
Prairie smoke
Prairie trillium
Purple corydalis
Purple trillium
Queen of the Prairie
Red turtlehead
Rose Mandarin
Rose trillium
Rose verbena
Rue anemone
Shooting star
Spotted cranesbill
Spring beauty
Swamp milkweed
Toadshade
Trailing arbutus
Twinflower
Two-leaved toothwort
Western bleeding heart
Wild ginger
Wine cups

YELLOW

Barren strawberry
Blue cohost
Bluebead lily
Canada goldenrod
Canada lily
Celandine poppy
Common cinquefoil
Common tansy
Cypress spurge
Downy yellow violet
Ginseng
Golden ragwort
Grass-leaved goldenrod
Hoary puccoon
Indian cucumber
Lady's mantle
Lakeside daisy
Large yellow lady's slipper
Marsh marigold
Merrybells
Moneywort
Nodding mandarin
Ox-eye
Prairie goldenrod
Silverweed
Smooth yellow violet
Solomon's seal
Stoneroot
Swamp candles
Trout lily
Wild oats
Wild senna
Yellow stargrass
Yellow trillium

ORANGE

Blackberry lily
Butterfly flower
Canada lily
Michigan lily
Tiger lily
Turk's-cap lily
Wild columbine
Wood lily

FALSE SOLOMON'S SEAL

1. Opuntia
2. Cereus
3. Opuntia streptacantha
4. Cereus candicans
5. Mammillaria
6. Cereus peruvians monstrosus
7. Cereus electracanthus
8. Mammillaria
9. Echinopsis formosa
10. Echinocactus Visnaga
11. Cereus peruvianus var.
12. Opuntia candelabriformis
13. Cereus strictus
14. Pilocereus senilis
15. Cereus Tweedii
16. Cereus chilensis

WILD GARDENS

Years ago the building of a wild place in the garden could indicate a leaning toward the natural habitats of native wild plants. Many naturalists and botanists used these gardens as identification and study places. The general idea was to build and maintain a place that had the same ecology as a parallel place in the wild. As the use of these wild gardens increased many gardeners who only grew the cultivated domestic varieties of flowers began to grow a few wild plants such as ferns and native orchids. Today this is a vast hobby and a big part of the horticultural business.

Most wild flowers are very special and need a great deal of care in an artificial garden. I suggest you read up on the subject and then try to build a place suggested by your reading. For example, ferns need shade and moisture and field flowers need a lot of sunlight and good ventilation. A lot of humus and a good garden loam will do for most of the native wild flowers of the northeast. The special mountain ecologies and arid locations for the west and the southwest are indeed unique. Only buy and grow what is natural and normal in your locale.

It was a practice years ago to go into the wild and collect the various plants needed. With the wild places of the country getting smaller and the wild plants getting thinner and thinner I suggest you buy from a wild plant dealer or collect seed and grow your own. The beauty of wild gardens is sort of overwhelming but do not dig if you can buy.

PROTECTING SHADE TREES

PROTECTING SHADE TREES DURING
HOME CONSTRUCTION OR WHILE
REBUILDING THE GARDEN

If you are buying a new home or building a new home or just moving in to an established house, and want to expand the garden, try and save the shade trees and larger plants. Design around them and try not to cut except where damage or destruction would otherwise result to the structure. Shade trees add thousands of dollars to the value of any residential property, not to mention the beauty of a sugar maple in the fall or a dogwood in the spring. Yet many homebuilders remove and cut before the new owner has had a chance of converse with a qualified landscape person.

Many trees can be saved with little expense and most big plants are worth the expense of saving. You cannot replace a 50-year-old tree. They do not sell them in most nurseries. Yes, I have heard of plantings of large plants by landscape architects for commercial works but the average gardener and homeowner is not in that league.

But some trees are worth the expense. How can you tell what should be paid to save a plant? A good check list for evaluating the trees to save and cost of saving them is:
1. Consider the location
2. Species
3. Size and Age
4. Vigor
Then consider the cost involved and the work necessary and make a decision based on a combination of all the above facts.

Location

The main consideration in location is whether the plant will fit into the landscape and provide shade where you want it. When a tree hinders the growth of the lawn or garden it is not worth the trouble to save it. If the plant acts as a windbreak during the winter months but prevents the summer breezes from freely circulating, then you have to choose between the two. Does the tree block a vista or does it hide an unpleasant view? Would you plant a tree in this location if none existed?

Considering all of the questions it may be hard to decide. If you have to call a professional landscape person in to make a rational decision, then do so. Do not try and judge for yourself such an important and costly step. A professional probably will see it another way or hopefully the right way. But once you cut a tree down that is it.

Species

This is of course a very personal thing. Find out all you can about the plant—the color of the foliage, the winter shape (without foliage), the growing habits of both the crown and the root sections. Many trees have surface roots (maple, dogwood, most evergreens) and may interfere with a lawn or even some flowering shrubs. Nothing is more frustrating than trying to plant bulbs or perennials in a mass of roots from a local shade tree or large evergreen. This has caused many neighbors to have a few words or worse when a large shade tree planted on the edge of a lot or fence blocked out sunlight, or the root section hindered building a perennial bed or even the planting of a few summer bulbs.

Size and Age

Many trees like the willow and lombardy poplar are famous for ripping up pipelines and sewers, for they need a lot of water. Consider these very carefully. Some trees are considered "dirty" by landscape people. This only means that the amount of leaves or seed pods means more work for you in the fall or spring.

Many trees are susceptible to plant diseases and insects. Ask about each plant and determine if that is what you want in that location.

Finally many trees will not transplant very easily. Maples are hard to move as are birch, beech, hickory, some oaks, and most needled and broadleaf evergreens. Moving or saving a large plant is a job for a professional tree specialist.

BHOTAN PINE.
(PINUS EXCELSA.)

TUNNEL BENEATH THE ROOT SYSTEMS

These drawings would probably kill the tree

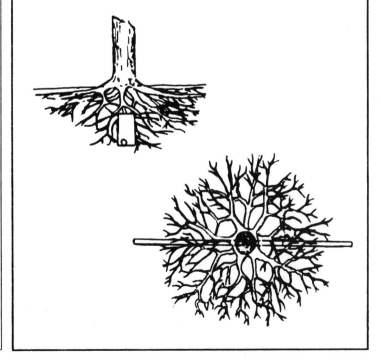

These drawings indicate the proper method of trenching

SCALE OF ⊢⊢⊢⊢⊢⊢⊢ FEET
10 20 30 40 50

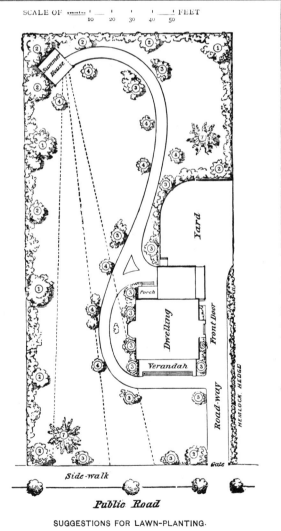

Side-walk

Public Road

SUGGESTIONS FOR LAWN-PLANTING.

1, LARGE LAWN TREES ; 2, TREES OF MODERATE GROWTHS ; 3, DECIDUOUS
SHRUBS OF MODERATE GROWTHS ; 4, RARE AND DWARF DECIDUOUS AND
EVERGREEN SHRUBS ; 7, EVERGREEN TREES.   LARGE SHRUBS EIGHT FEET
APART,—SMALL SHRUBS FOUR FEET APART,—HEDGE PLANTS TWO FEET
APART.   RULES TO BE VARIED SOMEWHAT, ACCORDING TO THE NATURE OF
THE PLANT USED.

Vigor

Very old trees do not transplant as easily as younger trees of the same species. A small tree is replaceable and sometimes cheaper to buy than to move. A smaller tree (like a small sugar maple) may be perfect in the location where it is growing now, but it will get to be over sixty feet. Consider the maturity of plants, not the actual size the plant is now. If a tree is located next to a building or near a driveway or walk, the plant will need a lot of pruning or will have to be removed as it grows too big for the location. It would be cheaper to remove it now rather than wait until it gets out of hand. Try to compare the plant under consideration with other plants and trees of the same species in the area.

After you have selected the plants that are to remain and culled out those that would cause trouble, or are not in the proper location for your overall design, then it is time to begin the protection procedure that is necessary to save them with minimum damage. The trees you want to save will have to be protected from damage that could result from the following:

1. Construction equipment and movement of equipment.

2. Grading the area either for lawn construction or pipelines.

3. Excavations for sewer or pipelines or stone walls that usually are built by the designer. This

PARSONS' SILVER FIR, WEEPING NORWAY SPRUCE, AND WEEPING LARCH.

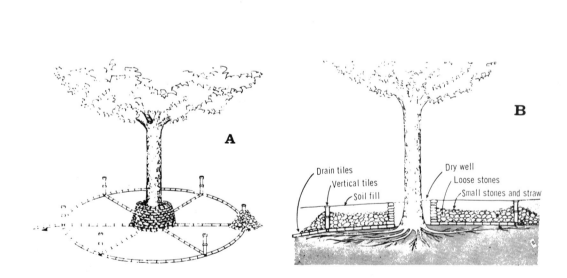

A tile system protects a tree from a raised grade. A, The tile is laid out on the original grade, leading from a dry well around the tree trunk. B, The tile system is covered with small stones to allow air to circulate over the root area.

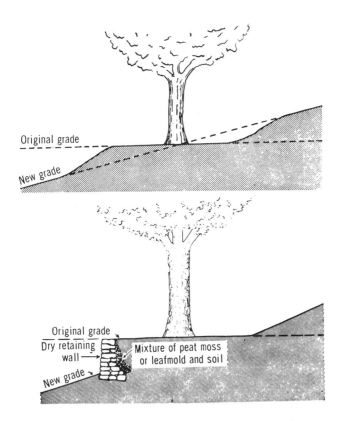

A retaining wall protects a tree from a lowered grade.

includes the patio and permanent stone walks and, if you are lucky enough, a swimming pool.

If the plant is located far enough away from the digging and the general construction of the house and stone work or the pipelines, all that is necessary is to protect it from the machines. If a tractor bumps into a plant it may cut the trunk or jar the root section. All you have to do is build a small fence out from the base of the plant about ten feet or so to prevent soil packing and structural damage to the plant itself. If you want to save a grouping of plants, build a fence around the whole area. Tell the worker on the job to be careful and tell the builder what you are toing to save.

Grade Changes

When the grade is lowered or raised around a tree it has to be protected for the following reasons. Trees need water, air and nutrients to survive. When the grade is changed either by adding soil or by removing soil the ecology of the location changes, thus putting the plant in jeopardy. This is a highly specialized field and the construction workers building the stone well, or building the house are usually not qualified to construct a proper tree well or grade wall. So I suggest a tree surgeon or an arborist with qualified background. When fill is added around the base of plants the surface roots are covered like a blanket and air and water circulation is hindered. If the fill is slight (three to six inches) most trees will survive.

GINKGO TREE, IRISH YEWS, AND WEEPING SOPHORA.

157

THE HOME GREENHOUSE

LORD AND BURNHAM
IRVINGTON-ON-HUDSON, NEW YORK

A WINDOW GREENHOUSE

   This is a very simple structure that can installed in any
window of the house. This window greenhouse is manufactured
by the LORD AND BURNHAN CO. and will be shipped to your
house. This is a perfect place to propagate seedlings for spring
and provide a space for your collection of high humidity tropical
plants.

LORD AND BURNHAM

TRICHOCENTRUM ALBO-PURPUREUM.

STANDARD SIZES FIT MOST WINDOWS

We make the Solar Window Greenhouse in 12 money-saving standard sizes that fit most windows . . . but custom sizes are also available.

After you've chosen the location you like best for your Solar Living Window, follow these easy A-B-C steps to select the right size:

A) Measure the width and height of the outer window opening where the screen fits. Add 2'' to the width and 1'' to the height to allow for overlap of the greenhouse on your window frame. This gives you the size of the smallest Solar you can install right on your window casing. (If your window opening is a few inches too large, it can be made smaller to suit a standard size Solar by nailing wood strips to the top and/or sides of the window frame.)

B) Measure the width and height of your outer window frame across the casing. Subtract 1'' from the width and 1/2'' from the height. This gives you the size of the largest Solar you can install on your window casing.

C) Order the Window Greenhouse whose width and height dimensions are in between the measurements you obtained in steps A and B.

ACCESSORIES FOR YOUR WINDOW GREENHOUSE

Heat—In moderate climates, just open house window in winter: heat from your home will keep greenhouse warm. In colder areas, install a small electric heater; only 10-1/2 x 5 x 3—3/4'', it has a built-in thermostat and fan, will boost the average-size window greenhouse temperature 20 degrees to 30 degrees: with house window closed and an outside temperature of 30 degrees, one 750/1500 watt heater gives your plants a comfortable 50 degrees to 60 degrees.

Fluorescent Light fixture clips to a shelf or front panel. Complete with cool white lamp. 20 watts, 26'' long.

Vinyl Plastic—attractive green color, in rolls 29'' wide x 25'' long. Smooth onto wet glass inside greenhouse with squeegee or stiff brush; reduces light 65%. Stays in place but removes easily in fall for storage and re-use. Must be cut to fit your greenhouse glass size. Order one

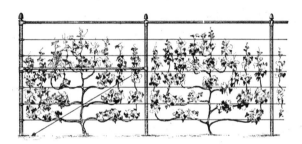

roll per window greenhouse.

Hygrometer/Thermometer—the dual purpose growing aid for all indoor gardeners.

Extra Shelves—after your window greenhouse is installed and planted, you may have room for an additional shelf. Complete with brackets. Specify greenhouse width.

Completely glazed—each panel has all the glass right in place, firmly sealed against weather and vibration with resilient vinyl glazing. Glass is bedded in a special waterproof caulking adhesive to insure against leaks and drafts. And Solar's vinyl glazing channel is inside—makes replacement of a broken lite (if it ever happens) easier and safer. Delivery is prepaid . . . and these exclusive features are included:

4-way adjustable roof sash with weather-tight hinge.

Insect screen sealed tight with vinyl on all sides.

Air/Flow shelving for plant "breathing"—2 with units 52''-84'' high; 1 with units 32''-48'' high.

Removable bottom pan holds gravel, sand, marble chips for natural humidity control. Complete assembly and operating instructions including What and How to Grow tips.

THE HOME GREENHOUSE

The small greenhouse can be an extension of the outdoors in the cold weather or a place to grow the more rare plants of the tropical rain forests. A greenhouse need not be a separate structure, apart from the rest of the house, but can be a continuation of the interior and outdoors. I prefer a small greenhouse to be hooked on to the house with an outside door for the warmer months. This way you have access to the plant world and world of plant color when the rest of the landscape is white and dormant.

A small greenhouse can be used to force spring bulbs like tulips, hyacinths, azaleas and even small shrubs like forsythia. I have seen dogwood in blossom in February in the greenhouse, and the smell of the flowers, when the greenhouse door is open to the house, invites entry for it is a spectacular sight to see the green and the colored flowers with a snowy background. A small greenhouse will provide you with so many extras in the field of horticulture that you will wonder how you ever lived without one. You may have a potting shed, a controlled space for orchids or violets, a storage space for tools and a place to sit and meditate under the palm tree. If you prefer grapes and melons, those too can be grown in the greenhouse, as can other small vegetable and fruit crops.

LATH-ROLLER BLIND.

Of course the small greenhouse is the perfect place to start the transplants for the summer vegetable and ornamental flower garden.

The greenhouse is a place of study. When you have a place to actually start the germination process and watch the plant grow to maturity, you have a built-in micro-climate. Depending on your preference and ability, the greenhouse can grow anything from very rare orchids to arid plants like succulents of the southwestern desert.

Greenhouse technology today is a very special kind of business. There are many greenhouse manufacturers that specialize in the home greenhouse. There are shapes and sizes to fit almost any architecture and most pocketbooks. The window greenhouse is also available. This is probably the smallest of the structures. If you have a regular sized window, you can buy a mini-greenhouse to put in the frame. This will serve as a miniature controlled space to grow plants that will not do well indoors because of low humidity. It is like an over-sized terrarium.

There are two kinds of home greenhouse, the attached that is usually hooked on to the house or garage, and the free standing. For the city gardener, with very limited space, a small attached greenhouse is probably the only one to consider. If you have a backyard, or a rooftop garden, you can extend the indoors in the form of a small inexpensive greenhouse either of glass or plastic. Let me say something about the plastic greenhouse. With today's technology, the plastic house is the most popular and of course less expensive than the glass house. Plastic means either rolls of polyethylene or sheets of plastic in the form of panels.

Heating is the overall problem of small greenhouses, or any greenhouse for that matter. Greenhouses can be classified according to temperature. The general rule of thumb is as follows:

1. The house house or tropical house . . . 65-75 degrees F. or higher.
2. The warm house . . . 55-65 degrees F.
3. The cool house . . . 45-55 degrees F.
4. The cold house or frame. . . . 35-45 degrees F.

Once you decide on the kind of structure you need and can handle for your space requirements and your gardening pleasure, I suggest you send to the manufacturer for price quotes, pamphlets on the kinds of structures available, and shipping costs. Due to the increase in sales in the small greenhouse field, many of the popular models seem to be back-ordered and there may be a waiting period for the model you choose.

This larger greenhouse provides almost a professional
level of floriculture. This larger house not only provides
a place to store tropical plants for the winter months but
with the right information you can grow and cultivate
many plants that are not ordinarily accessible to the average
gardener.

A greenhouse built right in to the structure of the home
is of course the ultimite greenhouse and propagating bed.
If you have the space and the money this is it.

LORD AND BURNHAM

163

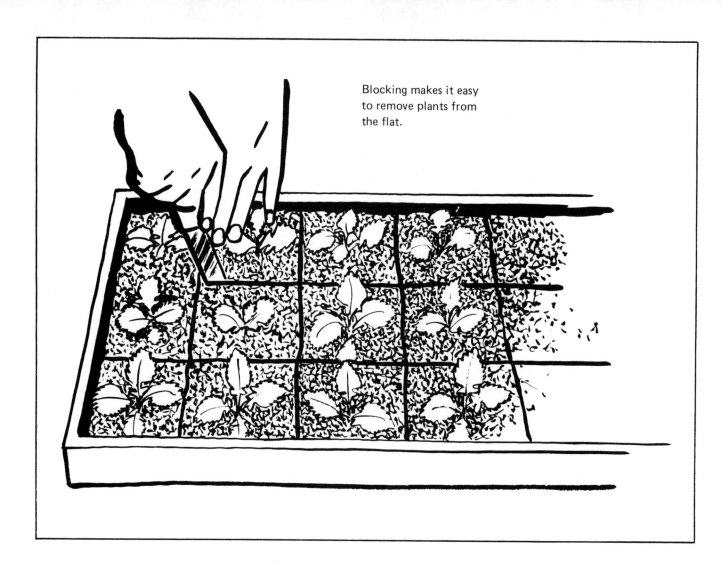

Blocking makes it easy to remove plants from the flat.

The Cold Frame

I do not think, generally speaking, that the cold frame is used or appreciated sufficiently by the average home gardener. If properly managed, and the technology is rather simple, so much can be done to help out your horticultural needs that, once you use one for a season, you will not know how to proceed without one in the years to follow. Besides the possibility of lengthening the seasons, you can safely carry perennials of a less hardy variety through the winters with ease.

You can build a cheap cold frame that has to be replaced every few years or you can build a permanent structure that is almost of commercial value. The cheap kind is just old window sash raised above a wooden frame or cinder block structure. There are a few examples of cold frames following so you can see what they look like. There is the heat of the sun, and in some cases where it is available, raw manure underneath the soil will provide the heat.

The cold frame is the perfect place to force bulbs for winter flowers. All bulbs must be forced in a cold place to establish roots before bringing them indoors for the final part of the show.

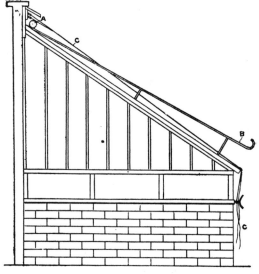

Fig. 30. TIFFANY ROLLER BLIND
(Sectional View).

References: – *a*, roller blind; *b*, light iron rod to elevate the blind; *c*, draw cord.

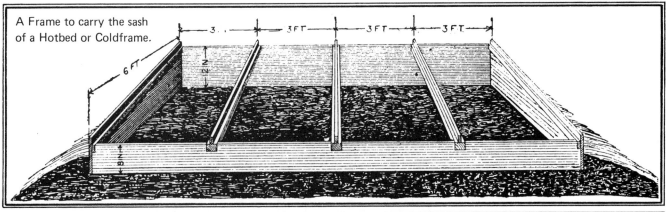

A Frame to carry the sash of a Hotbed or Coldframe.

6 FT · 3 · 3 FT · 3 FT · 3 FT

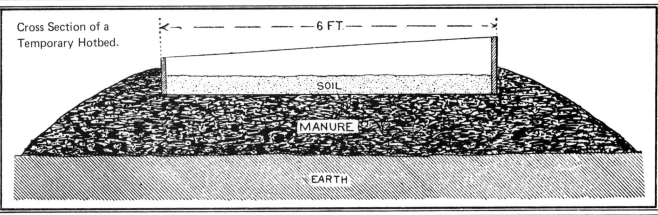

Cross Section of a Temporary Hotbed.

6 FT.

SOIL

MANURE

EARTH

Depth of Rooting

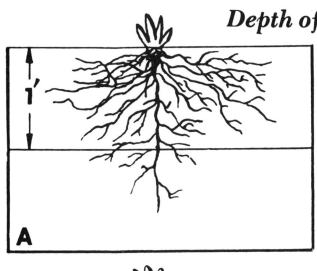

A

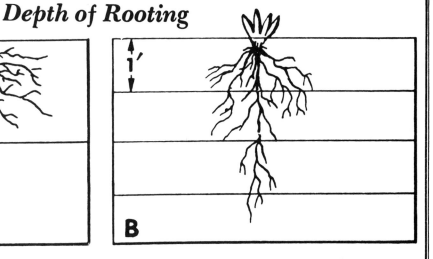

B

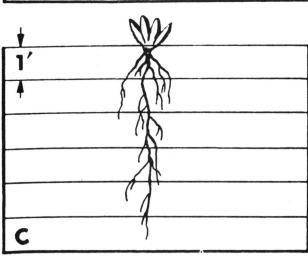

C

A. Shallow. Main root system is in the top 2 feet of soil. *Examples:* cabbage, cauliflower, lettuce, celery, sweet corn, onion, white potato, radish.

B. Moderately deep. Main root system is in top four feet of soil. *Examples:* snap bean, carrot, cucumber, eggplant, pea, pepper, summer squash.

C. Deep. Main root system is in top six feet of soil. *Examples:* globe artichoke, asparagus, cantaloupe, pumpkin, tomato, watermelon.

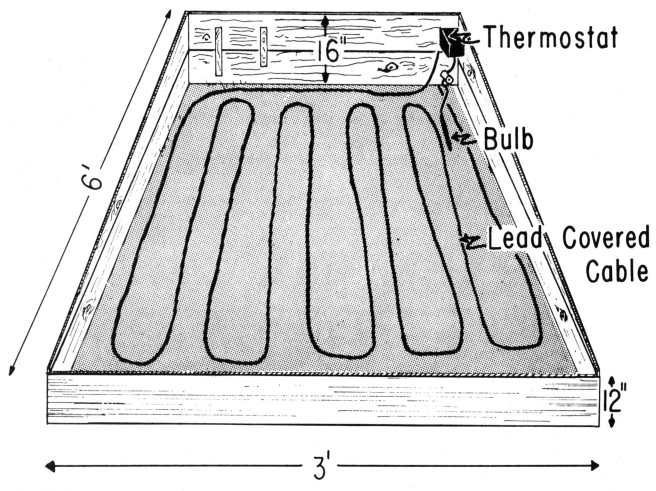

Electric hotbed (top) showing position of lead-covered cable thermostat and sensitive bulb for soil temperature. Cable to be covered with 3 to 4 inches of soil. Boards should be redwood.

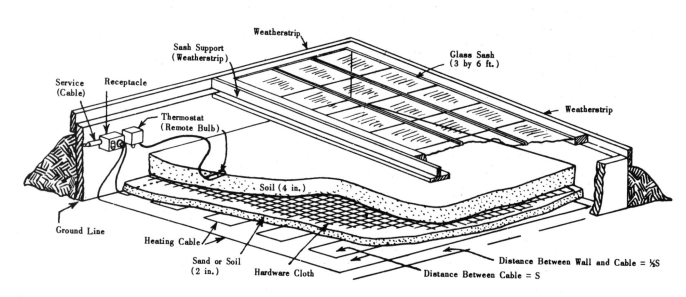

Cut-away drawing showing the construction
of an electrically heated hotbed.

Planting and care of selected garden annuals sown as seeds

Plant	Planting Time	Exposure	Germination Time	Plant Spacing
			(Days)	(Inches)
Ageratum	Late spring	Full sun	5	10-12
Amaranthus	Late spring	Semi-shade	10	10-12
Aster	Late spring	Full sun	8	12-14
Babies'-breath	Early spring	Full sun	10	10-12
Bachelor's Button	Early spring	Full sun	10	8-10
Calendula	Early spring	Full sun	10	8-10
Calliopsis	Late spring	Full sun	8	10-14
China Aster	Late spring	Shade or sun	8	10-12
Cockscomb	Late spring	Full sun	10	10-12
Cornflower	Early spring	Partial shade	10	12-14
Cosmos	Late spring	Full sun	5	10-12
Forget-me-not	Late spring	Full sun	8	10-12
		Semi-shade		
Four-o'clock	Late spring	Full sun	5	12-14
Gaillardia	Early-late spring	Full sun	20	10-12
Lupine	Early spring	Full sun	20	6-8
Marigold	Late spring	Full sun	5	10-14
Morning Glory	Late spring	Full sun	5	24-36
Nasturtium	Late spring	Full sun	8	8-12
Petunia	Early spring	Full sun	10	12-14
Phlox	Early spring	Full sun	10	6-8
Portulaca	Late spring	Full sun	10	10-12
Rudbeckia	Late spring	Full sun	20	10-14
		Semi-shade		
Salpiglossis	Early spring	Full sun	15	10-12
Scabiosa	Early-late spring	Full sun	10	12-14
Sweet Alyssum	Early spring	Full sun	5	10-12
Spider Plant	Early spring	Full sun	10	12-14
Strawflower	Early spring	Full sun	5	10-12
Sunflower	Late spring	Full sun	5	12-14
Sweetpea	Early spring	Full sun	15	6-8
Zinnia	Late spring	Full sun	5	8-12

167

Permanent flower beds and a flagstone floor set in a small greenhouse
makes an interesting sitting room. Combining the indoors
and outdoors is a universal idea in gardening and it works well here.

A decorative small greenhouse may be incorporated into your outside landscape. Build permanent flower beds around the small house to increase the beauty of the setting and provide color for your patio during the summer months.

LORD AND BURNHAM

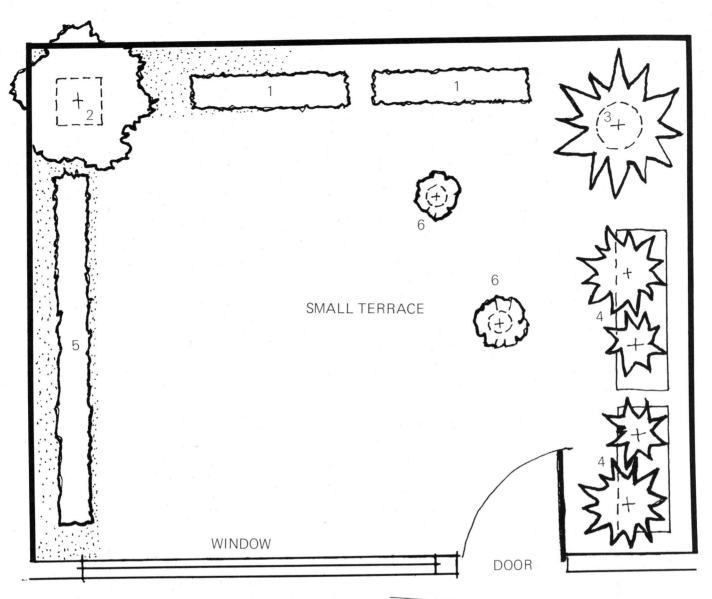

SMALL TERRACE

WINDOW

DOOR

1. Window boxes—annuals and hanging ivy or vinca.

2. Small deciduous tree (crab or redbud).

3. Black pine.

4. Two low growing evergreens (juniper horizontalis).

5. Annual box for vegetables.

6. Potted annuals.

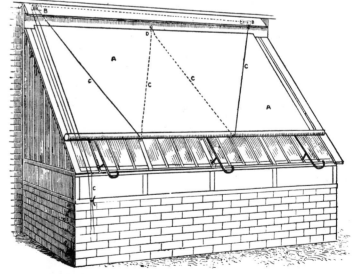

A Small Greenhouse for a City Terrace.

GARDEN DESIGNS

A penthouse terrace in New York City. The flower beds are permanent
stone structures with plenty of space to plant annuals and vegetables in
season.   The biggest problem on the terraces is the winter wind and as you
can see from the photo most of the plants are deciduous. Seeing that the
summer months are the most enjoyable, leave plenty of room for summer
color. Plant bulbs in the fall for spring color and then plant annuals for the
rest of the warm season.

Designing around existing plants increases the value of the landscape. This design
not only has a small rock garden but wide walks and flower beds. Never crowd
the grounds.

CITY ENTRANCE—LOTS OF SUN

1. Hybrid Rhododendrons

2. Spreading Yew

3. Red Cedar

4. Dwarf Pine

5. English Ivy

6. Rock

7. Redwood Box for Annuals

8. Permanent Sculpture

9. Fence

10. Gate

11. Walk

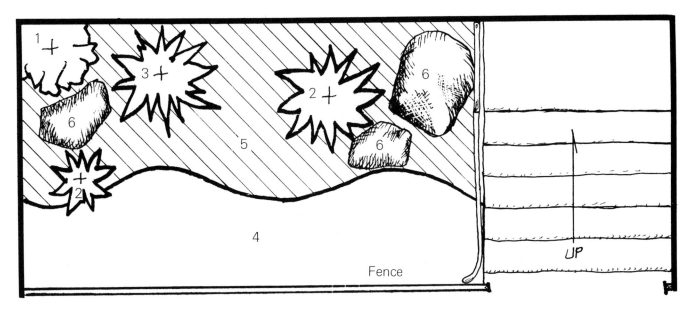

A MINI FRONTYARD ROCK GARDEN FOR
A CITY ENTRANCE

1. Andromeda

2. Bar Harbor Juniper

3. Spreading Yew

4. Ivy

5. Flower and Bulb Space

6. Rocks

173

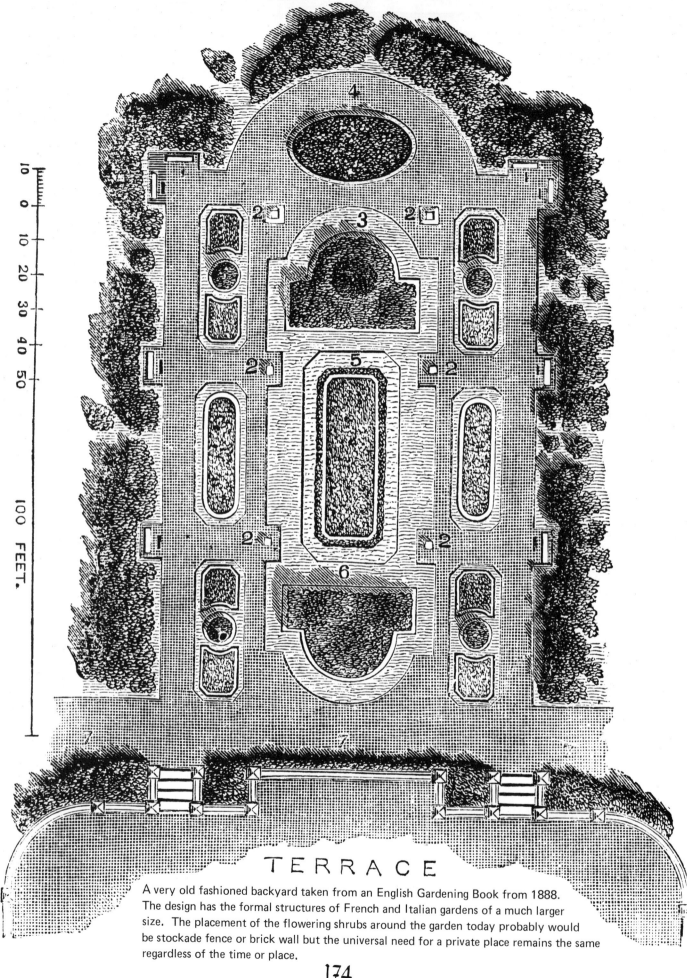

TERRACE

A very old fashioned backyard taken from an English Gardening Book from 1888. The design has the formal structures of French and Italian gardens of a much larger size. The placement of the flowering shrubs around the garden today probably would be stockade fence or brick wall but the universal need for a private place remains the same regardless of the time or place.

174

A SHADY CITY BACKYARD

1. Flowering Crab
2. Rhododendron
3. Andorra Juniper
4. Skimma
5. Flowering Cherry
6. Varigated Andromeda
7. Dwarf Barberry
8. Japanese Red Maple

9. Canadian Yew
10. Winged Euonymus
11. English Ivy
12. Redwood Box (Herbs)
13. Potted Plants (Begonias and Basil)
14. Flower Beds (Bulbs and Annuals)
15. Lawn (Annual Rye sown each spring)
16. Stonework

A SUBURBAN PATIO IN UPSTATE NEW YORK

This is the patio and backyard of a very famous Horticulturist and plant expert. As in all well designed patio areas there is always plenty of room to move about and party. The grouping of plants against the house has a texture and color quality that only an experienced landscape designer could have designed. The high point is an upright pine and the low growing junipers and groundcovers in front lend a sense of perfection. The rhododendron and andromeda finish the texture and complete the picture. A true masterpiece.

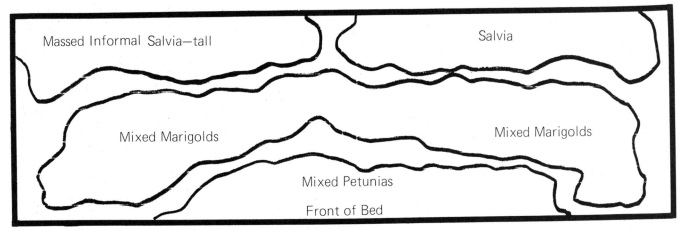

Massed Informal Salvia—tall

Salvia

Mixed Marigolds

Mixed Marigolds

Mixed Petunias

Front of Bed

ANNUAL FLOWER BEDS—SUNLIGHT

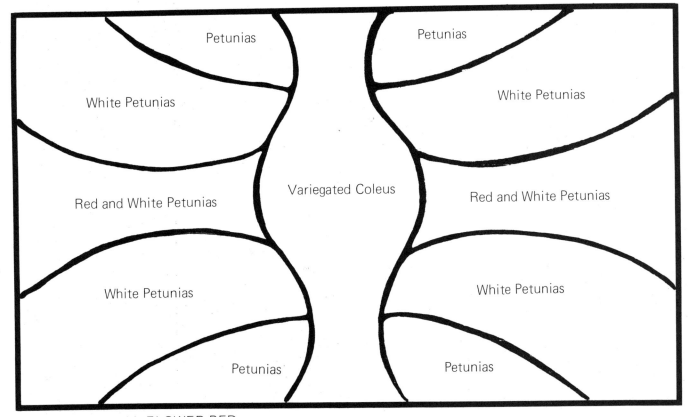

Petunias

Petunias

White Petunias

White Petunias

Variegated Coleus

Red and White Petunias

Red and White Petunias

White Petunias

White Petunias

Petunias

Petunias

FORMAL ANNUAL FLOWER BED

ANNUAL FLOWER BEDS—SHADE

Evergreen Background

White and Red Impatiens

White and Red Impatiens

Begonias mixed with Ivy

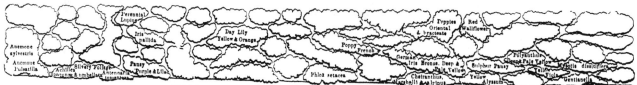

SUMMER.—State of the same border with the names of flowers in full bloom at that season.

SCALE OF FEET.

AUTUMN.—State of the same border with the names of the autumnal blooming plants

MASSED DESIGNS FOR PERENNIAL FLOWER BORDER

Always arrange taller plants against the wall or fence
and the other plants should gradually get smaller at
the front of the bed. The irregular patterns are
always more pleasing and the color blends together
without hard-edge effects.

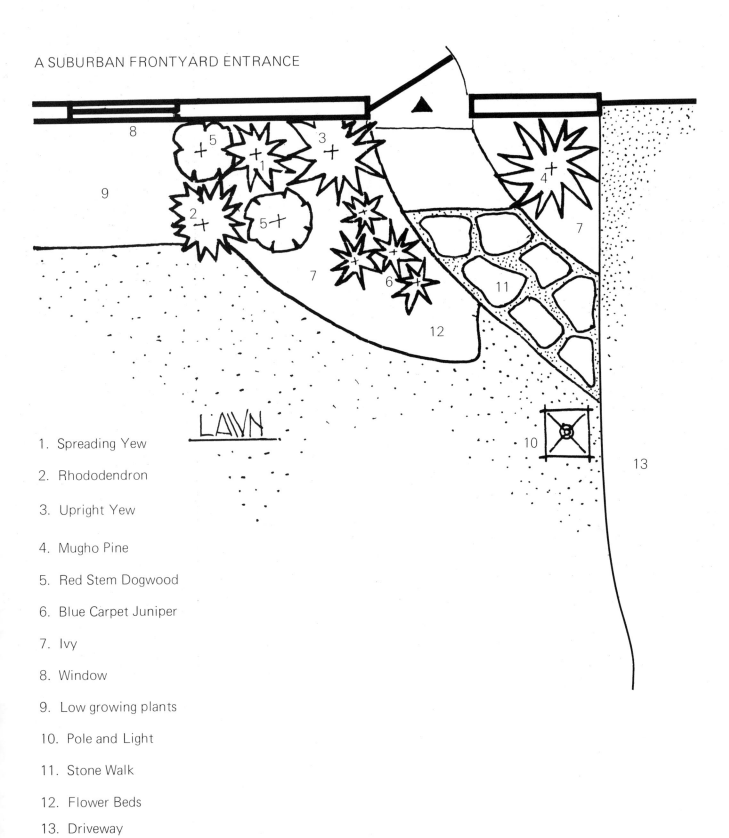

A SUBURBAN FRONTYARD ENTRANCE

LAWN

1. Spreading Yew

2. Rhododendron

3. Upright Yew

4. Mugho Pine

5. Red Stem Dogwood

6. Blue Carpet Juniper

7. Ivy

8. Window

9. Low growing plants

10. Pole and Light

11. Stone Walk

12. Flower Beds

13. Driveway

THE BACK OF THE BOOK... A WORD TOOLSHED

PLANTING AND SPACING STANDARDS

The following recommendations for planting and spacing are usually followed in private and institutional landscape work.

PLANTING HOLE SUGGESTIONS

Size of Shrub	Diameter and Depth of Planting Holes
1 to 2 ft.	16 in. by 10 in.
2 to 3 ft.	18 in. by 12 in.
3 to 4 ft.	20 in. by 14 in.
4 to 6 ft.	24 in. by 18 in.

Size of Trees	Diameter and Depth of Planting Holes
6 to 8 ft.	30 in. by 19 in.
1 to 1½ in. cal.	34 in. by 21 in.
1½ to 2 in. cal.	36 in. by 22 in.
2 to 2½ in. cal.	40 in. by 25 in.
2½ to 3 in. cal.	44 in. by 26 in.
3 to 4 in. cal.	52 in. by 30 in.
4 to 5 in. cal.	56 in. by 32 in.

AMERICAN SENNA.
(CASSIA MARYLANDICA.)

GROUND COVER SPACING

Type of Ground Cover	Suggested Spacing
Cotoneaster, spreading varieties	18 in. on Center
Euonymus radicans and varieties	12 in. on Center
Hedera helix and varieties	8 in. on Center
Juniperus horizontalis and varieties	18 in. on Center
Rosa wichuraiana hybrids	18 in. on Center
Vinca minor and varieties	8 in. on Center

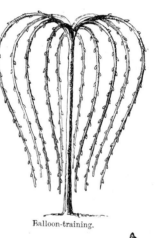

Balloon-training.

HEDGE PLANTING SPACING

Type of Hedge	Suggested Spacing
Berberis thunbergi and other Barberry	16 in. apart
Buxus suffruticosa	12 in. apart
Euonymus alatus and compactus	18 in. apart
Ilex crenata varieties	24 in. apart
Ligustrum ovalifolium and other Privet	18 in. apart
Pyracantha coccinea lalandi	24 in. apart
Taxus, upright varieties	24 in. apart
Thuja occidentalis nigra	24 in. apart

TREE SPACING

Type of Tree	Suggested Spacing
Small flowering and minor shade trees	20 ft. apart
Medium sized and columnar shade trees	30 ft. apart
Major shade trees	40 to 60 ft. apart
Screening trees	6 ft. apart

CHINESE CYPRESS.
(GLYPTOSTROBUS SINENSIS.)

PLANT HARDINESS ZONES

APPROXIMATE RANGE OF AVERAGE ANNUAL MINIMUM TEMPERATURES FOR EACH ZONE	
ZONE 1	BELOW -50° F
ZONE 2	-50° TO -40°
ZONE 3	-40° TO -30°
ZONE 4	-30° TO -20°
ZONE 5	-20° TO -10°
ZONE 6	-10° TO 0°
ZONE 7	0° TO 10°
ZONE 8	10° TO 20°
ZONE 9	20° TO 30°
ZONE 10	30° TO 40°

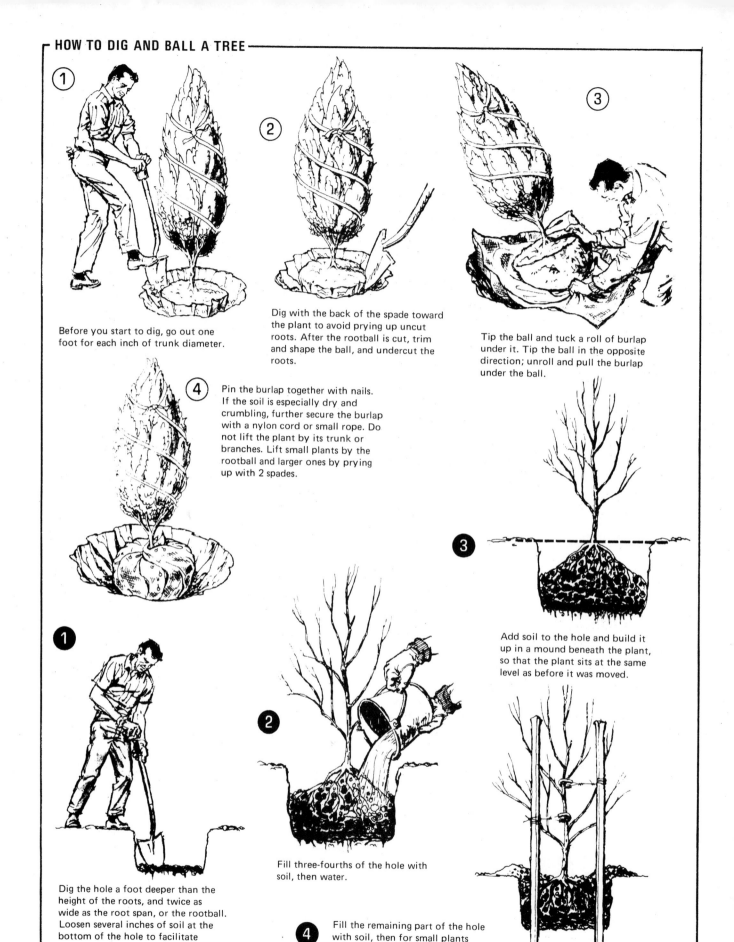

1 Before you start to dig, go out one foot for each inch of trunk diameter.

2 Dig with the back of the spade toward the plant to avoid prying up uncut roots. After the rootball is cut, trim and shape the ball, and undercut the roots.

3 Tip the ball and tuck a roll of burlap under it. Tip the ball in the opposite direction; unroll and pull the burlap under the ball.

4 Pin the burlap together with nails. If the soil is especially dry and crumbling, further secure the burlap with a nylon cord or small rope. Do not lift the plant by its trunk or branches. Lift small plants by the rootball and larger ones by prying up with 2 spades.

1 Dig the hole a foot deeper than the height of the roots, and twice as wide as the root span, or the rootball. Loosen several inches of soil at the bottom of the hole to facilitate drainage.

2 Fill three-fourths of the hole with soil, then water.

3 Add soil to the hole and build it up in a mound beneath the plant, so that the plant sits at the same level as before it was moved.

4 Fill the remaining part of the hole with soil, then for small plants drive in stakes to secure them. For securing large plants, use guy wires.

1. CARE OF PLANTS BEFORE PLANTING

(A) THOROUGHLY WATER PLANTS. ALL SURFACES MUST BE MOIST.

(B) SHADE PLANTS FROM DIRECT SUNLIGHT UNTIL THEY ARE TRANSPLANTED. DO NOT HOLD PLANTS ANY LONGER THAN NECESSARY SO ROOT DEVELOPMENT AND TIME OF GROWTH AND FLOWERING ARE NOT DELAYED.

2. PREPARATION OF PLANTS FOR PLANTING

TEAR UPPER LIP OFF THE POT.

REMOVE BOTTOM OF POT OR INSERT A STICK TO OPEN BOTTOM. KEEP POTS MOIST.

(A) PLANTS IN PEAT POTS OR PEAT PELLETS

KNOCK PLANTS OUT. DO NOT PULL ON STEM.

MAKE FINE CUTS 1/4 IN. DEEP IN SURFACE OF SOIL BALL IF ROOTS ARE MATTED.

REMOVE ALL DRAINAGE MATERIAL FROM BOTTOM.

(B) PLANTS IN CLAY OR PLASTIC POTS

KEEP BURLAP MOIST AT ALL TIMES. DO NOT PULL ON STEM MORE THAN NECESSARY. BALLED AND BURLAPPED PLANTS HAVE MANY FINE ROOT SYSTEMS THAT ARE EASILY DAMAGED.

(C) PLANTS BALLED AND BURLAPPED

4. CARE OF PLANTS AFTER PLANTING

(A) HAND PINCH 1/2 IN. OFF THE TIPS OF THE PLANTS WHEN THEY START TO GROW. DO NOT REMOVE LEAVES.

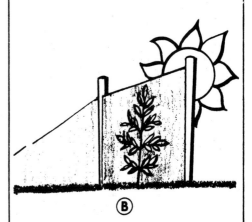

(B) SHADE PLANTS FOR THE FIRST SEVERAL DAYS IF THEY ARE EXPOSED TO DIRECT SUNLIGHT. REMOVE COVER IN THE AFTERNOON TO HELP PLANTS ADJUST TO THE NEW ENVIRONMENT.

3. INSERTING PLANTS IN SOIL

DO NOT MAKE A POCKET OR DEPRESSION AROUND THE PLANT. A DEPRESSION ALLOWS EXCESS WATER TO STAND.

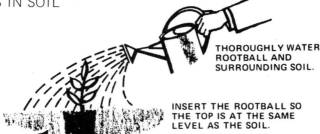

GROWING MEDIA

THOROUGHLY WATER ROOTBALL AND SURROUNDING SOIL.

INSERT THE ROOTBALL SO THE TOP IS AT THE SAME LEVEL AS THE SOIL.

APPLY A LIQUID FERTILIZER AT TIME OF PLANTING TO HELP THE PLANTS DEVELOP ROOTS. USE 1 TABLESPOON OF 16-52-10 PER GALLON OF WATER.

TULIP PLANTING GUIDE

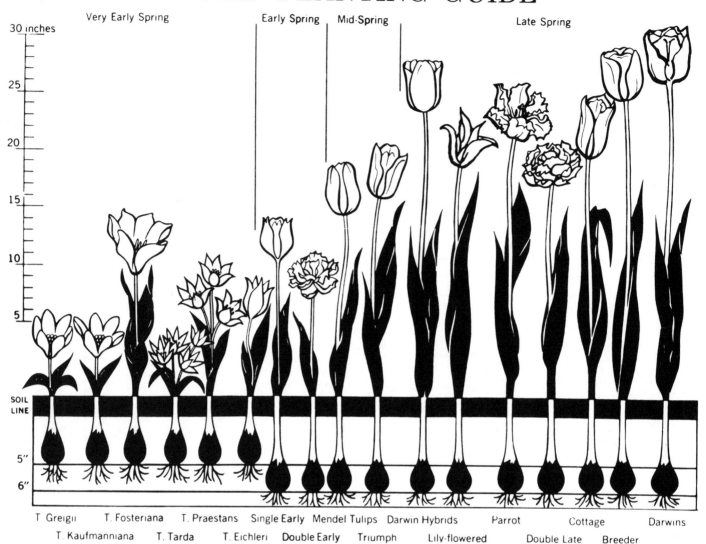

Very Early Spring — Early Spring — Mid-Spring — Late Spring

30 inches
25
20
15
10
5

SOIL LINE
5"
6"

| T. Greigii | T. Fosteriana | T. Praestans | Single Early | Mendel Tulips | Darwin Hybrids | Parrot | Cottage | Darwins |
| T. Kaufmanniana | T. Tarda | T. Eichleri | Double Early | Triumph | Lily-flowered | Double Late | Breeder | |

MINOR BULB GUIDE

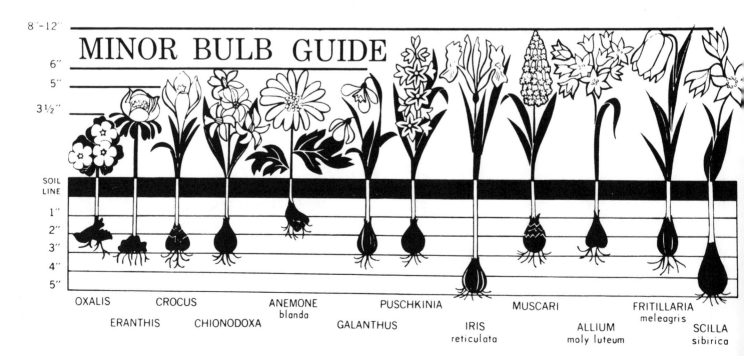

8"-12"
6"
5"
3½"

SOIL LINE
1"
2"
3"
4"
5"

| OXALIS | CROCUS | ANEMONE blanda | PUSCHKINIA | MUSCARI | FRITILLARIA meleagris |
| ERANTHIS | CHIONODOXA | GALANTHUS | IRIS reticulata | ALLIUM moly luteum | SCILLA sibirica |

FLAGSTONE AND
BRICK PATTERNS

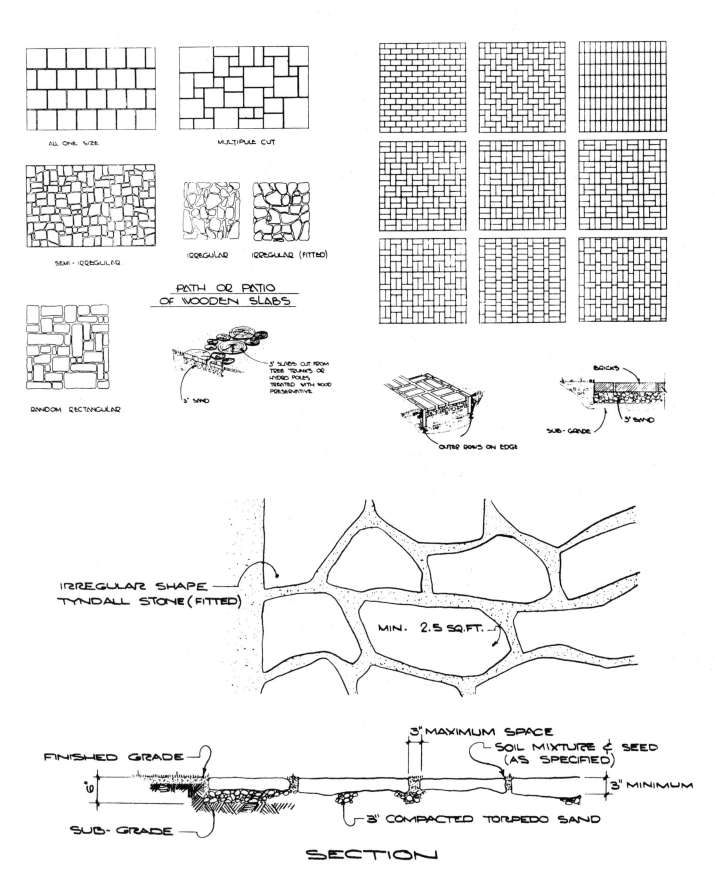

ALL ONE SIZE

MULTIPLE CUT

SEMI-IRREGULAR

IRREGULAR

IRREGULAR (FITTED)

RANDOM RECTANGULAR

PATH OR PATIO
OF WOODEN SLABS

3' SLABS CUT FROM
TREE TRUNKS OR
HYDRO POLES
TREATED WITH WOOD
PRESERVATIVE

3' SAND

OUTER ROWS ON EDGE

BRICKS

SUB-GRADE

3' SAND

IRREGULAR SHAPE
TYNDALL STONE (FITTED)

MIN. 2.5 SQ.FT.

3" MAXIMUM SPACE

SOIL MIXTURE & SEED
(AS SPECIFIED)

FINISHED GRADE

6"

3" MINIMUM

SUB-GRADE

3" COMPACTED TORPEDO SAND

SECTION

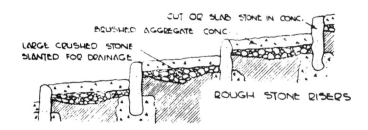

LARGE CRUSHED STONE
SLANTED FOR DRAINAGE

BRUSHED AGGREGATE CONC.

CUT OR SLAB STONE IN CONC.

ROUGH STONE RISERS

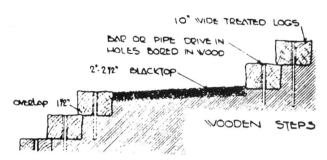

10" WIDE TREATED LOGS

BAR OR PIPE DRIVE IN
HOLES BORED IN WOOD

2"-2½" BLACKTOP

OVERLAP 1½"

WOODEN STEPS

BRICKS SET IN MORTAR

BRICKS SET IN SAND

BRICKS SET IN CONC.

TAMPED SAND BED
SLANTED FOR
DRAINAGE

BRICK RISERS

USE RAMP STEPS FOR LONG SLOPES

MAKE STEPS 2'-6" WIDE WITH 4"-7" RISERS
FLOOR THEM WITH SAND, BLACKTOP, BRICKS
GRAVEL OR WOOD.

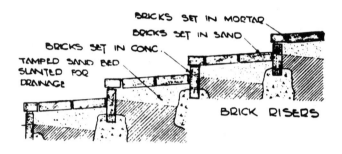

¾" FACING BOARD

2"x4" FRAME

2"x4" POSTS SET IN CONC.
FLOOR BOARDS ½" APART

BOARDWALK STEPS

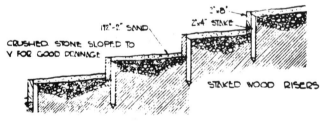

2"x8"

2"x4" STAKE

1½"-2" SAND

CRUSHED STONE SLOPED TO
V FOR GOOD DRAINAGE

STAKED WOOD RISERS

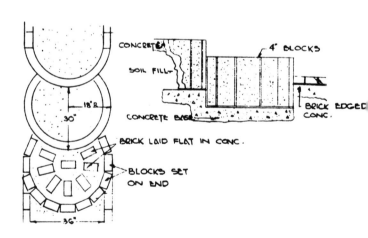

CONCRETE

4" BLOCKS

SOIL FILL

CONCRETE BASE

BRICK EDGED
CONC.

BRICK LAID FLAT IN CONC.

BLOCKS SET
ON END

18" R

30"

36"

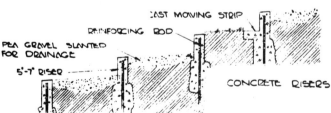

CAST MOWING STRIP

REINFORCING ROD

PEA GRAVEL SLANTED
FOR DRAINAGE

5"-7" RISER

CONCRETE RISERS

CONC. MAKES PERMANENT RISERS FOR
GRAVEL, BLACKTOP & CONC. STEPS. IF
LAWN IS USED, MOWING STRIP EASES CUTTING.

WALKS

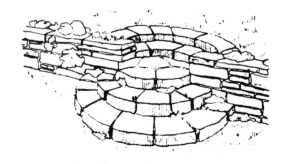

WALLS

RETAINING WALLS

Most interesting land has changes in slope and elevation that offer an opportunity or need for a retaining wall. If the wall is to be high and abrupt (A), the services of an engineer will be needed to design a structure that can safely resist the earth pressures which tend to push or tip it. A small wall, however, can be a challenging and artistic project (B) for the average amateur.

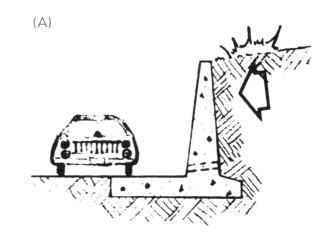

(A)

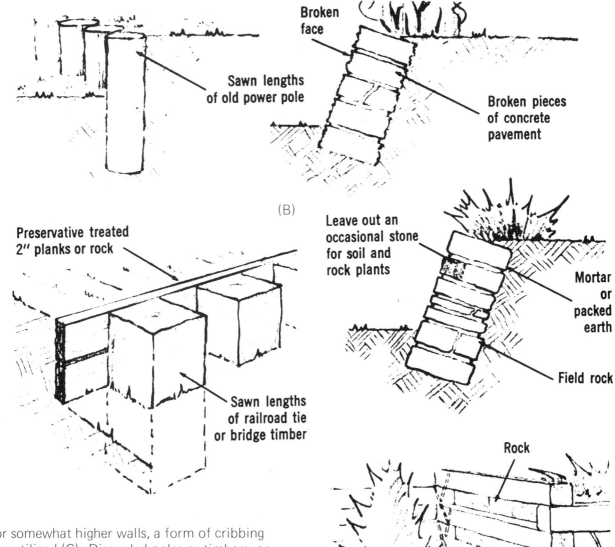

Sawn lengths of old power pole

Broken face

Broken pieces of concrete pavement

(B)

Preservative treated 2" planks or rock

Sawn lengths of railroad tie or bridge timber

Leave out an occasional stone for soil and rock plants

Mortar or packed earth

Field rock

For somewhat higher walls, a form of cribbing can be utilized (C). Discarded poles or timbers, or railroad ties, are cut, laid, and fastened in a manner similar to that used in pioneer log cabin construction. Those wooden materials that were originally pressure treated with wood preservatives (such as most railroad ties and power poles) are best used when direct contact with the earth is found to be necessary.

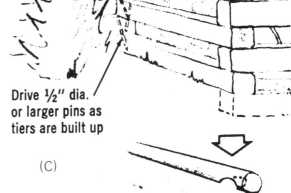

Rock

Drive ½" dia. or larger pins as tiers are built up

(C)

180

COMMON AND BOTANICAL NAMES OF FLOWERING PLANTS

Abyssianian Banana, Musa
Adams Needle, Yucca
Alleghany Vine, Adlumia
Alum Root, Heuchera
American Cowslip, Dodecatheon
American Senna, Cassia
Amethyst, Browallia
Artillery Plant, Pilea
Aurora's Bower, Gaillardia
Australian Glory Pea, Clianthus
Baby's Breath, Gypsophila
Bachelor's Button, Globe Amaranth
Balsam Apple, Momordica
Balsam Pear, Momordica
Banana Shrub, Magnolia
Barrenwort, Epimedium
Basket of Gold, Alyssum
Bath Flower, Trillium
Beard Tongue, Pentstemon
Bird's Nest Fern, Aspidium Nidus-Avis
Bishop's Weed, Aegopodium
Black-Eyed Susan, Thunbergia
Bleeding Heart, Dicentra
Blood Flower, Haemanthus
Bluebottle, Centaurea
Bluebottle, Grape Hyacinth
Blue Leadwort, Plumbago
Blue Lyme Grass, Elymus
Blue Saliva, S. patens
Blue Vetch, Grape Hyacinth
Bluet Houstonia
Boston Ivy, Ampelopsis
Bowman's Root, Gillenia
Bugle, Ajuga
Bugle Vine, Calampelis
Burning Bush, Euonymus
Butterfly Flower, Centrosema
Butterfly Flower, Schizanthus
Butterfly Orchid, Epidendrum
Butterfly Weed, Asclepias
Calico Bush, Kalmia
California Poppy, Eschscholtzia
Canterbury Bell, Campanula
Cape Hyacinth, H. Candicans
Cardinal Flower, Lobelia
Castor Bean, Ricinus
Cheneil Plant, Acalypha

Spiræa (Belmont, Carlow).

Chilian Glory Flower, Eccremocarpus
Chimney Bell Flower, Campanula
Chinese Bell Flower, Platycodon
Chinese Lantern Plant, Physalis
Chinese Matrimony Vine, Bougainvillea
Christmas Berry, Ardisia
Christmas Rose, Helleborus
Cinnamon Vine, Dioscorea
Cinquefoil, Potentilla
Climbing Fumitory, Adumia
Climbing Hawthorn, Actinidia
Cockscomb, Celosia
Columbine, Aquilegia
Cone Flower, Rudbeckia
Coral Plant, Erythrina
Corn Flower, Centaurea
Cowslip, Primula
Crane's Bill, Geranium
Creeping Mallow, Callirhoe
Crown Vetch, Coronilla
Cruel Plant, Physianthus
Cup and Saucer Plant, Campanula
Cup and Saucer Vine, Cobaea
Cup Flower, Nierembergia
Cushion Pink, Armeria
Dark Mullen, Verbascum
Day Lily, Hemerocallis
Devil in the Bush, Nigella
Double Buttercup, Ranunculus
Dropwort, Spiraea
Duck Plant, Aristolochia
Dutchman's Breeches, Dielytra
Dutchman's Pipe, Aristolochia
Dusty Miller Centaurea
Dusty Miller, Cineraria
Edelweiss, Gnaphalium
Emerald Feather, Asparagus
English Daisy, Bellis

Evening Glory, Ipomaea
Evening Primrose, Oenothera
Everlasting, Acroclinium
Everlasting, Ammobium
Everlasting, Globe Amaranth
Everlasting, Helichrysum
Everlasting, Lathyrus
Everlasting, Rhodanthe
Everlasting, Xeranthemum
Fair Maids of France, Ranunculus
False Chamomile, Boltonia
False Dragon Head, Physostegia
False Indigo, Baptisia
Feverfew, Matricaria
Fire on the Mountain, Euphorbia
Flame Flower, Tritoma
Fleur de Lis, Iris
Flora's Paint Brush, Cacalia

DOUBLE FLOWERING ALTHEA.
(HIBISCUS SYRIACUS, FL. PL.)

Florida Rattle Bos, Crotolaria
Floss Flower, Ageratum
Flowering Currant, Ribes
Flowering Dogwood, Cornus
Flowering Maple, Abutilon
Flowering Sage, Salvia
Flowering Spurge, Euphorbia
Forget-me-not, Myosotis
Fountain Plant, Acalypha
Four-o'clock, Marvel of Peru
Fringe Flower, Schizanthus
Garden Flower, Schizanthus
Gardener's Garter, Phalaris
Garland Flower, Daphne
Gas Plant, Dictamnus
Gay Feather, Liatris
Gilliflower, Cheiranthus
Globe Flower, Trollius
Glory Pea of Australia, Clianthus
Goat's Beard, Spiraea
Gold Lack, Wall Flower
Golden Bush Pea, Crotolaria
Golden Feather, Pyrethrum
Golden Honey Bell, Mahernia
Golden-leaved Elder, Sambucus
Golden Rod, Solidago
Golden Tuft, Alyssum
Great Reed, Arundo Donax
Great Sea Lavender, Limonium

Groundsel, Glechoma
Hawk's Beard, Crepis
Holly Fern, Crytomium
Honey Bell, Mahernia
Horn of Plenty, Datura
Horned Poppy, Glaucium
Horse Mint, Monarda
House Leek, Sempervivum
Humble Plant, Mimosa
Hyacinth Clematis, Clematis Davidiana
Jacobean Lily, Amaryllis
Jacob's Ladder, Polemonium
Japan Quince, Pyrus
Japanese Bell Flower, Platycodon
Japanese Beni, Caryopteris
Japanese Hop, Humulus
Japanese Ivy, Ampelopsis
Japanese Primrose, Cortusoidea
Japanese Primrose, Primula
Japanese Virgin's Bower, Clematis
Japanese Winter Cherry, Physalis
Jerusalem Cherry, Solanum
Jerusalem Cross, Lychnis
Kenilworth Ivy, Linaria
Lady Washington, Pelargonium
Larkspur, Delphinium
Lavender Cotton, Santolina
Lawn Pearlwort, Spergula
Lemon Verbena, Verbena

Leopard Plant, Farfugium
Lilac, Syringa
Lilly of the Palace, Agapanthus
Lily of the Palace, Amaryllis
Little Bo-Peep, Antirrhinum
Liverwort, Hepatica
London Tufts, Sweet William
Look at Me, Centrosema
Love Grove, Nemophila
Love in a Mist, Nigella
Love Lies Bleeding, Amaranthus
Lungwort, Martensia
Madagascar Periwinkle, Vinca
Maidenhair Fern, Adiantum
Mallow, Hibiscus
Maltese Cross, Lychnis
Mariposa Lily, Calochortus
Marsh Mallow, Hibiscus
Meadow Beauty, Rhexia
Meadow Sage, Salvia
Meadow Star, Spiroea
Mexican Fire Plant, Euphorbia
Mexican Lily, Amaryllis
Michaelmas Daisies, Aster
Monkey Flower, Mimulus
Monkshood, Aconitum
Moon Flower, Ipomeoa
Moonpenny Daisy, Chrysanthemum
Moonwort, Honesty

Morning Glory, Iopmoea
Mosses, Selaginellas
Moss Pink, Phlox
Moss Verbena, Verbena
Mother of Thousands, Saxifrage
Mountain Fleece, Polygonum
Mountain Fringe, Adlumia
Mountain Laurel, Kalmia
Mourning Bride, Scabiosa
Mouse-ear Chickweed, Cerastium
Moustache Plant, Caropteris
Musk Plant, Mimulus
Old Maid, Vinca
Old Man, Artemesia
Old Woman, Artemsia
Orchid Vine, Stigmaphyllon
Oriental Poppy, Papaver
Oswego Tea, Monarda
Painted Daisy, Chrysanthemum
Painted Leaf, Euphorbia
Painted Tongue, Salpiglossis
Pampas Grass, Gynerium
Pancratium, Ismene
Paris Daisy, Chrysanthemum
Passion Flower, Passiflora
Peacock Flower, Tigridia
Pearl Bush, Exochorda
Peppermint, Mentha
Periwinkle, Vinca

Seal Flower, Dielytra
Segar Plant, Cuphea
Sensitive Plant, Mimosa
Shaking Fern, Pteris
Shell Flower, Tigridia
Shooting Star, Dodecatheon
Shrubby Honeysuckle, Linicera
Silk Oak, Grevillea
Silver Bells, Halesia
Slipper Flower, Calceolaria
Smoke Tree, Rhus
Snapdragon, Antirrhinum
Sneezewort, Helenium
Snowball, Viburnum
Snowberry, Symphoricarpus
Snow in Summer, Cerastium
Snow on the Mountain, Euphorbia
Southern Wood, Abrotanum
Speedwell, Veronica
Spider Plant, Cleome
Spike Grass, Uniola
Spring Beauty, Claytonia
Starworts, Asters
Stone Crop, Sedum
Straw Flower, Helichrysum

Sulphur Fern, Gymnogramma
Sunflower, Helianthus
Sun Plant, Portulaca
Swan River Daisy, Brachycome
Swan River Everlasting, Rhodanthe
Sweet Olive, Olea
Sweet Sultan, Centaurea
Tassel Flower, Cacalia
Thrift, Armeria
Toad Flax, Linaria
Toad Lily, Castalia
Tobacco Plant, Nicotiana
Torch Lily, Tritoma
Tree Celandine, Bocconia
Trumpet Flower, Datura
Trumpet Vine, Bignonia
Umbrella Plant, Cyperus
Variegated Comfrey, Symphytum
Venus' Looking-Glass, Campanula
Virgin's Bower, Clematis
Wake Robin, Trillium
Wawhaw, Euonymus
Wax Plant, Hoya
Wax Plant, Mesembryanthemum

White Fringe, Chionanthus
Whitlow Grass, Draba
Wild Cucumber, Echinocystis
Wind Flower, Anemone
Winged Everlasting, Ammobium
Wolf's Bane, Aconitum

Wood Lily, Trillium
Woodruff, Aperula
Yellow Flax, Linum
Youth and Old Age, Zinnia
Zanzibar Balsam, Impatiens
Zebra Grass, Eulalia

BLOOMING SEASON OF VARIOUS
TREES, SHRUBS, AND PLANTS
T.—Tree. S.—Shrub. V.—Vine.
H.P.—Hardy Perennial. A.—Annual.
H.H.P.—Hardy Herbaceous Perennial.
E.—Evergreen.

APRIL
Akebia Quinata, H.P.V.
Alyssum Argenteum, H.P.
Anemone Blanda, H.P.
Bellis Perennis, H.P.E.
Dicentra—Bleeding Heart, H.H.P.
Dicentra-Dutchman's Breeches, H.P.
Dodecatheon, H.P.
Forsythia, Golden Bells, H.S.
Sanguinaria, Blood Root, H.H.P.
Saxifrage, H.P.
Uvularia—Bellwort, H.P.
Vinca, Periwinkle, Myrtle, H.P.E.
Violets, in var., H.P.E.

MAY
Adonis, H.P.
Ajuga, H.H.P.
Alyssum Argenteum, H.H.P.
Alyssum Saxatile, H.H.P.
Amsonia, H.H.P.
Aquilegia Argenteum, H.H.P.
Arum—Cuckoo Flower, H.H.P.
Aubretia, H.H.P.
Azalea, S.
Barberry, S.
Bellis—English Daisy, H.P.E.
Callicarpa Japonica, H.P.
Calycanthus—Sweet Shrub, H.P.S.
Chionanthus—White Wings, H.P.S.
Convallaria—Lily of the Valley, H.H.P.
Daphne, H.S.E.
Deutzia, H.P.S.
Dicentra, H.H.P.
Doronicum, H.H.P.
Double-flowered Almond, H.S.

Double-Flowered Crab, H.S.
Double-flowered Peach, H.S.
Epimedium, H.H.P.
Euonymus—Burning Bush, H.S.
Exochorda-Pearl Bush, H.S.
Genista, H.H.P.

Syringa—Lilac, H.T.
Tamarix, H.S.
Trillium, H.H.P.
Veronica, H.P.
Viburnum-Snowball, H.S.
Vinca, Myrtle, H.P.E.
Weigela, H.S.

Halesia—Snowdrop, H.T.
Hawthorn, H.T.
Honeysuckle—Bush, H.S.
Iris Aurea, H.H.P.
Iris Siberica, H.H.P.
Lychnis—Red Campion, H.H.P.
Ornithogalum—Bulbous, H.H.P.
Phlox Subulata, H.P.
Polemonium—Greek Valerian, H.P.
Polyanthus, H.P.E.
Potentilla, June to August, H.P.
Primula—English Primrose, H.P.E.
Pulmonaria—Lungwort, H.H.P.
Pyrus—(Cydonia) Japonica, H.P.S.
Ranunculus, Half H.P.
Rhododendrons, H.S.E.
Ribes, Flowering Currant, H.S.
Sanguinaria—Blood Root, H.H.P.
Spiraea Filipendula, H.H.P.
Spiraea Thunbergi, H.S.
Spiraea Van Houttei, H.S.

JUNE
Aconitum—Monkshood, H.H.P.
Alstromeria—Peruvian Lily, H.H.P.
Anchusa, H.H.P.
Anthemis, H.H.P.
Anthericum—St. Bruno's Lily, H.H.P.
Aquilegia, H.H.P.
Armeria, H.P.
Arum, H.P.
Astragalus—Milk Vetch, H.H.P.
Baptisia, H.P.
Bellis, H.P.E.
Buphthalmum, H.P.
Callirhoe, H.P.
Campanula, H.P.E.
Cassia, H.P.
Catalpa, H.T.
Centaurea, H.P.
Centranthus, H.P.
Coreopsis, H.P.
Cornus—Dogwood, H.T.

197

Coronilla, H.P.
Delphinium, H.H.P.
Deutzia Gracilis, H.S.
Deutzia—Pride of Rochester, H.S.
Digitalis, H.P.E.
Doronicum, H.P.
Dracocephalum, H.P.
Erigeron, H.P.
Heuchera, H.H.P.
Hollyhock, H.H.P.E.
Honeysuckle, H.V.
Hydrangea-Climbing, H.P.V.
Iris, H.H.P.
Jasminum, H.P.
Laburnum, H.T.
Lathyrus—Everlasting Pea, H.H.P.
Lilium Canadense, H.H.P. (bulb)
Lilium Canadense, H.H.P.E. (bulb)
Lilium Longiflorum, H.H.P. (bulb)
Linden, H.T.
Locust, H.T.
Lychnis Chalcedonica, H.H.P.
Lychnis Coronaria, H.H.P.
Lychnis Gigantea, H.H.P.
Magnolia, H.T.
Monarda, H.P.
Mountain Ash, H.T.
Papaver-Poppy, H.H.P.&A.
Pentstemon, Half H.P.

Philadelphus, H.T.
Potentilla, H.P.
Pyrethrum, H.H.T.
Ranunculus, H.P.
Rhododendron, H.P.E.
Rose, Hardy S.
Salpiglossis, A.
Schizanthus, A.
Sedum, H.P.
Spiraea, in var., H.P.
Sweet Alyssum, A.
Sweet Peas, A.
Sweet Scabiosa, H.P.
Sweet Sultan, A.
Veronica, T.P.
Vinca, E.V.
Violets, H.P.E.

JULY
Achillea, H.H.P.
Allium Angularis, H.P.
Anthemis, H.P.
Armeria, H.P.
Asphodel, H.P.
Aster Alpinus, H.P.
Bignonia Radicans, H.P.V.
Bocconia, H.P.
Campanula, H.P.E.
Candytuft, A.

Chrysanthemum Maximum, H.P.
Cobaea Scandens, Tender P.V.
Coreopsis, H.P.
Cosmos, A.
Dahlia, Tender P.
Datura, A.
Dictamnus, H.P.
Digitalis, H.P.E.
Dracocephalum, H.P.
Eccremocarpus, V.A.
Euphorbia, A.
Evening Primrose, H.P.
Funkia, P.
Gypsophila, A.
Iris—Japanese, H.P.
Liatris, H.P.
Lilium Auratum, H.P.
Linum, H.P.
Lychnis, H.H.P.
Perennial Phlox, H.H.P.
Phlox Drummondi, A.
Potentilla, H.P.
Salvia, Tender P.
Statice, H.P.
Thalictrum, H.P.
Thymus, H.P.
Vinca, Tender P.
Yucca, H.P.E.

AUGUST
Achillea, H.H.P.
Allium, H.P.
Armeria, H.H.P.
Asphodel, H.H.P.
Bellis, H.P.E.
Callirhoe, H.P.
Campanula, H.P.E.
Carnation, T.P.
Centranthus, H.P.
Clerodendron, H.P.
Cobaea, V.A.
Cosmos, A.
Delphinium, H.P.
Dianthus, H.H.P.
Digitalis, H.P.E.
Dolichos, V.A.
Eupatorium, H.P.
Euphorbia, A.
Funkia, H.H.P.
Helianthus, H.P.
Hibiscus, H.H.P.
Hollyhock, H.S.
Hydrangea, late in August, H.P.S.
Hypericum Moserianum, H.S.
Liatris, H.P.
Lilium Album, H.H.P.
Lilium Auratum, H.H.P.

Lilium Melpomene, H.H.P.
Lilium Roseum, H.H.P.
Lilium Rubrum, H.H.P.
Lobelia Carinalis, H.H.P.E.
Lychnis, H.H.P.
Monarda, H.P.
Oenothera, H.P.
Pentstemon, H.P.
Phlox, Perennial, H.H.P.
Platycodon, H.H.P.
Rudbeckia, H.H.P.
Salvia, Tender P.
Sedum, H.P.
Silphium, H.P.
Statice, H.P.
Vinca, Tender P.

SEPTEMBER

Althea, H.P.T.
Anchusa, H.P.
Anemone-Queen Charlotte, H.H.P.
Anemone-Whirlwind, H.H.P.
Asters, in var., A. & H.H.P.
Boltonia, H.P.
Clematis Paniculata, H.P.V.
Erianthus, H.P.
Eulalia, H.P.
Eupatorium, A.H.P.
Euphorbia, A.
Gladiolus, Bulbs
Golden Rod, H.H.P.
Hibiscus, H.P.&T.P.
Hydrangea, H.P.
Ipomaea, A.
Lobelia Cardinalis, H.H.P.E.
Pampas Grass, Half H.P.
Rudbeckia, H.P.
Salvia, T.P.
Statice, H.P.
Tritoma, Tender P.
Vinca, Tender P.

ALL SUMMER

Ageratum, A.
Antirrhinum, T.P.
Armeria, A.
Balsam, A.
Bartonia, P.
Begonia, Tuberous, T.P.
Begonia, Vernon, T.P.
Brachycome, P.
Browallia, T.A.
Canary Bird Vine, A.
Candytuft, A.
Canna, Tender P. Rhizomes
Celosia, A.
Centrosema, H.P.
Clarkia, A.
Cleome Pungens, A.
Cobaea Scandens, A.
Collinsia, A.
Cosmos, A.
Crotolaria, A.
Cypress Vine, A.
Delphinium, H.P.
Gloxinia, T.P.
Hyacinthus Candicans, H.P.
Ipomaea, A.
Maurandya, P.
Nasturtium, A.
Pansy, P.

Petunia, A.
Portulaca, A.
Rose, Hardy or Half Hardy S.
Sweet Pea, A.
Sweet Scabiosa, A.
Sweet Sultan, H.P.
Thunbergia, T.P.
Verbena, T.P.
Veronica, H.P.
Vinca, T.P.
Vincetoxicum, H.P.

Stock-ten week
Sweet William
Tradescantia
Trifolium
Tunica
Verbascum
Veronica
Virginia Stock
Viscaria
Vittadenia
Whitlavia
Zinnia

TIME FOR GERMINATION OF SEEDS

From Three to Five Days

Ageratum
Ammobium
Aster
Celosia
Centaurea
Chrysanthemums
Cypress Vine
Gilla
Hollyhock
Lavatera
Layia Elegans
Leptosyne Maritima
Marigold
Mimulus
Mina Lobata
Salvia
Sedum
Silene Shasta
Spherogyne
Stevia

In Five to Seven Days

Acacia
Amaranthus
Arabis Alpina
Beta
Brompton Stock
Bromus
Browallia
Candytuft
Cannabis
Carnations
Centaurea
Chelone
Chrysanthemum Indicum
Cineraria
Clitoria
Coleus
Coreopsis Lanceolata
Crucianella
Cuphea
Cynoglossum
Dahlia

Daisy	Antirrhinum
Eschscholtzia	Armeria
Eupatorium	Balsams
Gaillardia	Begonia
Geranium	Calceolaria
Gypsophila	Campanula, Annual
Hablitzia	Canna
Helenium	Capsicum
Helianthus	Commelyna Coelestis
Helichrysum	Deutzia
Hibiscus	Digitalis
Iberis Gibraltarica	Dracocephalum
Linaria Reticulata	Erianthus
Lobelia	Gaura
Lupinus	Gloxinia
Lychnis	Gnaphalium
Malva Moschata	Hibiscus Syriacus
Mathiola	Humulus Japonica
Mesembryanthemum	Kaulfussia
Mignonette	Lychnis
Morning Glory	Morina
Nicotiana	Pansy
Picotee	Pansy, Viola
Pink	Papaver
Salpiglossis	Pentstemon
Schizanthus	Petunia
	Phacelia
	Phlox Drummondi
In Eight to Ten Days	Poinsettia
Abutilon	Potentilla
Achimines	Pyrethrum
Agrostemma	Rudbeckia

Thunbergia
Tropaeolum
Valeriana
Verbena
Zea

In Ten to Twelve Days

Achillea
Alonsoa
Alyssum Saxatile
Anchusa
Aquilegia
Argemone
Artemisia
Asphodelus
Aubrietia
Bidens
Calandrinia
Calonyction
Campanula
Feverfew
Galtonia
Geum
Gypsolphila
Helianthemum
Linaria
Ipomopsis
Scutellaria
Silphium
Spiraea

In Twelve to Fifteen Days

Anemone Sylvestris
Antigonon
Asters, Per.
Callirhoe
Campanula Tenorei
Datura
Didiscus
Gazanopsis
Gourds
Hunnemannia
Lantana
Mandevillea
Maurandya
Myosotis
Nicotiana
Nierembergia
Peas
Perilla
Petunia, Double
Platycodon
Polemonium
Ranunculus
Ricinus
Thalictrum
Torenia
Verbena Venosa

In Fifteen to Twenty Days
Acanthus
Agapanthus
Anemone
Antigonon
Armeria Maritima
Calla
Cobaea
Cuphea
Dictamnus
Geranium Sanguineum
Heliotrope
Hemerocallis
Impatiens Sultana
Iris
Liatris Spicata
Primula Sinensis
Rivina Humilis
Smilax, Boston
Solanum Robustum

In Twenty to Thirty-five Days
Adlumia
Baptisia Australia
Berberis Vulgaris
Campanula Fragilis
Campanula Leutweiana
Campanula Macrantha
Campanula Nobilis

Clematis Diversifolia
Clematis Integrifolia
Clianthus Dampieri
Delphinium Nudicaule
Funkia
Gentiana Acaulis
Hibiscus Speciosa
Humea Elegans
Musa Ensete
Phlox, Perennial
Phormium
Physianthus
Tritoma Uvaria
Yucca

One Year or More
Adlumia
Ampelopsis
Anthericum
Clematis, in variety
Dictamnus
Fuchsia
Geranium Sanguineum
Iris
Lilies
Lupinus Polyphyllus
Musa
Tradescantia
Viola Odorata

FRAGRANT FLOWERS OR LEAVES

Baby's Breath
Large Purple-fringed Orchis
Smaller Purple-fringed Orchis
Hepatica (occasionally)
Purple Marsh Clematis
English Violet
Wild Phlox
Catnip
Pennyroyal
Wild Thyme
Peppermint
Spear Mint
Wild Mint
Dittany
Pasture Thistle
Pink Moccasin Flower
Showy Orchis
Rose Pogonia
Arethusa
Calopogon
Night-flowering Catchfly
Bouncing Bet
Purple-flowering Raspberry
Queen-of-the-Prairie
Wild Rose
Red Clover
Musk Mallow
Prince's Pine
Bog Wintergreen
Pink Azalea
White Azalea
Trailing Arbutus
Sabbatia
Fly-trap Dogbane

Four-leaved Milkweed
Field Bindweed
Wild Bergamot
Twin-flower
Joe-Pye Weed (slightly)
Wild Spikenard (slightly)
White-fringed Orchis
Ladies' Tresses
Lizard's Tail
Bladder Campion
White Water Lily
Laurel Magnolia
Squirrel Corn
White Sweet Clover
Wild Grape
Sweet White Violet
Canada Violet
Sweet-Cicely
Sweet Pepperbush
Pyrola
Shin-leaf
Wintergreen
Button-bush
Partride Vine
Elder
Clammy Everlasting
Bellwort
Adder's Tongue
Small Yellow Lady's Slipper
Spice-bush
Yellow Sweet Clover
Yellow Wood-sorrel
Evening Primrose
Horse-balm

Horned Bladderwort
Honeysuckles
Fragrant Golden-rod
Ground-nut
Pine Sap
Oswego Tea

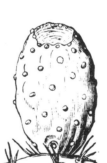

UNPLEASANTLY SCENTED

Purple Trillium
Black Cohosh
Mandrake
Jamestown Weed
Salt-marsh Fleabane
Camomile
Carrion-flower
Barberry
Skunk Cabbage
Hound's Tongue
Beech-drops

ANNUAL CHART OF TRADE NAMES AND VARIETIES IN COMMON USE

Plant	Varieties	Color	Height (inches)	Comments
Ageratum (Flossflower)	Blue Blazer	deep blue	5	compact, free blooming
	Blue Chip	blue	12	large flower clusters bloom from early summer to frost
	Blue Heaven	blue	6	dwarf plants, large leaves and flowering heads.
	North Sea	deep blue	8	blooms freely
	Royal Blazer	radiant deep blue	5	compact, free blooming
	Summer Snow	pure white	5	early blooming
Alyssum	Carpet of Snow	snowy white	2½	early, free flowering
	New Carpet of Snow	white	3-4	extra dwarf
	Rosie O'Day	deep rose-pink	4	blooms two months after seeding, blooms until frost
	Royal Carpet	deep violet-blue	2-4	doesn't transplant easily
	Tiny Tim	snow white	3	blooms early
Amaranthus	Early Splendor	rosy-crimson	36	earlier, more brilliant than old Molten Fire
	Flaming Fountain	brilliant red	36	slender, ribbon-like leaves
	Tricolor splendens (Joseph's Coat)	yellow, green, and red	36	side branches contain as much color as the main shoot.
Balsam	Double Bush-Flowering mixture	scarlet and mixed	14	bright green foliage, camellia-like flowers
	Tom Thumb or Dwarf Bush mixture	mixed	12	dwarf compact leaves, flowers freely producing
Basil (ornamental)	Dark Opal	lavender-white	15	excellent for borders
Begonia (Fibrous-rooted)	*Hybrids* *Pink and Rose*			
	Caravelle Pink	blush pink	8-10	large flower and large leaf
	Caravelle Rose	bright rose	8-10	large flower and large leaf
	Linda	rich rose	6-8	resists disease, adverse weather

Also available in separate colors.

Plant	Varieties	Color	Height (inches)	Comments
	Patria	clear rose	6-8	bronze foliage
	Pink Charm	rich pink	6-8	ideal for large scale landscape planting
	Rose Comet	really pink	6-8	bronze foliage
	Pink Comet	light pink	6-8	bronze foliage
	Pink Tausendschoen	bright pink	8-10	dwarf, rich green foliage
	Red			
	Caravelle Red	bright orange scarlet	8-10	large flower and large leaf
	Matador	light scarlet with white center	8-10	very vigorous for outdoors
	Othello	scarlet orange	9-10	deep waxy, bronze foliage
	Red Comet	fiery scarlet	9-10	bronze foliage
	Scarletta	scarlet red	6-8	uniform, dwarf habit
	Red Tausendschoen	clear red	8-10	blooms profusely
	White			
	Viva	pure white	6-8	weather resistant
	White Comet	white	9-10	bronze foliage
	White Tausendschoen	pure white	6-8	bright green foliage

207

Mixtures				
Galaxy Mixed	mixed colors	6-8	bronzed leaves, often appears metallic	
Organdy Mixture	red, pink, white	9-10	predominantly green foliage, about 20% of plants have bronze foliage	
Inbreds				
Red				
Ball Red	scarlet-red	4-6	reddish-green leaves	
Dwarf Indian Maid	scarlet	4-6	compact	
White				
Snowbank	glistening-white	4-6	large, dense-growing	
Bicolor				
Flamingo	white with pink edge	4-6	bicolor	
Novelties				
Singles--Cindrella	rose-white	8-10	extra large flowers with golden centers	
Doubles--Christmas Candle	deep rose	12	green foliage	
White Christmas	white	12	green foliage	

Bells of Ireland (*Molucella laevis*)		green, white	24	good for flower arranging

Browallia	Blue Bells Improved	amethyst-blue	8-10	very free flowering
	Silver Bells	snowy white	8	blooms all summer until frost

Calendula (Pot Marigold)	Orange Coronet	bright orange	12	produce abundance of flowers throughout summer
	Pacific Beauty Mixed	mixed or separate	18	withstand summer heat

Calliopsis	Dwarf Mixture	mixed or separate	9-12	flowers on short stems

Carnation (annual)	Chabaud Giants Mixed	scarlet, crimson, pink, rose, white and yellow	18	large, full double, fringed flowers
	Dwarf Fragrance Mixed	mixed	13-15	highly fragrant, double flowers

Castor Bean (*Ricinus*)	Black Beauty (Cambodgensis)	dark brown turn deep green	60	vigorous plants
	Crimson Spire	purplish leaves, red stems, stalks	72	leaves change from purple to bronzy green
(Seeds are poisonous)	Zanzibariensis mixed	various colors	96	

Celosia (Cockscomb)	*Cristata type*			
	Fireglow	velvety orange-carmine	20-24	large, globular, 6-inch + flower heads
	Floradale	red	16	large center comb with medium side combs
	Jewel Box (mixture)	white, light yellow to pink, red, purple	6-8	extra dwarf, large combs
	Prairie Fire	bright red	18	uniform, hedge-like plants
	Toreador	bright red	24	bright green foliage
	Yellow Toreador	yellow	24	bright green foliage, a spot of Toreador
	Coral Gardens Mixed (individual colors include)		10	
	Empress Improved	velvety crimson-red	10	
	Gladiator Improved	bright yellow gold	10	
	Kardinal Improved	shining orange-scarlet	10	immense bloom, dwarf plants
	Rose Empress	bright rose	10-12	large combs, reddish leaves

Plumosa type			
	Crusader	glistening red	24	bronze foliage, dwarf version of Forest Fire
	Dwarf Fiery Feather	fiery red	12	attractive pyramid formation
	Dwarf Golden Feather	deep golden yellow	14	pyramid formation
	Forest Fire Improved	scarlet	30	early flowering, large plumes
	Golden Gem	gold	9	miniature type of Golden Feather
	Golden Torch	golden yellow	24	bushy, green plants
	Golden Triumph (AAS '68)	tawny gold	24	vigorous, many plumes, good for cut flowers
Centaurea (Cornflower)	Jubilee Gem	blue	12	bright blue cornflower
	Little Boy Blue	bright blue	24-30	standard blue
	Polka Dot Mixture	blue, maroon, red, rose-pink, lavender, and white	15-18	showy dwarf mixture, improvement over Jubilee Gem in color, doubleness and bushy plant habit
	Snow Ball (AAS '69)	white	12-16	neat well-branched almost ball-shaped plants
	Tall Mixture	variety of colors	24	
Cheiranthus allioni	Siberian Wallflower	orange	18	free blooming
Chrysanthemum (annual)	Autumn Glory	full color range	5-6	stays dwarf, can be sown early, up to May
Cleome (Spiderflower)	Helen Campbell	pure white	42	large thorny border plant
	Rose Queen	deep bright rose	42	strong color which is held throughout the season
Coleus (from seed)	Rainbow Mixture	all colors	24	shade plants, select for color and leaf texture desired
	(Many others being introduced yearly)			
Convolvulus (Morning Glory)	Dwarf Royal Ensign	royal blue	12	dwarf bush
	Early Call Rose (AAS '70)	rose	84	early flowering, 4-inch flowers, remain open into day
Cosmos	Bright Lights Mixture	yellow, gold, red	36	multipetaled flowers, 2 inches wide, a blend of Goldcrest, Sunset and a new bright yellow.
	Early Sensation Mixture	all colors	36	extra-large flowers and extreme earliness
	Goldcrest	gold	24-36	flowers cover plants early until frost
	Sunset (AAS '66)	orange-scarlet	36	bright vermillion blooms, showy hedge from early summer, semi-double flowers
Cynoglossum (Chinese Forget-me-not)	Firmament	indigo blue	15	good for borders, edgings and rock gardens, long stiff upright stems
Dahlia (from seed)	Border Jewels	good color range	14-18	compact, reliable, early blooming
	Early Bird Mixed	bright colors	15	extra early, very dwarf, double and semi-double strain
	Unwin's Dwarf Mixture	vivid reds through soft pinks, yellow and orange to pale buff	24	popular for bedding and cut flowers

Daisies (miscellaneous)	Dahlborg Daisy	gold	8	dainty, ferny foliage, for close edgings, bedding or rock gardens
	Tahoka Daisy	lilac-blue petals golden-yellow center	20	bushy compact flowering plants, fern-like foliage, flowers are 2 inches across
Delphinium	Connecticut Yankees Mixed* (AAS '65)	wide color range	30-36	good in beds, borders, and medium-tall backgrounds, and excellent cutting, may need staking
Dianthus (Annual Pinks)	Baby Doll	wide color range	8	large-flowered dwarf single mixture with plain edged flowers.
	Bravo	flaming scarlet-red	8	compact upright plant type
	China Doll (AAS '70)	salmon, red, and white	12-18	vigorous growing plants, flowers profusely.
	Gaiety, single and double	wide color range	12	fringed and laciniated single flowers of unusual size and colorings
	Queen of Hearts (AAS '72)	brilliant scarlet red	12-15	vigorous, uniform, mass bloom
	Red Empress	deep red	12	ideal cutting stems
Digitalis (Foxglove) (First year flowering)	Foxy (AAS '67)	rose, heliotrope, cream, white and rose-red	36	sow early, not later than March, may need staking
Dimorphotheca (Cape Marigold)	Aurantiaca Mixed	yellow, buff, orange	12	3½-inch single flowers
	Glistening White	pure white petals shiny black center	8	black eyes, edged violet
Dusty Miller	Cineraria maritima 'Diamond'	white	10	an improved strain, compact even growth.
	Silver Dust	silvery white	8	very dwarf strain, finely cut.
	Silver Lace (Silver Feather)	silver gray	6-8	neat compact, with very finely cut leaves resembling delicate lace.
Eschsoholtzia (California Poppy)	Mission Bells Mixed	rose and white, scarlet and yellow orange and gold, pink and amber, solid colors	12	bloom early, abundant, dainty, free-flowering plants.
Euphorbia	Mexican Fire Plant (E. Heterophylla)	bright red	24	upper foliage is blotched bright red
	Snow-on-the-Mountain (E. variegata)	white and green	24	snowy white bracts top "mountain" of green.
Four O'Clocks (Mirabilis)	Four O'Clock Mixture	red, pink, lilac, yellow, white, several colors on one plant	24	flowers open in afternoon or all day if cloudy, easily grown, blooms July until frost.
Gaillardia (1st year flowering)	Lollipops Mixed	all colors	10-14	sweet 2-2½ inch ball-shaped double flowers
	Lorenziana Double Sunshine Mixed	all colors	10-14	large flowers in breath-taking array of colors
Gazania	Splendens Grandiflora Mixture	orange with shades of yellow and white	8	vigorous plants constantly in bloom

Geranium (F$_1$ hybrid) (from seed)	*Carefree Series*			
	Bright Pink (AAS '68)	pink	24	medium early
	Deep Salmon (AAS '68)	darker pink	20	early, large clusters, free flowering
	Fickle Scarlet	bright scarlet white center	20	
	Light Salmon	light salmon	19	
	Red and Scarlet	red and scarlet	20	early, large clusters, free flowering
	New Era Series			
	Bright Red	bright red	20	medium early, free flowering and very showy.
	Coral	rich coral salmon	20	abundant bloom, medium early with large flower clusters
	Light Salmon	soft, luminous	20	medium zone leaf, early free-flowering
	Medium Salmon	clear medium salmon	20	zonal leaf ring, early free flowering
	Scarlet	bright scarlet-red	21	medium early, large flower clusters free flowering
	Scarlet with White Eye	brilliant scarlet with large white eye	26	late, extra-large clusters.
	Double Dip Series			
	Cherry	red	16	5 inch flower globes tightly packed with double florets, temptingly born above dark green foliage.
	Peach	creamy peach	16	5-inch flower globes, tightly packed with double florets, temptingly borne above dark green foliage
	Raspberry	bright pink	16	5-inch flower globes tightly packed with double florets, temptingly borne above dark green foliage
	Strawberry	red	16	5-inch flower globes, tightly packed with double florets, temptingly borne with dark green foliage
	Sprinter (Fleuroselect '73)	bright scarlet	18	free flowering, two weeks earlier and dwarfer

Grasses (Ornamental)	Blue Fescue (*Festuca ovina* 'Glauca')	blue grass	12	dense glaucous tuffs
	Fountain Grass (*Pennisetum ruppeli*)	strikingly colored	48	12-inch spikes are strikingly colored, leaves narrow, 2 ft. long.
Helianthus (Sunflower)	Sungold	golden yellow	72	freely borne, 100% double
	Teddy Bear	bright yellow	36	Dwarf sunflower, double chrysanthemum-like blooms up to 5 inches across on bushy uniform 3 ft. plants with many lateral branches
Helichrysum (Strawflower)	Giant Formula Double Mixture	many colors	36	Exceptionally large flowers
	Tom Thumb Dwarf Mixture	all colors	12-18	
Heliopsis	Summer Sun	golden	4	double flowers borne on long strong stems from July through late September
Heliotrope	Dwarf Regale Mixture	clear-colored strain	15	dwarf, produced extremely large flower heads.
	Marine	deep violet-blue	24	giant umbels
Hibiscus (1st year flower)	Southern Belle (AAS '71)	crimson, red, rose, pink, white and white with red eye	48-72	huge blooms, 7 or more inches across, flowers the same season as seeds sown
Hollyhock (annual)	Silver Puffs (AAS '71)	silvery pink	24	bushy plants produce short flower spikes
	Summer Carnival (AAS '72)	scarlet, deep rose, pink, white, yellow	60-72	vigorous, flowers from seed the first year, and plants winter over and bloom well for many years
Hunnemannia (Mexican Tulip Poppy)	Sunlite	bright yellow	24	tulip-like flowers, fine for cutting.
Impatiens (Sultana)	Baby Mixed	many colors	6	uniform, free flowering
	Elfin Mixture	bright vivid colors	8-10	self branching at base, no pinching required
	Imp Mixture	variety of colors	15	large round flowers even in hot weather up to 2 inches across, excellent for difficult shady area
	Shade Glow Mixture	mixed colors	10	quicker, better germination, faster more uniform growth, earlier, larger more abundant bloom
Kochia (Summer Cypress	Summer Cypress	Green turning to red in late fall	30-36	fine for summer hedges, feathery foliage
Lobelia	Blue Gown	deep blue	6	free flowering
	Cambridge Blue	clear light blue	4	fine for edgings, rock gardens, and borders
	Crystal Palace	intense deep blue	6	fine variety, fine edger
	Rosamond	red with white eyes	4	good for edging
	String of Pears Mixture	mixture	6	blended form separate colors
	White Lady	clear glistening white	6	good for edgings and borders

Marigold	*Dwarf*			
	Apollo	glowing orange	14	bushy compact plant (dwarf giant double)
	Bolero (AAS '70)	bright maroon petals, tinged gold center	12-18	early bloom, free flowering, compact habit, flowers 1½ to 2¼ inches. (Dwarf French)
	Dainty Marietta	golden yellow	12	extra dwarf compact flowers (single, medium dwarf)
	King Tut	golden yellow crest, deep red guard petals	8	large 2½-inch flowers (super double)
	Lemondrop	lemon yellow flowers	9	dwarf compact plants with medium small, fully double flowers
	Moonshot	brilliant yellow	14	3-inch double blooms, very early (dwarf, giant double)
	Petite Mixed	variety of bright colors	12	early flowering with a profusion of blooms (extra dwarf double)
	7-Star Gold	gold	18	uniform bushy compact plants, large flowering mule marigold
	Red Brocade	dark mahogany-red gold on outer edges	14	2-inch flowers on compact ball-shaped plants (French double)
	Spanish Brocade	rich gold, deep red flowers	8-10	abundant, large 2½ inch flowers (French double)
	Sparky	gold edged and marked with red	8-10	original strain, compact plants 2½-inch flowers (French double)
	Yellow Nugget	bright yellow	12	free flowering, everblooming bushy plants, blooms are 2 inches, last all summer (dwarf French)
	Golden Gem (Signet type)	rich golden orange	12	free flowering, fine lacy foliage
	Irish Lace		6	unique, foliage type marigold for edging
	Tall			
	Diamond Jubilee	primrose yellow	18-24	4-inch flowers, long lasting, hedge type
	Golden Jubilee (AAS- '67)	nice golden yellow	24	3-4 inch flowers, hedge-type
	Orange Jubilee (AAS- '68)	bright orange	24	uniform, 3 to 4-inch flowers, hedge-type
	First Lady (AAS- '68)	yellow	18	erect, compact plant, carnation-like blooms.
	Gold Lady	golden yellow	18	carnation-type blooms almost hide the semi-dwarf plants, hedge type
	Orange Lady	bright deep orange	18	fully double flowers measuring up to 3½ inches, plants bear more than 50 blooms, hedge type
	Gold Galore (AAS- '72)	solid gold	18	hedge-type, outstanding in vigor and uniformity, hedge type
	Climax Mixed	many shades	24-36	almost globular blooms up to 5 inches across, fully double
	Gold Coin Mixture	from light orange to pure gold	30	large extra double flowers 3½ to 4 inches, fine for cut flowers
	Happy Face (AAS- '73)	golden-yellow	24	flowers early and freely on bushy plants

Matricaria (Feverfew)	Double White Improved	pure white	24	fully-double flowers, long stems
	Golden Ball	golden yellow	8	like tiny chrysanthemums
	Snow Ball	pure white	10	double rounded flowers
	White Stars	white	8	extra dwarf, broad guard petals around button type centers
Nasturtium	Double Gleam Mixture	array of many colors, yellows to reds	36	extra large
	Jewel Mixture	mixture of colors in cherry rose class	12	free flowering, blooms held above neat domes of foliage
Nicotiana (Flowering tobacco)	Crimson Bedder	deep crimson	18	long tubular florets, compact habit
	Idol	red	8-10	first true dwarf red
	Lime Sherbert (Lime green, Lime-light)	cool green	12-18	vigorous, refreshing color
	White Bedder	pure white	12	dwarf compact, fragrant flowers

SEA LAVENDER.

ORIENTAL POPPY.
(PAPAVER BRACTEATUM.)

SLENDER LEAVED PEONY.

Nierembergia (Dwarf cupflower)	Purple Robe	violet-blue	6	dwarf plants, flowering throughout the summer, sow before most bedding plants for an early start
Oxypetalum	Southern Star	silvery blue	15	wide arching sprays
Pansy	Clear Crystals	red, purple, blue	8	no blotching, free flowering, rounded compact plants, weather resistant
	Color Carnaval	wide color range	6	vigorous, strong growing husky plants
	Majestic Giants Mixed	bright color range	7	4-inch flowers
	Jumbo Mixture	well-balanced blend of pastel colors	6	early vigorous, long stemmed and very large-flowered
	Roggli Elite Swiss Giants Mixture	rich colors	5-7	for flower size uniformity, and habit these are one of the finest, all have dark bloches
	Azure Blue	blue	6	showy, rich blooms all summer
Penstemon (Annual Beard Tongue)	Rainbow or Sensation Mixture	red, rose, pink lavender	30	showy spikes of bugle-shaped flowers
Perilla (Crinkled Coleus)	Frutescens (Nankinensis) Crispa	same as coleus	18	quicker and easier from seed than Coleus

Petunia (Grandiflora Single)	Bicolor			
	Astro	white and brilliant red	12	uniform pattern, 3½-inch flowers
	Bingo Improved	wine-red and white	12	good clear pattern plus extra vigor
	Cavalier	rich salmon and white	12	early nicely-fringed blooms of varying pattern
	Cherry Blossom	cherry red and pure white	12	medium sized flowers freely producing on vigorous plants
	Fiesta	bright rose and white	12	good weather and botrytis resistance
	Gay Paris	wine-purple and white	12	free flowering
	Minstrel Improved	rich violet-blue and white	10	dwarfer than other bicolors and has a darker pattern under certain weather conditions
	Roulette	red and white	12	blooms early, flowers are 3½ inches
	Zig-Zag	deep rose and white	12	uniform plant, free flowering
	Razzle-Dazzle (Mixture)	red, deep rose, deep blue and crimson	12	popular mixture to achieve a dazzling effect
	White and Cream Yellow			
	Apollo	white	12-15	short and early blooming, heavy textured, 3 to 3½-inch flowers
	Glacier	glistening icy white, chartreuse in center	12-15	heavy textured flowers, compact plants
	White Ensign	white	13	huge, fringed, bold 4½-inch flowers
	White Magic	white	12	lightly fringed flowers, compact plants
	White Sails	white	12	one of the most popular grandifloras
	Sunburst	clear lemon-white	12	attractively fringed, semi-upright plants, 3-inch flowers

Pink and Rose

Happiness	carmine-pink	15	large-flowered
Pink Cameo	rose-pink	12	3¼-inch flowers, unusually stocky plants, highly weather resistant
Pink Lace	light pink, rose-pink veins	10	free blooming, heavily fringed
Pink Magic	bright rose pink	18	very weather resistant, ruffled, plain edged, extra large flowers, no veins.
Pink Paradise	soft rose pink	14	early and free flowering, large 4-inch flowers
Pink Snow	light pink	12	3 to 3½-inch flowers bloom early on compact mound shaped plants
Rose Cloud	deep red	12	early spring to frost, blooms 4 to 5 inches across

Red, Crimson and Orange

Ace of Hearts	rich deep scarlet	12	flowers are 3½ inches, foliage is dark green
Candy Apple	scarlet red	13	early and free flowering, more rain resistant than most red varieties
El Toro	rich red	12	early and dwarf but bloom is not abundant and lacks resistance
Matador (Toreador)	rich magenta-crimson	14	vigorous bulky habit
Red Clous	deep red	12-14	very early, extra large-flowered blooms, 4 inches across
Red Magic	orange-red	14	upright rather loose growth, flowers not large but produced freely, early
Tangerine	bright tangerine-orange white throats	12	free flowering, compact habit
Red Baron	bright red	12	early flowers and intense color

Salmon

Balerina	intense glowing	12	large frilled flowers with deeper veins, withstands adverse weather well.
Bridesmaid	soft pink salmon, small gold throat	12	one of the earliest salmons, free flowering
Flamboyant	bright flamingo-pink with small creamy white throat	14	flowers are 2¼ inches and up
Harvest Moon	light salmon orange	12-14	free blooming compact plants
Maytime	light salmon pink	12	produces an abundance of flowers
Polynesia	cool salmon	12	early blooming and profuse, with tight, compact habit
Tickled Pink	pink and white throats	12	held facing upward on compact dark green plants

Blue and Purple

Blue Charm	blue	12	free flowering blossoms are star-shaped
Blue Jeans	blue with violet cast	12	star-shaped bloom
Blue Lace	orchid blue	16-18	star-shaped, 3-inch wide-throated flowers
Blue Magic	deep violet-blue	18	3-inch flowers on dwarf compact plants which are vigorous and free-flowering
Mariner	deep ocean blue	10-12	cover themselves with big flowers (3½ inches of ocean blue)
Sky Magic	silvery sky-blue	14	earliest, most free-flowering, plain-edged light blue
Sugar Daddy	orchid-purple	15	large-flowered cascade type with 4-inch flowers

Salmon			
Coral Bells	bright coral with white throat	12	flowers all season
Coral Satin	coral-rose	12	highly weather resistant
Gypsy	deep coral-salmon	12	medium early, 2 3/4-inch flowers
Pink Joy	medium salmon-pink	12	very free flowering
Sundance	clear glowing salmon	12	tight, compact, mounded growth
Pink Bountiful	soft, salmon-pink	12	abundance of bloom, clear and unfading
Blue and Purple			
Blue Lagoon	medium blue	15	a very prolific hybrid
Blue Mist	heavenly blue	14	tremendous production of bloom
Candy Plum	blue	12	blooms early and 2½-inch flowers
Plum Purple	glowing purple, centers lighter at edges	12	heavily veined, 2½-inch flowers
Purple Joy	deep violet	12	dwarf habit, free flowering
Purple Satin	blue-purple	10	perfect habit, heavily textured blooms
Sugar Plum	orchid-pink	12	heavily veined in deep color, excellent weather resistant
Petunia (Multiflora Double)	Delight Mixture	wide range, including blue	12	well matched for habit and doubleness
	Empress Mixed Colors	mixture of colors	12	good double flowers
	Sweet Tarts (Bonanza) Mixture	various colors	12	carnation flowers
Petunia (Grandiflora Double)	Canadian Mixture	complete range of petunia colors	12	a fine blend of Canadian varieties, large flowers, nicely ruffled
	Fanfare Mixture	rose, lavender, orchid, wine purple and white	12	all uniformly early, solid and variegated colors
	Glorious Mixture	all Pan-American colors	12	good range of colors
	Victorious Mixture	wide color arnge	12	formula mixture of Japanese varieties
	Circus (AAS-'72)	salmon-red, white bicolor	12	maintains variegation throughout season
Phlox drummondi (Annual Phlox)	Beauty Mixture	mixed colors	6-8	rounded compact bushes, blooms twice the size of others
	Glamour	mid-salmon	12	plants are vigorous and uniform
	Ideal Bedding Mixture	bright mixture	7-8	uniform in its dwarf habit
	Twinkle Mixed	variety of colors	6	large as the taller type, brilliant flowers and profuse bloomers, dainty starred flowers
Portulaca (Rose Moss)	Grandifora Double Mixture	all colors	6	very showy, produces 85-90% true double flowers
	Red Jewel and White Jewel	white or red	6	single flowers are four times the size of ordinary varieties
	Single large-flowering Mixed	variety of colors	6	good color selection
	Sunnyside Strain	all colors	6	new improvement in improved doubleness and large-sized flower

Petunia (Balcony and Cascade)	Chiffon Cascade	light pink	14	wind and rain resistant
	Coral Cascade	coral-rose	14	slightly compact plants
	Pink Cascade	bright clear pink	15	large flowers from 4½ to 5 inches
	Red Cascade	brilliant deep red	14	flowers are slightly ruffled
	White Cascade	white	14	flowers blanket large areas
	Red Avalanche	bright red	14	early, 3½-inch flowers
	White Avalanche	pure white	14	3 3/4-inch blooms

Petunia (Multiflora Single)	*Bicolor*			
	Festival	ruby red, well defined white star, yellow throats	14	large 2 3/4-inch flowers
	Lollipop	rose pink and white	14	early large flowers
	Pinwheel	scarlet-salmon	12	very early, 2 3/4-inch flowers
	Polaris	violet-blue white star	17	good contrast
	Satellite	bright rose with a star	14	free flowering
	Star Joy	deep rose with white star	14	very early, holds color well
	Starfire Improved	red and white	12	free flowering
	White and Cream Yellow			
	Paleface	pure white with a creamy throat	15	white 2½-inch flowers, free flowering
	Polar Cap	pure white	13	very large flowered and freeblooming
	Snowdrift	pure white	13	large flowers, 3¼-inch flowers
	White Bountiful	white	13	smaller flowered but blooms are more plentiful than Snowdrift. 2-2 3/4-inch flowers
	White Joy	pure white	13	fine branching habit and very free blooming, blooms early, 3-inch flowers
	White Satin	white	14	free flowering with good compact habit
	Brass Band	clear yellow	14	free-flowering, 2 3/4-inch blooms
	Pink and Rose			
	Cherokee	warm mid-rose	13	bears flowers in profusion on plants with excellent habit
	Cover Girl	medium bright rose	12	early and extremely free flowering, 2½-inch flowers
	Pink Cheer	glowing pink	13	big 3-inch flowers, early
	Pink Satin	deep rose	13	large satiny flowers
	Plum Pink	rose pink	12	very dwarf, high degree of weather tolerance
	Rose Joy	clear rose pink	12	early, free blooming habit
	Sugar Pink	deep pink on light pink	12	weather tolerance of Sugar Plum
	Red and Orange			
	Comanche	fiery vivid scarlet-red	14	2½-inch across on dwarf plants
	Orange Bells	orange-scarlet	13	unique variety, compact and free-flowering
	Red Cap	intense red	12	early flowering with 2 3/4-inch flowers
	Red Joy Improved	bright scarlet-red	12	one of the largest flowered red multifloras
	Red Satin	fire-engine red	12	flowers are 2 to 2½ inches and late
	Victory	intense scarlet	13	big 3¼-inch flowers

Rubeckia (Coneflower)	Gloriosa Double Daisy	golden yellow	36	blooms 4 inches across, double and brown-eyed semi-double
	Gloriosa Golden Daisy	golden yellow	24-30	spectacular 5½-inch flowers with dark velvety centers
	Gloriosa Daisy, Pinwheel	mahogany and gold	30	5-inch flowers, bicolored, vigorous
Salpiglossis	Splash	wide color range	30	many flowering stems and exceptionally large flowers
Salvia splendens (Scarlet Sage)	America (Globe of Fire)	brilliant scarlet	26	round bushy plants covered with well-filled upright spikes.
	Blaze of Fire	brilliant scarlet	15	spikes cover dwarf plants, from early in season to frost
	Extra Early Bonfire	red	24	about 10 days earlier than Bonfire on somewhat shorter plants
	Fireball (Scarlet Pygmy)	red	10	extra early blooming and more dwarf habit
	Red Pillar (Hot Jazz)	blazing scarlet	15	great numbers of long tight-packed spikes
	St. John's Fire	bright scarlet-red	10-12	very uniform, compact and upright
Salvia farinacea (Mealycup Sage)	Regal Purple	deep violet-blue	24	blooms in mid-season
	Regal White	pure white	24	good for bedding and cutting
	Royal Blue	deep blue	36	very tall, improved strain of Blue Bedder.
Sanvitalia procumbens (Creeping zinnia)		yellow	12	ideal annual ground cover
Scabiosa (Pincushion Flower)	Imperial Giant Mixed	white, pink, deep red, salmon, blue, and lavender	30	flowers are large, colors are rich and varied, and stems are long
Snapdragon	Bright Butterflies	red, rose, white yellow, bronze, cherry, light pink	24	open throats with a flared lip, like foxgloves
	Carioca Mixed	white, yellow, bronze, pink, and red	10-12	base-branching plants are domeshaped and very uniform
	Floral Carpet Mixture	mixed colors	6-8	extra dwarf bushy plants
	Frontier Mixed Colors	white, orchid, crimson, rose, orange, flame, yellow	20-24	half-tall hybrids
	Knee-High Mixture	red, bronze, pink, and yellow	18-24	early flowering mixture
	Little Darling (AAS-'71)	mixed color	12	semi-dwarf, butterfly form of Bright Butterflies
	Madame Butterfly	colored mixture of scarlet, crimson rosy-orange, yellow pink, light golden bronze, magenta red	24-30	base branching plants have 10 or more large, well-placed, all-double spikes open
	Pinnacle Mixture	cherry, crimson, bronze, red, white, scarlet-orange and others	30	bloom early, making several crops of spikes possible in one season
	Promenade Mixture	lively color range	12	dwarf, bush-flowering snaps with attractive spikes

Snapdragon	Rockets Mixed	bronze, cherry, golden, orchid, pink, red, and others	30-36	long spikes with many closely spaced florets
	Sprite Mixture	variety of clear colors	14-18	semi-dwarf, uniform, compact base-branching habit produces numerous medium length spikes
	Supreme Doubles Mixed	scarlet, yellow rose and white	36	tall, tapered spikes packed with full double, ruffled, florets
Sweet Pea (Dwarf Bush Form)	Knee-Hi Mixed	all colors mixed	30	early large-flowered, heat resistant variety, five to seven flowers per stem
	San Francisco (AAS-'67)	salmon-cream-pink	30	ideal for cutting, bedding or massed planting
Talinum paniculatum (Jewels of Omar, Coral Flower)		deep waxy green foliage, pink flowers	12-18	flowers open every afternoon, effecting a pink haze, plants withstand summer heat
Tithonia (Mexican Sunflower)	Torch	brilliant orange-scarlet	40-48	long stemmed single blooms are produced in late summer
Torenia (Wishbone Flower)	Compacta Blue	light blue	8-12	compact bushy plants bloom during the summer and fall.
Verbena	Amethyst	lavender-blue	6	low cushion-like plants
	Blaze (AAS-'68)	bright scarlet	6-10	very free flowering, dwarf, compact plants
	Crystal	snow-white	6	large flowers, dwarf spreading
	Delight	coral-pink suffused salmon	8-10	dwarf spreading
	Ideal Florist Mixture	wide range of unusual colors	8	early flowering, spreads up to 18 inches
Vinca Rosea (Periwinkle)	Little Mixture	white, rosy-pink, rose	10	formula blend of Little Bright Eye, Little Pinkie, Little Blanche, Little Delicata
	Little Blanche	pure white	10	compact plants, glossy green leaves
	Little Bright Eye	white, rose-red eye	10	dwarf and very compact
	Little Delicata	pale pink, red eye	10	very delicate color, ideal companion for Little Bright Eye and Little Pinkie
	Little Pinkie	rosy pink	10	dwarf compact habit, glossy green leaves
	Polka Dot (AAS-'69)	white with red eye	4-6	annual ground cover, spreads 2 feet or more, weather resistant
	Rose Carpet	rose with deep red eye	4-6	dwarf spreading habit
Zinnia	Carved Ivory (AAS-'72)	ivory-colored	30	uniform, vigorous, and productive, blooms 5 inches wide, cactus type
	Lipstick	crimson	30	flowers in a thick ball-shaped form
	Nectarine	rose-pink	24-36	cactus-type flowers
	Rosy Future (AAS-'69)	rose pink	24	spectacular 5½ to 6-inch, ball-shaped flowers
	Tangerine	bright orange	36	2 to 2½-inch flowers on tall, well branched plants
	Torch (AAS-'69)	brilliant glowing orange	24	large 5½ to 6-inch cactus-flowers of thick ball-shaped form, quilled double bloom
	Wild Cherry (AAS-'68)	cherry-rose	30	cactus-flowered zinnia, flowers up to 6 inches across, plants are vigorous, bushy and prolific
	Winesap	deep scarlet-red	30	flowers up to 6 inches across

Zinnia

Yellow Zenith	clear mid-yellow	24	cactus type, very free flowering
Fruit Bowl Mixture	cherry-rose, scarlet-red, pink, yellow, cream and orange	24-30	very uniform for large flower size
Zenith Mixture	all colors	30	cactus-type, flowers very freely on vigorous uniform, bushy dark green leaved plants
State Fair Mixture (tetraploid)	complete color range	30-36	5 to 6 inches across, thick blooms and broad petals
Peter Pan Pink (AAS '71)	coral-pink	10-12	vigorous, uniform in growing habit and flowering
Peter Pan Plum (AAS '71)	lavender-rose or plum	10-12	3 to 4-inch flowers, vigorous, uniform in growth habit and flowering
Peter Pan Scarlet (AAS '73)	brilliant scarlet	10-12	double, uniform and free flowering
Cherry Buttons (AAS '69)	cherry-coral	10-12	profuse blooms, long lasting, fully double 1½ to 1 3/4-inch, wiry stem
Pink Buttons	salmon-pink	12	uniform compact plant
Paint Brush Mixed Colors	full color range	16-18	dahlia-shaped flowers
Old Mexico	bicolored; mahogany red and shades of gold	12-15	husky plants, highly disease resistant
Zinnia linearis	myriad golden orange with lemon strip	8	beautiful border or edging plant, blooms in six weeks, excellent color all summer
Cupid Mixture	white, orange scarlet and pink	24	similar to pompoms or small button-type
Lilliput Mixture	many	24	small, full, button-type flowers, well suited for cutting or garden display
Zinnia pumila (Cut and come again)	many	36	between giants and lilliputs in flower size, well-branched plants

Common name	Height (Inches)	Hardiness (Zone)	Type	Soil and light	Comments
Barrenwort .... *Epimedium alpinum; E. grandiflorum; E. pinnatum*	12	4–8	Woody herb	Tolerates almost any soil	Dense foliage; lasts into winter; white, yellow, lavender flowers
Bearberry .... *Arctostaphylos uvursi*	6–10	2–9	Evergreen shrub	Excellent in stony, sandy, acid soils	Low; hard to transplant; bright red fruit
Bergenia, heartleaf .... *Bergenia cordifolia*	12	5–10	Creeping, clumpy perennial; thick rootstocks	Sun or partial shade	Pink flowers; thick, heavy foliage
Broom .... *Genista pilosa; G. sagittalis*	6–12	5–9	Deciduous shrub	Well-drained soil; sun	Flowers are pea shaped
Bugleweed .... *Ajuga reptans*	4–8	5–9	Perennial herb	Tolerates most soils	Densely packed plants; blue-purple flowers; rapid grower
Capeweed .... *Phyla nodiflora*	2–4	9–10	Creeping perennial herb	Sand and waste areas	Low-growing; spreads rapidly; cut like grass; light pink flowers
Coralberry .... *Symphoricarpos orbiculatus*	to 36	3–9	Deciduous shrub	Thrives in poor soils	Rapid growth by underground stems; requires yearly pruning
Cotoneaster .... *Cotoneaster adpressa*	6–30	5–10	Semi-evergreen herb	Full sun, reseed	Stems will layer subject to fire blight
C. apiculata		5–9			
C. dammeri					
C. horizontalis		6–10			
C. microphylla		7–10			
Cowberry .... *Vaccinium vitis-idaea*	to 12	5–9	Small evergreen shrub	Acid soil	Small pink flowers, dark-red berries
Creeping lilyturf .... *Liriope spicata*	to 12	5–10	Matted herb	Extreme heat, dry soil, stands salt spray	Dense mat, dark green leaves, purple flowers
Creeping lippia .... *Phyla nodiflora* var. *canescens*	2–4	5–10	Creeping perennial	Any soil, sun	White, lilac flowers
Creeping thyme .... *Thymus serpyllum*	to 3	5–10	Subshrubby with creeping stems	Tolerates dry soils, sun	Substitute for grass, extremely variable
Crownvetch .... *Coronilla varia*	12–24	3–7	Herb	Dry, steep banks, sun	Small pink flowers
Daylily .... *Hemerocallis*	18–60	3–10	Root, fleshy and tuberous parts	Sun, dry to boggy soils	Few problems; summer flowers
Dichondra .... *Dichondra repens*	1–2	9 and 10	Evergreen perennial	Sunny or shady locations	Poor drought resistance; rarely needs clipping; spreads rapidly
Dwarf bamboo .... *Sasa pumila, S. veitchii, and Shibataea kumasaca*		6–10	Low shrub	Sun; sandy soil	Foliage brown in winter; fire hazard; grass substitute
English ivy .... *Hedera helix*	6–8	5–9	Evergreen vine	Sun or shade	Clip leaves to control leaf spots
Forsythia species .... *Forsythia* spp.	Trim to 18	5–9	Deciduous shrub	Sun, well-drained soil	Stems root easily; yellow flowers in spring
Galax .... *Galax aphylla*	6	5–7	Evergreen, stemless perennial herb	Moist, rich, acid soil, shade	White flowers in spring; leaves turn bronze in fall
Germander .... *Teucrium chamaedrys*	to 10	6–10	Small woody perennial	Sun or partial shade	Winter damage without protection
Ground-ivy .... *Glechoma hederacea*	3	3–9	Trailing perennial	Sun or shade; any soil	Becomes a pest in lawn if not trimmed; forms a low mat
Heath .... *Erica carnea*	6–12	5–8	Evergreen shrub	Poor, acid soils, sun	Pink, purple, red, white varieties
Heather .... *Calluna vulgaris*	6–24	4–7	Evergreen shrub	Acid soil, well-drained, low fertility, sun	Shear plants each spring
Holly, Japanese .... *Ilex crenata*	Keep to 24	6–10	Evergreen shrub	Sun or semi-shade	Slow growing; small bank plantings
Hollygrape, dwarf .... *Mahonia repens*	to 10	6–9	Evergreen shrub	Sun or shade, any type soil	Yellow flowers

Plant	Height	Zone	Type	Conditions	Remarks
Honeysuckle, Japanese .... *Lonicera japonica*	to 10	5–9	Twisting, trailing vine	Sun or partial shade	Prune yearly to keep in bounds; a semi-evergreen with white turning to yellow flowers
Iceplant .... *Cephalophyllum, Carpobrotus, Delosperma, Drosanthemum, Malephora, Lampranthus*	4–6	10	Low succulent	Sun; well-drained soil	Temporary ground cover in cold climates; brilliant colored flowers open in full sunlight
Japanese spurge .... *Pachysandra terminalis*	to 6	5–8	Evergreen herb	Semi-shade under tree	Spreads by underground stems
Juniper .... *Juniperus horizontalis* *J. sabina* *J. procumbens* *J. chinensis* *J. conferta*	12–18 trim to 36	3–10	Evergreen conifer	Sun; dry areas	Yearly pruning of upright forms; wide range of foliage colors; some turn purple in winter
Lantana .... *Lantana sellowiana;* *L. montevidensis*	6–10	8–10	Trailing shrub	Sun, high salt tolerance	Wide range of flower colors
Lily-of-the-valley .... *Convallaria majalis*	6–10	4–9	Rootstock	Rich, moist, high organic soil; partial shade	Fragrant white bell-shaped flowers
Lilyturf dwarf (Mondograss) ...... *Ophiopogon japonicus*	to 10	7–10	Matted herb	Any soil, sun or shade	Spikes of pale lilac flowers
Moss sandwort .... *Arenaria verna*	3	2–9	Perennial herb	Fertile soil, moist; partial shade	Requires some winter protection
Moss, pink .... *Phlox subulata*	6	4–10	Evergreen perennial	Porous soil; sun	Flowers are shade of pink and white
Periwinkle .... *Vinca minor* (small leaves) *V. major* (large leaves)	6–8	5–10	Trailing herb	Avoid high nitrogen fertilizer, poorly drained soils	Purple, blue, and white flowers
Plantain lily .... *Hosta* spp.	12–16	4–10	Tufted plant with broad leaves	Moist, well-drained soils; shade	Needs frequent division
Polygonum, dwarf .... *Polygonum cuspidatum* var. *compactum*	12–24	4–10	Stout perennial	Rocky or gravelly soil; sun	Foliage turns red in fall
Rose, memorial .... *Rosa wichuraiana*	6–12	5–9	Semi-evergreen low-growing shrub	Banks and sand dunes	2-inch white flowers
St.-Johns-wort .... *Hypericum calycinum*	9–12	6–10	Semi-evergreen shrub	Semi-shade; sandy soil	Yellow flowers in summer; red foliage in autumn
Sand Strawberry .... *Fragaria chiloensis*	10–12	6–10	Perennial herb	Suitable for most soils	Spreads rapidly
Sarcococca .... *Sarcococca hookeriana*	to 72	6–10	Evergreen shrub	Shade	Shear for height control; small white flowers, large leaves
South African daisy .... *Gazania rigens*	6–9	9–10	Evergreen perennial	Avoid high nitrogen fertilizers; poorly drained soils	Light green foliage; orange flowers
Stonecrop, goldmoss .... *Sedum acre*	4	4–10	Evergreen perennial	Dry areas	Forms mats of tiny foliage
Strawberry geranium .... *Saxifraga sarmentosa*	15	7–9	Perennial herb	Partial shade; rock gardens, heavy clay soils	Spreads by runners
Thrift .... *Armeria maritima*	6	5–9	Perennial herb	Sandy soil; full sun	Small pink flowers in spring
Wandering-Jew .... *Zebrina pendula*	6–9	10	Tender herb	Shade, acid or alkaline soils	Roots easily
Wintercreeper .... *Euonymus fortunei*	2–4	5–10	Clinging evergreen vine	Sun; shade; ordinary soil	Rapid, flat growth; subject to scale insects
Wintergreen .... *Gaultheria procumbens*	4	5–7	Creeping evergreen	Acid soil; moist shady areas	Creeps over area
Yarrow .... *Achillea millefolium*	2–3	5–9	Fern-like perennial herb	Adapted to poor, dry soil; full sun	Remains green even during drought

Earliest dates, and range of dates, for safe spring planting of vegetables in the open

Crop	Planting dates for localities in which average date of last freeze is—						
	Jan. 30	Feb. 8	Feb. 18	Feb. 28	Mar. 10	Mar. 20	Mar. 30
Asparagus [1]	Feb. 1-Apr. 15	Feb. 10-May 1		Mar. 15-June 1	Mar. 15-June 1	Feb. 1-Mar. 1	Feb. 15-Mar. 20.
Beans, lima	Feb. 1-Apr. 1	Feb. 1-May 1	Mar. 1-May 1	Mar. 1-May 1	Mar. 20-June 15	Apr. 1-June 15	Apr. 15-June 20.
Beans, snap	Jan. 1-Mar. 15	Jan. 1-Mar. 15	Feb. 1-May 1	Mar. 10-May 15	Mar. 15-May 15	Mar. 15-May 25	Apr. 1-June 1.
Beet	Jan. 1-30	Jan. 1-30	Jan. 1-Feb. 15	Jan. 15-Feb. 15	Feb. 1-Mar. 15	Feb. 15-Mar. 15	Mar. 1-20.
Broccoli, sprouting [1]	Jan. 1-30	Jan. 1-30	Jan. 1-30	Feb. 1-Mar. 1	Feb. 15-Mar. 15	Feb. 15-Mar. 15	Mar. 1-20.
Brussels sprouts [1]	Jan. 1-15	Jan. 1-Feb. 10	Jan. 15-Feb. 25	Feb. 1-Mar. 1	Feb. 15-Mar. 15	Feb. 15-Mar. 15	Mar. 1-20.
Cabbage [1]	(²)	(²)	(²)	Jan. 1-Feb. 25	Jan. 25-Mar. 1	Feb. 10-Mar. 1	Feb. 15-Mar. 10.
Cabbage, Chinese					(²)	(²)	(²)
Carrot	Jan. 1-Mar. 1	Jan. 1-Mar. 1	Jan. 15-Mar. 1	Feb. 1-Mar. 1	Feb. 10-Mar. 15	Feb. 15-Mar. 20	Mar. 1-Apr. 10.
Cauliflower [1]	Jan. 1-Feb. 1	Jan. 1-Feb. 1	Jan. 1-Feb. 10	Jan. 20-Feb. 20	Feb. 1-Mar. 1	Feb. 10-Mar. 10	Feb. 20-Mar. 20.
Celery and celeriac	Jan. 1-Feb. 1	Jan. 1-Feb. 1	Jan. 10-Feb. 20	Feb. 1-Mar. 1	Feb. 20-Mar. 20	Mar. 1-Apr. 1	Mar. 15-Apr. 15.
Chard	Jan. 1-Apr. 1	Jan. 1-Apr. 1	Jan. 10-Apr. 1	Feb. 1-May 1	Feb. 15-May 15	Feb. 20-May 1	Mar. 1-May 25.
Chervil and chives	Jan. 1-Mar. 1	Jan. 1-Feb. 1	Jan. 1-Feb. 1	Jan. 15-Feb. 15	Feb. 10-Mar. 10	Feb. 10-Mar. 10	Feb. 15-Mar. 15.
Chicory, witloof					June 1-July 1	June 1-July 1	June 1-July 1.
Collards [1]	Jan. 1-Feb. 15	Jan. 1-Feb. 15	Jan. 1-Mar. 15	Jan. 15-Mar. 15	Feb. 1-Apr. 1	Feb. 15-Mar. 15	Jan. 15-Mar. 15.
Cornsalad	Jan. 1-Feb. 15	Jan. 1-Feb. 15	Jan. 1-Mar. 15	Feb. 1-Mar. 15	Jan. 15-Mar. 15	Feb. 15-May 15	Jan. 25-Mar. 15.
Corn, sweet	Feb. 1-Mar. 15	Feb. 1-Mar. 15	Feb. 1-Feb. 15	Feb. 15-Mar. 15	Feb. 20-Mar. 20	Mar. 20-May 15	Mar. 1-Apr. 1.
Cress, upland	Jan. 1-Feb. 1	Jan. 1-Feb. 1	Jan. 15-Feb. 15	Feb. 15-Apr. 15	Feb. 15-Apr. 15	Apr. 1-May 1	Apr. 10-May 15.
Cucumber	Feb. 15-Mar. 15	Feb. 10-Mar. 15	Feb. 15-Apr. 15	Mar. 1-Apr. 15	Mar. 15-Apr. 15	Apr. 10-May 15	Apr. 15-May 15.
Eggplant [1]	Feb. 1-Mar. 1	Feb. 10-Mar. 15	Feb. 20-Apr. 1	Mar. 10-Apr. 15	Mar. 15-Apr. 15	Mar. 15-Apr. 15	Mar. 10-Apr. 10.
Endive	Jan. 1-Mar. 1	Jan. 1-Mar. 1	Jan. 15-Mar. 1	Feb. 1-Mar. 1	Feb. 15-Mar. 15	Mar. 1-Apr. 1	Feb. 15-Mar. 10.
Fennel, Florence	Jan. 1-Mar. 1	Jan. 1-Mar. 1	Jan. 15-Mar. 1	Feb. 1-Mar. 1	Feb. 15-Mar. 15	Mar. 1-Apr. 1	Mar. 1-Apr. 1.
Garlic [1]	(²)	(²)	(²)	(²)	(²)	Mar. 1-Apr. 1	Feb. 15-Mar. 15.
Horseradish [1]						Feb. 1-Mar. 1	Feb. 10-Mar. 10.
Kale	Jan. 1-Feb. 1	Jan. 1-Feb. 1	Jan. 10-Feb. 1	Feb. 1-20	Feb. 10-Mar. 1	Feb. 20-Mar. 10	Mar. 1-20.
Kohlrabi	Jan. 1-Feb. 1	Jan. 1-Feb. 1	Jan. 1-Feb. 1	Jan. 20-Feb. 15	Feb. 1-Mar. 1	Feb. 10-Mar. 10	Feb. 20-Mar. 10.
Leek	Jan. 1-Feb. 1	Jan. 1-Feb. 1	Jan. 1-Feb. 1	Jan. 15-Feb. 15	Jan. 25-Mar. 1	Feb. 1-Mar. 1	Feb. 15-Mar. 15.
Lettuce, head [1]	Jan. 1-Feb. 1	Jan. 1-Feb. 1	Jan. 1-Mar. 1	Jan. 15-Feb. 15	Feb. 1-20	Feb. 15-Mar. 10	Mar. 1-20.
Lettuce, leaf	Feb. 15-Mar. 15	Feb. 15-Mar. 15	Feb. 15-Apr. 15	Feb. 15-Mar. 15	Feb. 15-Apr. 1	Feb. 15-Apr. 1	Feb. 15-Apr. 15.
Muskmelon	Jan. 1-Mar. 1	Jan. 1-Mar. 1	Feb. 15-Apr. 15	Mar. 1-Apr. 15	Mar. 15-Apr. 15	Apr. 1-May 1	Apr. 10-May 15.
Mustard	Feb. 15-Apr. 1	Feb. 15-Apr. 1	Jan. 1-June 1	Mar. 10-June 1	Mar. 20-June 1	Feb. 20-Apr. 15	Mar. 1-Apr. 1.
Okra	Jan. 1-15	Jan. 1-Mar. 1	Jan. 1-June 1	Feb. 10-June 1	Feb. 20-June 15	Apr. 10-June 15	Apr. 10-June 15.
Onion [1]	Jan. 1-15	Jan. 1-15	Jan. 1-15	Jan. 1-Feb. 15	Feb. 1-Feb. 15	Feb. 10-Mar. 10	Feb. 15-Mar. 15.
Onion, seed	Jan. 1-15	Jan. 1-15	Jan. 1-15	Jan. 1-Feb. 15	Feb. 1-Mar. 1	Feb. 15-Mar. 15	Feb. 20-Mar. 15.
Onion, sets	Jan. 1-30	Jan. 1-30	Jan. 1-30	Jan. 15-Mar. 15	Feb. 1-Mar. 15	Feb. 15-Mar. 20	Mar. 1-Apr. 1.
Parsley			Jan. 1-Mar. 1	Jan. 15-Mar. 15	Feb. 1-Mar. 10	Feb. 20-Mar. 15	Feb. 10-Mar. 20.
Parsnip			Jan. 1-June 1	Mar. 1-June 1	Mar. 1-July 1	Apr. 1-July 1	Apr. 15-June 1.
Peas, garden	Jan. 1-Feb. 15	Jan. 1-Feb. 15	Jan. 1-Mar. 1	Mar. 1-May 1	Apr. 1-June 1	Apr. 10-June 1	Apr. 1-June 1.
Peas, black-eye	Feb. 15-May 1	Feb. 15-Apr. 15	Mar. 15-May 1	Mar. 15-May 15	Mar. 1-May 15	Jan. 20-May 1	Feb. 20-Mar. 20.
Pepper [1]	Feb. 1-Apr. 1	Feb. 1-Apr. 1	Mar. 1-May 1	Mar. 15-May 1	Apr. 1-June 1	Apr. 10-June 1	Jan. 1-Jan. 1.
Potato	Jan. 1-Feb. 15	Jan. 1-Feb. 15	Jan. 15-Mar. 1	Feb. 1-Mar. 1	Feb. 10-Mar. 15	Jan. 20-May 1	Feb. 15-May 1.
Radish	Jan. 1-Apr. 1	Jan. 1-Apr. 1	Jan. 1-Apr. 1	Jan. 1-Apr. 1	Jan. 1-Apr. 15	Jan. 20-May 1	Apr. 1-May 1.
Rhubarb [1]							
Rutabaga							
Salsify	Jan. 1-Feb. 1	Jan. 1-Feb. 10	Jan. 15-Feb. 20	Jan. 15-Mar. 1	Jan. 15-Feb. 15	Jan. 15-Feb. 15	Feb. 1-Mar. 1.
Shallot	Jan. 1-Feb. 1	Jan. 1-Feb. 1	Jan. 1-Feb. 1	Jan. 15-Mar. 1	Feb. 1-Mar. 1	Feb. 15-Mar. 15	Mar. 1-15.
Sorrel	Jan. 1-Feb. 1	Jan. 1-Mar. 1	Jan. 15-Mar. 10	Feb. 1-Mar. 10	Feb. 20-Mar. 10	Feb. 10-Mar. 20	Mar. 15-Apr. 1.
Soybean	Mar. 1-June 30	Mar. 1-June 30	Mar. 10-June 30	Mar. 20-June 30	Apr. 10-June 30	Apr. 20-June 30	Apr. 20-June 30.
Spinach	Jan. 1-Feb. 15	Jan. 1-Feb. 15	Jan. 1-Mar. 1	Jan. 1-Mar. 1	Jan. 15-Mar. 15	Jan. 15-Mar. 15	Feb. 1-Mar. 1.
Spinach, New Zealand	Feb. 1-Apr. 15	Feb. 1-Apr. 15	Feb. 1-Apr. 15	Mar. 15-May 15	Apr. 1-May 15	Apr. 1-May 15	Apr. 10-June 1.
Squash, summer	Feb. 15-May 15	Mar. 1-May 15	Mar. 15-May 15	Mar. 15-May 15	Apr. 1-June 1	Apr. 10-June 1	Apr. 20-June 1.
Sweetpotato		Feb. 15-Apr. 15	Mar. 1-Apr. 20	Mar. 15-Apr. 20	Mar. 20-May 10	Apr. 10-May 20	Apr. 20-June 1.
Tomato	Feb. 1-Apr. 1	Feb. 20-Apr. 10	Mar. 1-Apr. 20	Mar. 10-May 1	Mar. 20-May 10	Apr. 10-May 20	Apr. 20-Mar. 20.
Turnip	Jan. 1-Mar. 1	Jan. 1-Mar. 1	Jan. 10-Mar. 1	Jan. 20-Mar. 1	Feb. 1-Mar. 1	Feb. 10-Mar. 10	Feb. 20-Mar. 20.
Watermelon	Feb. 15-Mar. 15	Feb. 15-Apr. 1	Feb. 15-Apr. 15	Mar. 1-Apr. 15	Mar. 15-Apr. 15	Apr. 1-May 1	Apr. 10-May 15.

[1] Plants.
(²) Generally fall-planted (table 5).

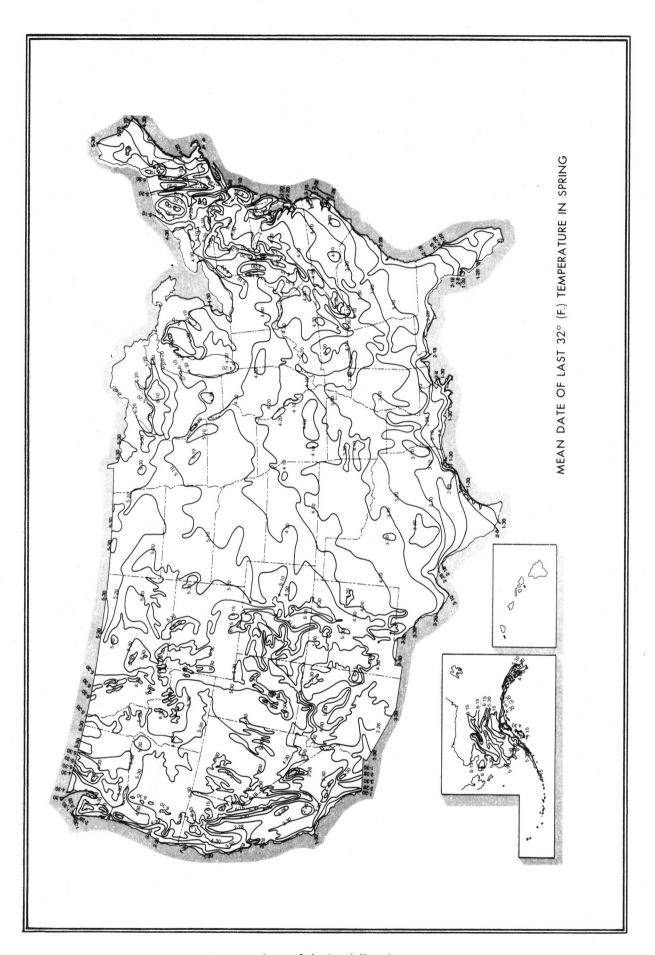

Average dates of the last killing frost in spring.

—Earliest dates, and range of dates, for safe spring planting of vegetables in the open—Continued

Crop	Planting dates for localities in which average date of last freeze is—						
	Apr. 10	Apr. 20	Apr. 30	May 10	May 20	May 30	June 10
Asparagus[1]	Mar. 10–Apr. 10	Mar. 15–Apr. 15	Mar. 20–Apr. 15	Mar. 10–Apr. 30	Apr. 20–May 15	May 1–June 1	May 15–June 1.
Beans, lima	Apr. 1–June 30	May 1–June 20	May 15–June 15	May 25–June 15			
Beans, snap	Apr. 10–June 30	Apr. 25–June 30	May 10–June 30	May 10–June 30	Apr. 15–June 30	May 1–June 15	May 15–June 15.
Beet	Mar. 10–June 1	Mar. 20–June 1	Apr. 1–June 15	Apr. 15–June 15	Apr. 25–June 15	May 1–June 15	May 20–June 10.
Broccoli, sprouting[1]	Mar. 15–Apr. 15	Mar. 25–Apr. 20	Apr. 1–May 1	Apr. 15–June 1	May 1–June 15	May 10–June 10	May 20–June 10.
Brussels sprouts[1]	Mar. 15–Apr. 15	Mar. 25–Apr. 20	Apr. 1–May 1	Apr. 15–June 1	May 1–June 15	May 10–June 15	May 20–June 1.
Cabbage[1]	Mar. 1–Apr. 1	Mar. 15–Apr. 10	Mar. 15–Apr. 10	Apr. 1–May 15	May 1–June 1	May 10–June 15	May 20–June 1.
Cabbage, Chinese	(²)	(²)	(²)				
Carrot	Mar. 10–Apr. 20	Apr. 1–May 15	Apr. 10–June 1	Apr. 20–June 15	May 1–June 1	May 10–June 15	May 20–June 1.
Cauliflower[1]	Mar. 1–Mar. 20	Mar. 15–Apr. 20	Apr. 10–May 10	May 10–June 15	May 20–June 1	June 1–July 1	June 1–July 15.
Celery and celeriac	Apr. 1–Apr. 20	Apr. 10–May 1	Apr. 15–May 1	Apr. 20–June 15	June 1	June 1–July 15	June 1–July 15.
Chard	Mar. 15–June 15	Apr. 1–June 15	Apr. 15–June 15	Apr. 20–June 15	May 10–June 15	May 20–June 1	May 15–June 1.
Chervil and chives	Mar. 1–Apr. 1	Mar. 1–Apr. 15	Apr. 1–May 1	Apr. 10–May 1	Apr. 15–May 15	May 1–June 1	June 1–15.
Chicory, witloof	June 10–July 1	June 15–July 1	June 15–July 1	June 1–20	June 1–July 1	June 10–July 1	May 20–June 15.
Collards[1]	Mar. 1–June 1	Mar. 10–June 1	Apr. 1–June 1	Apr. 15–June 1	May 1–June 1	May 10–June 1	May 15–June 15.
Cornsalad	Feb. 1–Apr. 1	Feb. 15–Apr. 1	Apr. 1–June 1	Apr. 15–June 1	May 1		
Corn, sweet	Apr. 10–June 1	Apr. 25–June 15	May 10–June 15	May 10–June 1	May 15–June 1	May 20–June 1	May 20–June 15.
Cress, upland	Mar. 10–Apr. 15	Mar. 20–May 1	Apr. 10–May 1	Apr. 20–May 20	May 15–June 1	May 15–June 1	
Cucumber	Apr. 20–June 1	May 1–June 15	May 15–June 15	May 20–June 15	June 1–15		
Eggplant[1]	May 1–June 1	May 10–June 1	May 15–June 1	May 20–June 15	June 1–15		
Endive	Mar. 15–Apr. 15	Apr. 1–May 1	Apr. 15–May 15	Apr. 15–May 15	May 1–30	May 1–30	May 15–June 1.
Fennel, Florence	Mar. 15–Apr. 15	Apr. 1–May 1	Apr. 15–May 15	Apr. 15–May 15	May 1–30	May 1–30	May 15–June 1.
Garlic	Feb. 20–Mar. 20	Mar. 10–Apr. 1	Apr. 1–May 1	Apr. 15–May 15			
Horseradish[1]	Mar. 10–Apr. 10	Mar. 20–Apr. 20	Apr. 1–30	Apr. 15–May 15	Apr. 20–May 20	May 1–30	
Kale	Mar. 10–Apr. 10	Mar. 20–Apr. 10	Apr. 1–May 10	Apr. 10–May 1	Apr. 20–May 20	May 1–30	May 15–June 1.
Kohlrabi	Mar. 10–Apr. 10	Mar. 20–May 1	Apr. 1–May 1	Apr. 10–May 10	Apr. 20–May 20	May 1–30	May 15–June 1.
Leek	Mar. 1–Apr. 1	Mar. 15–Apr. 15	Apr. 1–May 1	Apr. 15–May 15	Apr. 1–May 20	May 1–30	May 1–15.
Lettuce, head[1]	Mar. 10–Apr. 1	Mar. 20–Apr. 15	Apr. 1–May 1	Apr. 15–May 15	May 1–June 20	May 1–30	May 15–June 1.
Lettuce, leaf	Mar. 15–May 15	Mar. 20–May 15	Apr. 1–June 1	Apr. 15–May 15	Apr. 15–June 30	May 10–June 30	May 20–June 30.
Muskmelon	Apr. 20–June 1	May 1–June 15	May 15–June 15	May 15–June 15	June 1	May 10–June 30	May 20–June 30.
Mustard	Mar. 10–Apr. 20	Mar. 20–May 1	Apr. 1–May 10	Apr. 15–June 1	Apr. 15–June 1	May 10–June 30	May 20–June 30.
Okra	Apr. 20–June 15	May 1–June 1	May 1–June 1	May 20–June 10	June 1–20	May 1–30	May 20–June 30.
Onion[1]	Mar. 1–Apr. 1	Mar. 15–Apr. 10	Apr. 1–May 1	Apr. 10–May 1	Apr. 20–May 15	May 1–30	May 10–June 10.
Onion, seed	Mar. 1–Apr. 1	Mar. 15–Apr. 10	Apr. 1–May 1	Apr. 10–May 1	Apr. 15–May 15	May 1–30	May 1–June 10.
Onion, sets	Mar. 1–Apr. 1	Mar. 10–Apr. 10	Apr. 1–May 1	Apr. 10–May 1	Apr. 20–May 15	May 1–30	May 10–June 10.
Parsley	Mar. 10–Apr. 10	Mar. 20–Apr. 20	Apr. 1–May 1	Apr. 15–May 15	May 1–20	Apr. 10–June 1	May 10–June 15.
Parsnip	Mar. 10–Apr. 10	Mar. 20–Apr. 20	Apr. 1–May 1	Apr. 15–May 15	May 1–20	Apr. 10–June 1	May 1–June 1.
Peas, garden	Feb. 20–Mar. 20	Mar. 10–Apr. 10	Mar. 20–May 10	Apr. 1–May 15	Apr. 15–June 1	May 10–June 1	May 10–June 10.
Peas, black-eye	May 1–July 1	May 10–June 15	May 15–June 1	May 15–July 1	June 1	May 1–June 15	May 20–June 10.
Pepper[1]	May 1–June 1	May 10–June 1	May 15–June 1	May 20–June 10	June 1		
Potato	Mar. 10–Apr. 1	Mar. 15–Apr. 10	Mar. 15–June 10	Apr. 1–June 15	Apr. 15–June 15	June 1–15	May 1–June 1.
Radish	Mar. 1–May 1	Mar. 10–May 10	Apr. 1–June 1	Apr. 1–June 1	Apr. 15–June 15	May 1–15	May 15–June 1.
Rhubarb[1]	Mar. 1–Apr. 1	Mar. 10–Apr. 10	Mar. 20–May 10	Apr. 1–May 1	Apr. 15–May 10	May 1–20	May 20–June 10.
Rutabaga		Mar. 10–Apr. 10	May 1–June 1	May 1–June 1	May 1–20	May 10–20	
Salsify	Mar. 10–Apr. 15	Mar. 20–May 15	Apr. 1–May 15	Apr. 15–June 1	Apr. 15–June 1	May 1–June 1	May 15–June 1.
Shallot	Mar. 1–Apr. 1	Mar. 15–Apr. 15	Apr. 1–May 1	Apr. 10–May 1	Apr. 1–May 10	Mar. 1–15	May 15–June 15.
Sorrel	Mar. 1–Apr. 15	Mar. 15–May 1	Apr. 1–May 15	Apr. 15–June 1	May 1–June 1	May 1–June 1	May 20–June 1.
Soybean	May 1–June 30	May 10–June 20	May 15–June 15	May 15–June 15	May 25–June 10	Apr. 20–June 15	May 1–June 10.
Spinach	Feb. 15–Apr. 1	Mar. 1–Apr. 15	Mar. 20–Apr. 20	Apr. 1–June 15	Apr. 10–June 15	Apr. 20–June 15	May 1–June 15.
Spinach, New Zealand	Apr. 20–June 1	May 1–June 15	May 1–June 15	May 10–June 15	May 20–June 15	June 1–20	June 10–20.
Squash, summer	May 1–June 1	May 1–May 30	May 1–30	May 10–June 10	May 20–June 15	June 1–15	June 15–30.
Sweetpotato	May 1–June 1	May 10–June 10					
Tomato	Apr. 20–June 1	May 5–June 10	May 10–June 15	May 15–June 10	May 25–June 15	May 15–30	June 15–30.
Turnip	Mar. 1–Apr. 1	Mar. 1–Apr. 15	Mar. 1–May 1	Apr. 1–June 1	Apr. 1–June 15	Apr. 1–June 15	May 15–June 15.
Watermelon	Apr. 20–June 1	May 1–June 15	May 15–June 15	June 1–June 15	June 15–July 1	June 15–June 15	

[1] Plants.
[2] Generally fall-planted (table 5).

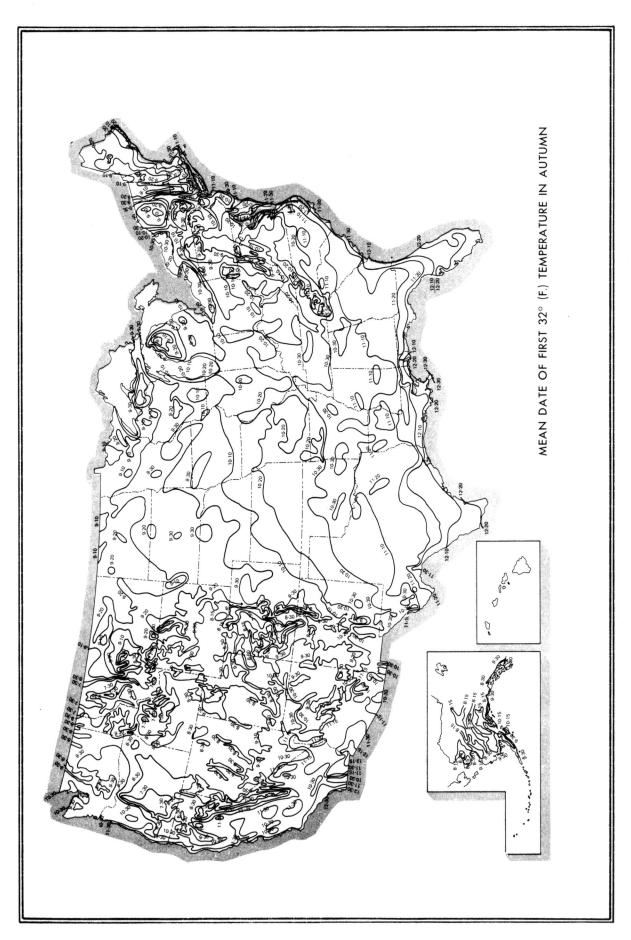

MEAN DATE OF FIRST 32° (F.) TEMPERATURE IN AUTUMN

Average dates of the first killing frost in fall.

White Beets.

Spanish Potatoes.

Wild Leek.

Colly flowers

Kidney Beans

Latest dates, and range of dates, for safe fall planting of vegetables in the open

Crop	Planting dates for localities in which average dates of first freeze is—					
	Aug. 30	Sept. 10	Sept. 20	Sept. 30	Oct. 10	Oct. 20
Asparagus [1]					Oct. 20–Nov. 15	Nov. 1–Dec. 15.
Beans, lima				June 1–15	June 1–15	June 15–30.
Beans, snap		May 15–June 15	June 1–July 1	June 1–July 10	June 15–July 20	July 1–Aug. 1.
Beet	May 15–June 15	May 15–June 15	June 1–July 1	June 1–July 10	June 15–July 25	July 1–Aug. 5.
Broccoli, sprouting	May 1–June 1	May 1–June 1	May 1–June 15	June 1–30	June 15–July 15	July 1–Aug. 1.
Brussels sprouts	May 1–June 1	May 1–June 1	May 1–June 15	June 1–30	June 15–July 15	July 1–Aug. 1.
Cabbage [1]	May 1–June 1	May 1–June 1	May 1–June 15	June 1–July 10	June 1–July 15	July 1–20.
Cabbage, Chinese	May 15–June 15	May 15–June 15	June 1–July 1	June 1–July 15	June 15–Aug. 1	July 15–Aug. 15.
Carrot	May 15–June 15	May 15–June 15	June 1–July 1	June 1–July 10	June 15–July 20	June 15–Aug. 1.
Cauliflower [1]	May 1–June 1	May 1–July 1	May 1–July 1	May 10–July 15	June 1–July 25	July 1–Aug. 5.
Celery [1] and celeriac	May 1–June 1	May 15–June 15	May 15–July 1	June 1–July 5	June 1–July 15	June 1–Aug. 1.
Chard	May 15–June 15	May 15–July 1	June 1–July 1	June 1–July 5	June 1–July 20	June 1–Aug. 1.
Chervil and chives	May 10–June 10	May 1–June 15	May 15–June 15	(2)	(2)	(2)
Chicory, witloof	May 15–June 15	May 15–June 15	May 15–June 15	June 1–July 1	June 1–July 1	June 15–July 15.
Collards [1]	May 15–June 15	May 15–June 15	May 15–June 15	June 15–July 15	July 1–Aug. 1	July 15–Aug. 15.
Cornsalad	May 15–June 15	May 15–July 1	June 1–Aug. 1	July 15–Sept. 1	Aug. 15–Sept. 15	Sept. 1–Oct. 15.
Corn, sweet			June 1–July 1	June 1–July 1	June 1–July 10	June 1–July 20.
Cress, upland	May 15–June 15	May 15–July 1	June 15–Aug. 1	July 15–Sept. 1	Aug. 15–Sept. 15	Sept. 1–Oct. 15.
Cucumber			June 1–15	June 1–July 1	June 1–July 1	June 1–July 15.
Eggplant [1]				May 20–June 10	May 15–June 15	June 1–July 1.
Endive	June 1–July 1	June 1–July 1	June 15–July 15	June 15–Aug. 1	July 1–Aug. 1	July 15–Sept. 1.
Fennel, Florence	May 15–June 15	May 15–July 15	June 1–July 1	June 1–July 1	June 15–July 15	June 15–Aug. 1.
Garlic	(2)	(2)	(2)	(2)	(2)	(2)
Horseradish [1]	(2)	(2)	(2)	(2)	(2)	(2)
Kale	May 15–June 15	May 15–June 15	June 1–July 1	June 15–July 15	July 1–Aug. 1	July 15–Aug. 15.
Kohlrabi	May 15–June 15	June 1–July 1	June 1–July 15	June 15–July 15	July 1–Aug. 1	July 15–Aug. 15.
Leek	May 1–June 1	May 1–June 1	(2)	(2)	(2)	(2)
Lettuce, head [1]	May 15–July 1	May 15–July 1	June 1–July 15	June 15–Aug. 1	July 15–Aug. 15	Aug. 1–30.
Lettuce, leaf	May 15–July 15	May 15–July 15	June 1–Aug. 1	June 1–Aug. 1	July 15–Sept. 1	July 15–Sept. 1.
Muskmelon			May 1–June 15	May 15–June 1	June 1–June 15	June 15–July 20.
Mustard	May 15–July 15	May 15–July 15	June 1–Aug. 1	June 15–Aug. 1	July 15–Aug. 15	Aug. 1–Sept. 1.
Okra			June 1–20	June 1–July 1	June 1–July 15	June 1–Aug. 1.
Onion [1]	May 1–June 10	May 1–June 10	(2)	(2)	(2)	(2)
Onion, seed	May 1–June 1	May 1–June 10	(2)	(2)	(2)	(2)
Onion, sets	May 1–June 1	May 1–June 10	(2)	(2)	(2)	(2)
Parsley	May 15–June 15	May 1–June 15	June 1–July 1	June 1–July 15	June 15–Aug. 1	July 15–Aug. 15.
Parsnip	May 15–June 1	May 1–June 15	May 15–June 15	June 1–July 1	June 1–July 10	(2)
Peas, garden	May 10–June 15	May 1–July 1	June 1–July 15	June 1–Aug. 1	(2)	(2)
Peas, black-eye					June 1–July 1	June 1–July 1.
Pepper [1]			June 1–June 20	June 1–July 1	June 1–July 1	June 1–July 10.
Potato	May 15–June 15	May 1–June 15	May 1–June 15	May 1–June 15	May 1–June 15	June 15–July 15.
Radish	May 1–July 15	May 1–Aug. 1	June 1–Aug. 15	July 1–Sept. 1	July 15–Sept. 15	Aug. 1–Oct. 1.
Rhubarb [1]	Sept. 1–Oct. 1	Sept. 15–Oct. 15	Sept. 15–Nov. 1	Oct. 1–Nov. 1	Oct. 15–Nov. 15	Oct. 15–Dec. 1.
Rutabaga	May 15–June 15	May 15–June 15	June 1–July 1	June 1–July 1	June 15–July 15	July 10–20.
Salsify	May 15–June 1	May 10–June 10	May 20–June 20	June 1–20	June 1–July 1	June 1–July 1.
Shallot	(2)	(2)	(2)	(2)	(2)	(2)
Sorrel	May 15–June 15	May 15–June 15	June 1–July 1	June 1–July 15	July 1–Aug. 1	July 15–Aug. 15.
Soybean				May 25–June 10	June 1–25	June 1–July 5.
Spinach	May 15–July 1	June 1–July 15	June 1–Aug. 1	July 1–Aug. 15	Aug. 1–Sept. 1	Aug. 20–Sept. 10.
Spinach, New Zealand				May 15–July 1	June 1–July 15	June 1–July 1.
Squash, summer	June 10–20	June 1–20	May 15–July 1	June 1–July 1	June 1–July 15	June 1–July 20.
Squash, winter			May 20–June 10	June 1–15	June 1–July 1	June 1–July 1.
Sweetpotato					May 20–June 10	June 1–15.
Tomato	June 20–30	June 10–20	June 1–20	June 1–20	June 1–20	June 1–July 1.
Turnip	May 15–June 15	June 1–July 1	June 1–July 15	June 1–Aug. 1	July 1–Aug. 1	July 15–Aug. 15.
Watermelon			May 1–June 15	May 15–June 1	June 1–June 15	June 15–July 20.

[1] Plants.
[2] Generally spring-planted (table 4).

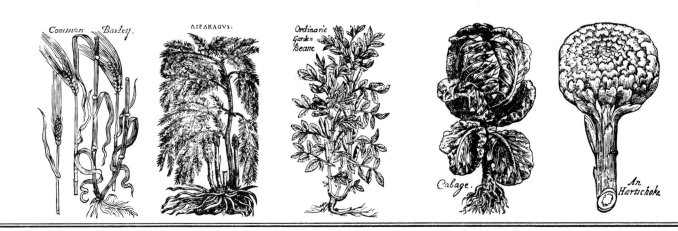

Crop	Planting dates for localities in which average date of first freeze is—					
	Oct. 30	Nov. 10	Nov. 20	Nov. 30	Dec. 10	Dec. 20
Asparagus [1]	Nov. 15–Jan. 1	Dec. 1–Jan. 1				
Beans, lima	July 1–Aug. 1	July 1–Aug. 15	July 15–Sept. 1	Aug. 1–Sept. 15	Sept. 1–30	Sept. 1–Oct. 1.
Beans, snap	July 1–Aug. 15	July 1–Sept. 1	July 1–Sept. 10	Aug. 15–Sept. 20	Sept. 1–30	Sept. 1–Nov. 1.
Beet	Aug. 1–Sept. 1	Aug. 1–Oct. 1	Sept. 1–Dec. 1	Sept. 1–Dec. 15	Sept. 1–Dec. 31	Sept. 1–Dec. 31.
Broccoli, sprouting	July 1–Aug. 15	Aug. 1–Sept. 1	Aug. 1–Sept. 15	Aug. 1–Oct. 1	Aug. 1–Nov. 1	Sept. 1–Dec. 31.
Brussels sprouts	July 1–Aug. 15	Aug. 1–Sept. 1	Aug. 1–Sept. 15	Aug. 1–Oct. 1	Aug. 1–Nov. 1	Sept. 1–Dec. 31.
Cabbage [1]	Aug. 1–Sept. 1	Sept. 1–15	Sept. 1–Dec. 1	Sept. 1–Dec. 31	Sept. 1–Dec. 31	Sept. 1–Dec. 31.
Cabbage, Chinese	Aug. 1–Sept. 15	Aug. 15–Oct. 1	Sept. 1–Oct. 15	Sept. 1–Nov. 1	Sept. 1–Nov. 15	Sept. 1–Dec. 1.
Carrot	July 1–Aug. 15	Aug. 1–Sept. 1	Sept. 1–Nov. 1	Sept. 15–Dec. 1	Sept. 15–Dec. 1	Sept. 15–Dec. 1.
Cauliflower [1]	July 15–Aug. 15	Aug. 1–Sept. 1	Aug. 1–Sept. 15	Aug. 15–Oct. 10	Sept. 1–Oct. 20	Sept. 15–Nov. 1.
Celery [1] and celeriac	June 15–Aug. 15	July 1–Aug. 15	July 15–Sept. 1	Aug. 1–Dec. 1	Sept. 1–Dec. 31	Oct. 1–Dec. 31.
Chard	June 1–Sept. 10	June 1–Sept. 15	June 1–Oct. 1	June 1–Nov. 1	June 1–Dec. 1	June 1–Dec. 31.
Chervil and chives	(2)	(2)	Nov. 1–Dec. 31	Nov. 1–Dec. 31	Nov. 1–Dec. 31	Nov. 1–Dec. 31.
Chicory, witloof	July 1–Aug. 10	July 10–Aug. 20	July 20–Sept. 1	Aug. 15–Sept. 30	Aug. 15–Oct. 15	Aug. 15–Oct. 15.
Collards [1]	Aug. 1–Sept. 15	Aug. 15–Oct. 1	Aug. 25–Nov. 1	Sept. 1–Dec. 1	Sept. 1–Dec. 31	Sept. 1–Dec. 31.
Cornsalad	Sept. 15–Nov. 1	Oct. 1–Dec. 1	Oct. 1–Dec. 1	Oct. 1–Dec. 31	Oct. 1–Dec. 31	Oct. 1–Dec. 31.
Corn, sweet	June 1–Aug. 1	June 1–Aug. 15	June 1–Sept. 1			
Cress, upland	Sept. 15–Nov. 1	Oct. 1–Dec. 1	Oct. 1–Dec. 1	Oct. 1–Dec. 31	Oct. 1–Dec. 31	Oct. 1–Dec. 31.
Cucumber	June 1–Aug. 1	June 1–Aug. 15	June 1–Aug. 15	July 15–Sept. 15	Aug. 15–Oct. 1	Aug. 15–Oct. 1.
Eggplant [1]	June 1–July 1	June 1–July 15	June 1–Aug. 1	July 1–Sept. 1	Aug. 1–Sept. 30	Aug. 1–Sept. 30.
Endive	July 15–Aug. 15	Aug. 1–Sept. 1	Sept. 1–Oct. 1	Sept. 1–Nov. 15	Sept. 1–Dec. 1	Sept. 1–Dec. 1.
Fennel, Florence	July 15–Aug. 15	July 15–Aug. 15	Aug. 15–Sept. 15	Sept. 1–Nov. 15	Sept. 1–Dec. 1	Sept. 1–Dec. 1.
Garlic	(2)	Aug. 1–Oct. 1	Aug. 15–Oct. 1	Sept. 1–Nov. 15	Sept. 15–Nov. 15	Sept. 15–Nov. 15.
Horseradish [1]	(2)	(2)	(2)	(2)	(2)	(2)
Kale	July 15–Sept. 1	Aug. 1–Sept. 15	Aug. 15–Oct. 15	Sept. 1–Dec. 1	Sept. 15–Dec. 31	Sept. 1–Dec. 31.
Kohlrabi	Aug. 1–Sept. 1	Aug. 15–Sept. 15	Sept. 1–Oct. 15	Sept. 1–Dec. 1	Sept. 15–Dec. 31	Sept. 1–Dec. 31.
Leek	(2)	(2)	Sept. 1–Nov. 1	Sept. 1–Nov. 1	Sept. 1–Nov. 1	Sept. 15–Nov. 1
Lettuce, head [1]	Aug. 1–Sept. 15	Aug. 15–Oct. 15	Sept. 1–Nov. 1	Sept. 1–Dec. 1	Sept. 15–Dec. 31	Sept. 15–Dec. 31.
Lettuce, leaf	Aug. 15–Oct. 1	Aug. 25–Oct. 1	Sept. 1–Nov. 1	Sept. 1–Dec. 1	Sept. 15–Dec. 31	Sept. 15–Dec. 31.
Muskmelon	July 1–July 15	July 15–July 30				
Mustard	Aug. 15–Oct. 15	Aug. 15–Nov. 1	Sept. 1–Dec. 1	Sept. 1–Dec. 1	Sept. 1–Dec. 1	Sept. 15–Dec. 1.
Okra	June 1–Aug. 10	June 1–Aug. 20	June 1–Sept. 10	June 1–Sept. 20	Aug. 1–Oct. 1	Aug. 1–Oct. 1.
Onion [1]		Sept. 1–Oct. 15	Oct. 1–Dec. 31	Oct. 1–Dec. 31	Oct. 1–Dec. 31	Oct. 1–Dec. 31.
Onion, seed			Sept. 1–Nov. 1	Sept. 1–Nov. 1	Sept. 1–Nov. 1	Sept. 15–Nov. 1.
Onion, sets		Oct. 1–Dec. 1	Nov. 1–Dec. 31	Nov. 1–Dec. 31	Nov. 1–Dec. 31	Nov. 1–Dec. 31.
Parsley	Aug. 1–Sept. 15	Sept. 1–Nov. 15	Sept. 1–Dec. 31	Sept. 1–Dec. 31	Sept. 1–Dec. 31	Sept. 1–Dec. 31.
Parsnip	(2)	(2)	Aug. 1–Sept. 1	Sept. 1–Nov. 15	Sept. 1–Dec. 1	Sept. 1–Dec. 1.
Peas, garden	Aug. 1–Sept. 15	Sept. 1–Nov. 1	Sept. 1–Nov. 1	Oct. 1–Dec. 1	Oct. 1–Dec. 31	Oct. 1–Dec. 31.
Peas, black-eye	June 1–Aug. 1	June 15–Aug. 15	July 1–Sept. 1	July 1–Sept. 10	July 1–Sept. 20	July 1–Sept. 20.
Pepper [1]	June 1–July 20	June 1–Aug. 1	June 1–Aug. 15	June 15–Sept. 1	Aug. 15–Oct. 1	Aug. 15–Oct. 1.
Potato	July 20–Aug. 10	July 25–Aug. 20	Aug. 10–Sept. 15	Aug. 1–Sept. 15	Aug. 1–Sept. 15	Aug. 1–Sept. 15.
Radish	Aug. 15–Oct. 15	Sept. 1–Nov. 15	Sept. 1–Dec. 1	Sept. 1–Dec. 31	Aug. 1–Sept. 15	Oct. 1–Dec. 31.
Rhubarb [1]	Nov. 1–Dec. 1					
Rutabaga	July 15–Aug. 1	July 15–Aug. 15	Aug. 1–Sept. 1	Sept. 1–Nov. 15	Oct. 1–Nov. 15	Oct. 15–Nov. 15.
Salsify	June 1–July 10	June 15–July 20	July 15–Aug. 15	Aug. 15–Sept. 30	Aug. 15–Oct. 15	Sept. 1–Oct. 31.
Shallot	(2)	Aug. 1–Oct. 1	Aug. 15–Oct. 15	Aug. 15–Oct. 15	Sept. 15–Nov. 1	Sept. 15–Nov. 1.
Sorrel	Aug. 1–Sept. 15	Aug. 15–Oct. 1	Aug. 15–Oct. 15	Sept. 1–Nov. 15	Sept. 1–Dec. 15	Sept. 1–Dec. 15.
Soybean	June 1–July 15	June 1–July 25	June 1–July 30	June 1–July 30	June 1–July 30	June 1–July 30.
Spinach	Sept. 1–Oct. 1	Sept. 15–Nov. 1	Oct. 1–Dec. 1	Oct. 1–Dec. 31	Oct. 1–Dec. 31	Oct. 1–Dec. 31.
Spinach, New Zealand	June 1–Aug. 1	June 1–Aug. 15	June 1–Aug. 15			
Squash, summer	June 1–Aug. 1	June 1–Aug. 10	June 1–Aug. 20	June 1–Sept. 1	June 1–Sept. 15	June 1–Oct. 1.
Squash, winter	June 10–July 10	June 20–July 20	July 1–Aug. 1	July 15–Aug. 15	Aug. 1–Sept. 1	Aug. 1–Sept. 1.
Sweetpotato	June 1–15	June 1–July 1	June 1–July 1	June 1–July 1	June 1–July 1	June 1–July 1.
Tomato	June 1–July 1	June 1–July 15	June 1–Aug. 1	Aug. 1–Sept. 1	Aug. 15–Oct. 1	Sept. 1–Nov. 1.
Turnip	Aug. 1–Sept. 15	Sept. 1–Oct. 15	Sept. 1–Nov. 15	Sept. 1–Nov. 15	Oct. 1–Dec. 1	Oct. 1–Dec. 31.
Watermelon	July 1–July 15	July 15–July 30				

Latest dates, and range of dates, for safe fall planting of vegetables in the open

```
                KEY              Sh = Shade           *   = Tender Perennial
        A = Annual               Pr = Poor Soil       S   = Propagation by Seed
        B = Biennial             G  = Good Soil       Div =      "     by Division
        P = Perennial            D  = Dry Location    C   =      "     by Cuttings
        S = Sun                  M  = Moist Location  L   =      "     by Layering
```

Watir Angelica.

NAME Common & Botanical		Ht.	Soil	Prop.	Culinary	Decorative	Medicinal
*ALLIUM				S			
(Allium senescens	P	24"	S	Off-		Lilac	
glaucum)			D	sets		flowers	
ANGELICA			Mod-sh		Rhubarb		
(Angelica	B	4'-	G	Fresh	Candy	Arrange-	Tea
archangelica)		6'	M	S	Wine	ments	Poultices
ARTEMISIA SILVER						Arrange-	
KING (Artemisia	P	3'	S	Div		ments	
albula)			Pr			Rock	
SILVER MOUND		12"	D	Div		garden	
(A. schmidtiana							
nana)							
BALM, LEMON			Mod		Fr. cups	Attractive	
(Melissa	P	24"	Sh	Div	Fr.drinks	to bees	Tea
officinalis)			Pr		Liqueurs		
BASIL, BUSH			G	S	Tomato	Edging	Stimulant
(Ocimum minimum)	A	12"	S	C	Macaroni	House	Nervine
PURPLE			G		Vinegar	plant	
(O. m. purpureum)		12"	S	S	Same		
SWEET			S				
(O. basilicum)		24"	G	S	Same		
*BAY, SWEET		3'-	S		Soups	Tub plant	
(Laurus nobilis)	P	6"	G	C	Stews	in cool	Narcotic
					Fish	room	
BEE BALM,					Fr.salads	Attractive	
BERGAMOT	P	36"	S	Div	Wine cups	to humming	Tea
(Monarda didyma)			G		App.jelly	birds	
WILD BERGAMOT		36"	S	Div			
(M. fistulosa)			G			Same	
BETONY,		2'-					
(Stachys		3'					
officinalis)						Border	
BURNET			S				
(Sanguisorba	P	18"-	Pr	S	Salad	Border	Astringent
minor)		24"	D		Vinegar		Hemorrhage
*CARDAMON			Sh			House	
(Amomum cardamon)	P		G	Div		Palm-like	
CATNIP		2'-	G	S			Tea
(Nepeta cataria)	P	3'	D	C			Stimulant
				Div			for cats
*AFRICAN BABY'S						Border	
BREATH (Chaes-	P	8"	S	C		Resembles	
nostoma fasti-			G			Sweet	
giatum)						Alyssum	
CHAMOMILE		1"-	S	S		Gr. cover	
(Anthemis nobilis)	P	12"	Pr	Div		Daisy fl.	Tea
CHIVES, ONION					Omelets		
(Allium schoen-	P	12"	S	S	Ch.spread	Edging	
oprasum)			G	Div	Mashed pot.		
CHIVES, GARLIC						Fragrant	
(Allium tub-	P	20"	S	S	Salads	wh. fl.	
erosum)			G	Div		heads	
CICELY, SWEET				S	Seafood		
(Myrrhis	P	2'-	Sh	Div	Salads	Border	
odorata)		3'	M				
*CINNAMOMUM			Sh			Shrub for	
camphora	P		M	S		pot	
COSTMARY:BIBLE					Iced	Leaf as	
LEAF (Chrysan-	P	3½'	S	Div	drinks	book	Tea
themum balsamita)					Ale	mark	
*DITTANY OF CRETE			S			Pot plant	
(Origanum dict-	P	12"	Pr	C		Arrange-	
aminus)			D			ments	

Cat~Mint Common.

Cives

230

Common headed or set Leck.

Calaminta Americana.

Fennell.

NAME Common & Botanical		Ht.	Soil	Prop.	USES Culinary	Decorative	Medicinal
ELECAMPANE		5'-	S	S	Candy		Cough med.
(Inula helenium)	P	10'	M	Div	Vermouth		Veterinary
FENNEL, SWEET		24"-			Salads		
(Foeniculum	P	60"	S	S	Seafoods		Eye lotion
vulgare)					Breads		
GERMANDER						Edging	
(Teucrium	P	12"	S	C		Rock	
chamaedrys)						garden	
*(T. fruticans)	P	30"	G	C		Pot plant for ghse.	
GOOD KING HENRY				G			
(Chenopodium	P	18"	S	S	Easter as		Laxative
bonus-henricus)			G	Div	greens		
*HELIOTROPE, FR.		2'-	S	S		Fragrant garden or	
(Heliotropium	P	4'	G	C		pot plant	
arborescens)							
HELIOTROPE, GARDEN (Valer-	P	4'-	G	S		Garden	Tea
ina officinalis)		5'	M			favorite	Rat bait
*HOREHOUND							Tea
(Marrubium	P	18"	S	S	Candy		Syrup
vulgare)			D				
HYSSOP						Edging	Infusion
(Hyssopus	P	12"-	S	S		Attractive	Induces per-
officinalis)		18"				to bees	spiration
							Removes col-
							or from
							bruises
HYSSOP, ANISE					Cold drink	Attractive	
(Agastache	P	3'	S	S	Fr. cup	to bees	
anethiodora)			G		Potpourri		
LADY'S MANTLE			S-Sh			Dr. & fr.	
(Alchemilla	P	18"	G	S		arrange-	
vulgaris)				Div		ments	
LAMB'S EARS			S	S		Arrange-	
(Stachys lanata)	P	12"	G	Div		ments	
LAVENDER, ENG.			S				
(Lavendula	P	18"	Pr	S		Dried	
officinalis)			D	C			
*FERN LEAF	P	24"	S	S		Pot Plant	
(L. multifida)			G	C		Garden in	
*FRENCH	P	2'-	M			summer	
(L. stoechas)		3'	S				
			Pr	S			
			D	C		Same	
*FRINGED			S				
(L. dentata)	P		G	C			
			M				
LEEKS			S		Sub. for		
(Allium porrum)	P	24"	S	Div	Chives	Garden	
*LICORICE PLANT		20"-				Gray fol.	
(Helichrysum	P	30"	S	C		Arrange-	
petiolatum)						ments	
LOVAGE			Sh		Soups		
(Levisticum	P	6'	G	S	Salad		
officinale)			M	Div	Celery flvr		
MARJORAM, SHOWY				Div		Garden	
(O. pulchellum)	P	18"	S	C	Pizza	Ornamen-	
						tal	
*SWEET				S	Egg salad		
(Majorana	P	10"	S	C	Meats	Rock	
hortensis)			D	S	Soups	garden	
WILD			S		Spaghetti		Oil on cot-
(Origanum	P	24"	S	Div	Salad		ton for
vulgare)				C	Tomatoes		toothache

233

NAME Common & Botanical		Ht.	Soil	Prop.	Culinary	Decorative	Medicinal
MINT, APPLE			S-Sh		Iced tea		
(Mentha rotun-	P	30"	M	Div	Lamb	Woolly leaf	Tea
difolia)					App.sauce		
CORSICAN					Creme de	Rock	
(M. requieni)		1"	S-Sh	Div	Menthe	garden	
CURLY							Tea
(M. crispa)	P	2"	S-Sh	Div	Jellies	Gr. cover	
			M	C		Arrange.	
ORANGE			M	Div	Gives can-		
(M. citrata)	P	18"	S-Sh	C	ned veg.		Tea
PEPPER					fr. flvr.		
(M. piperita)	P	24"	S-Sh	Div	Candy		Cough med.
			M	C	Liqueurs		Toothpaste
PINEAPPLE			S-Sh	Div	Salads		
(M. rotundifolia		18"	M	C	Cold		
variegata)					drinks		
SILVER	P	18"	S-Sh	Div		Arrange-	
			M	C		ments	
SPEAR			S-Sh	Div	Jellies		
(M. spicata)	P	18"	M	C	Juleps		Tea
					Candy		
MINT, STONE			S	S		Dry	
(Cunila	P	16"				places	
origanoides)			D	Div			
MUGWORT, SWEET			S	S			
(Artemisia	P	4'	S	Div		Arrange-	Epilepsy
lactiflora)			M	C		ments	
*OREGANO					Spaghetti		
(Origanum	P	2'	S	C	Pizza		
onites)					Salad		
PARSLEY, CURLY					Garnish		
(Petroselinum	B	6"	S	S	Soup		Dispel
crispum)			M		Stew		fever
PENNYROYAL			S-Sh			Ground	
(Mentha pulegium)		5"	M	Div		cover	
*ROSEMARY					Roast		
(Rosmarinus	P	6'	S	S	chicken	House	Tea
officinalis)			M	C	Pork	plant	
*PROSTRATE					Biscuits		
(R. o. prostrata)	P			C	Same	Bonsai	
RUE			S		Cr.cheese	Arrange-	
(Ruta graveolens)	P	2'	Pr	S	Sandwich	Ments	Disinfec-
						May cause	tant
						rash	
SAGE, CLARY			S			Garden	
(Salvia sclarea)	B	4'	D	S	Wine		
GARDEN			S	S	Poultry	Low hedge	Tea
(S. officinalis)	P	2½'	M	Div	Sausage	Attracts	
DWARF GARDEN		6"-	S	C		bees & hum-	
(S. o. nana)	P	8"	M	Div	Same	mingbirds	
*GOLDEN						Pretty	
(S. o. aureus)	P	12"	M	C	Same	foliage	
*PINEAPPLE			S		Cold	House	Tea
(S. rutilans)	P	24"	M	C	drinks	plant	
					Fr. cups		
*TRICOLOR					Desserts		
(S. officinalis	P	12"	S	C		Pretty	
tricolor)						foliage	
SANTOLINA, GRAY						Border	
(S. chamaecypar-	P	18"	S	C		Rock	
issus)			D	L		garden	
SANTOLINA, GREEN			S	C			
(S. virens)	P	24"	D	L		Same	
SAVORY, WINTER			S	C			
(Satureja mon-	P	12"				Edging	
tana)			Pr	L			
SENNA						Lg.speci-	
(Cassia mari-	P	5'-	S	S		men for	Laxative
landica)		6'	Pr	Div		border	Tea
SKIRRET			G		Edible		
(Sium sisarum)	P	3'	D	Div	root	Foliage	
SORRELL, FRENCH			S	S	Soups		
(Rumex scutatus)	P	3'	M	Div	Salad		
SOUTHERNWOOD			S	C			
(Artemisia	P	3'	D	Div			
abrotanum)							

Spear Mint.

Common Basil.

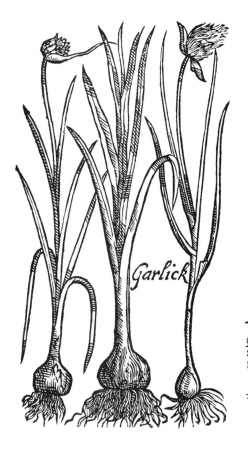

Garlick

Dill.

Dandelion.

NAME Common & Botanical		Ht.	Soil	Prop.	USES Culinary	Decorative	Medicinal
STRAWBERRY, RUNNERLESS (Baron von Solemaker)	P	6"	S-Sh G M	S			
TANSY, COMMON (Tanacetum vulgare)	P	4'- 5'	S	S Div		Arrangements	Infusion considered dangerous
FERN LEAF (T. v. crispum)	P	2'				Broader, more curl	
TARRAGON (Artemisia dracunculus)	P	2'	S G	Div C	Steak Fish Vinegar		
THYME, CARAWAY (Thymus herba-barona)		6"	S	Div C	Beef	Rock gard. Gr. cover, sandy banks	
CREEPING (T. serphyllum) Pk.,wh.,crimson	P	3"	S D	Div C		Between flagstones	
CREEPING GOLDEN	P	4"	S D	Div C		Rock gard. Gr. cover	
ENGLISH (T. vulgaris)	P	8"	S D	Div C	Fish Stews Pork Cooking	Fragrance	Cough medicine Tooth-aches
FRENCH (T. vulgaris)							
GOLDEN LEMON (T. v. aureus)		8"	S D	Div C		Foliage	
LEMON (T. v. citrio-dorus)		8"	S D	Div C	Jellies Cooking	Arrangements	Tea
SILVER LEMON (T. v. argenteus)		8"	S	Div	Cooking	Arrange-Foliage	Tea
WOOLLY (T. serphyllum lanuginosus)	P	3"	S D	Div C		Grey gr. cover be-tween flagstones	
HALL'S WOOLLY	P	4"	S D	Div C		Ground cover	
WOOLLY STEMMED (T. lanicaulis)	P	8"	S D	Div C		Rock garden Trailing	
*VERBENA, LEMON (Lippia citri-dora)	P	To 6'	S M	C		Potpourri Finger-bowls	Tea
WOODRUFF, SWEET (Asperula odor-ata)	P	8"	Sh. G M	Div C	Wines Snuff "Maiwein"	Fragrant ground cover	Tea
WORMWOOD, COMMON (Artemisia absinthium)	P	4'	S Pr D	S	Absinthe	Excellent seashore plant	Liniments
ROMAN (A. pontica)	P	18"		Div		Border Arrange-ments	

233

HERBS TO REPEL INSECTS

HERB	INSECTS REPELLED OR USES	(COMPANION PLANTING) SUGGESTED PLANTING WITH
BASIL	Flies	Tomatoes
BEE BALM	Growth and Flavor	Anywhere in Garden
BORAGE	Tomato Worm	Tomatoes and Strawberries
CATNIP	Flea Beetle	In the Border
CHAMOMILE, ROMAN	Growth and Flavor	Cabbage and Onions
CHERVIL	Growth and Flavor	Radishes and Elsewhere
CHIVES	Growth and Flavor	Between rows of Carrots
DILL	Improves growth	Cabbage
FLAX	Potato Bug	Between rows of Potatoes
GARLIC	Japanese Beetle	
	Improves Growth and Health	Roses and Raspberries
HORSERADISH	Potato Bug	Potatoes
HYSSOP	Cabbage Moth	Cabbage and Grapes
LEEKS	Carrot Fly	
	Growth and Flavor	Celery and Carrots
LOVAGE	Health and Flavor	In the Garden
MARIGOLDS	Nematodes and Cucumber	In the Garden
	Beetles	In the Garden
MARJORAM, SWEET	Health and Flavor	
MINT	Cabbage Moth	Cabbage
	Health and Flavor	Carrots
ONION	Carrot Fly	
PENNYROYAL	Carrot Fly	As Ground Cover
	Flies and Mosquitoes	Tomatoes in Groups
POT MARIGOLD	Tomato Worm and General	
	Garden Pests	Peas and Leaf Lettuce
RADISH	Beetles	Cabbage, Beans and Carrots
ROSEMARY	Growth and Flavor	
	Cabbage Moth, Bean	Roses and Raspberries
RUE	Beetles and Carrot Fly	
SAGE	Japanese Beetle	Cabbage and Carrots
	Cabbage Moth and Carrot Fly	
SAVORY, SUMMER	Bean Beetles	Onions and Beans
	Growth and Flavor	
SOUTHERNWOOD	Cabbage Moth	In the Garden Anywhere
	Growth and Flavor	
TANSY	Japanese Beetle, Ants and	Raspberries and Roses
	Flying Insects	
THYME	Cabbage Worm	Cabbage and in the Garden
WORMWOOD	Growth and Flavor	Cabbage and in the Garden

234

Production Information for Several Fruit Types

Fruit Type	Feet of Space Between Rows	Feet of Space Between Plants	Bearing Age Years	Average Yield Per Plant	Life Expectancy Years
Apple					
Semi Dwarf					
(M 7, MM 106)	18	15	4	6 bu	25
Dwarf (M 9, M 26)	14	6	4	2 bu	20
Blueberry	6	4	3	8 pt	10 to 15
Blackberry	8	3	2	3 pt	6 to 8
Currant	8	4	3	10 pt	15
Elderberry	10	6	2	15 lb	10
Gooseberry	8	4	2	8 pt	10
Grape	10	8	3	15 lb	15
Pear					
Standard	25	20	5	5 bu	25
Dwarf	18	12	4	2 bu	15
Plum	18	15	4	60 lb	20
Raspberry					
Red	8	2	2	3 pt	12
Black	8	4	2	4 pt	8
Purple	8	4	2	6 pt	8
Fallbearing cultivars	8	2	2	3 pt	8
Strawberry					
Regular	4	2	1	3 pt	3
Fallbearing cultivars	3	1	4 mo.	1 pt	2

PEAR TREE TRAINED ON WALL

PLANTS FOR SPECIAL SOILS OR CONDITIONS

Some plants that are desirable for special conditions are specified in the following lists:

For bright sunshine with plenty of fertility and moisture: Over 4 feet high, castor-bean, cosmos, sunflower, sorghum, feterita, milo, and Indian corn; over 3 feet, Josephs coat, love-lies-bleeding, feather cockscomb, orange sunflower, princesfeather, spiderflower, and summer-cypress; 30 inches, cornflower, larkspur, scabiosa, scarlet sage, strawflower, and zinnia; 24 inches, balsam, calliopsis, China-aster, summer chrysanthemum, cockscomb, coneflower, four-o'clock, gaillardia, Aztec marigold, playcodon, poppy, salpiglossis, snapdragon, and snow-on-the mountain; 18 inches, Jobs-tears, mignonette, and stock; 12 inches, calendula, California-poppy, calliposis, candytuft, French marigold, petunia, Drummond phlox, pink, and Iceland poppy; under 12 inches, ageratum, cockscomb, lobelia, portulaca, sweet alyssum, and verbena.

Of easiest culture under ordinary garden conditions: Over 4 feet, sunflower; about 3 feet, Josephs-coat, love-lies-bleeding, heliopsis, and princesfeather; about 30 inches, cornflower, strawflower, gaillardia, marigold, poppy, and snow-on-the-mountain; about 18 inches, mignonette; about 12 inches, Cape-marigold, calendula, California-poppy, balsam, candytuft, petunia, Drummond phlox, pink, dwarf nasturtium, portulaca, and sweet alyssum.

On light fertile soil: Gaillardia, marigold, Drummond phlox, and portulaca.

On light soil, not too rich: Cockscomb and feather cockscomb.

On poor soil: Love-lies-bleeding, princes-feather, Josephs-coat, Cape-marigold, godetia, dwarf nasturtium, portulaca, grass-pink, sweet alyssum, garden balsam, and calliopsis.

On lands near the seacoast: Plants from the three foregoing lists, depending on the fertility of the soil, together with the castor-bean, sunflower, heliopsis, spiderflower, cornflower, strawflower, zinnia, calliopsis, snow-on-the-mountain, four-o'clock, stock, calendula, California-poppy, petunia, and sweet alyssum.

In partial shade: Basketflower, sweet-sultan, clarkia, platycodon, godetia, Drummond phlox, pansy, sweet alyssum, lupine, and forget-me-not.

Especially responding to rich soil: Castor-bean, scarlet sage, balsam, and China-aster.

To cut for everlastings: Rose everlasting, feathered cockscomb, globe-amaranth, and strawflower.

Not adapted to the South except for late and early spring: Salpiglossis, pansy, and forget-me-not.

Plants that can be started to advantage in

hotbeds and coldframes for early flowering, whether they are to be used for bedding purposes or for cut flowers; Ageratum, China-aster, calliopsis, castor-bean, calendula, cosmos, cockscomb, chrysanthemum, godetia, lobelia, marigold, petunia, grasspink, scarlet sage, spiderflower, and verbena.

Some plants that may be sown in beds in the open ground and later transplanted to their permanent locations are ageratum, calendula, calliopsis, China-aster, clarkia, cockscomb, dahlia, gaillardia, godetia, lobelia, mignonette, pansy, pink, snapdragon, spiderflower, stock, and zinnia. Most of these may be sown earlier in a hotbed or coldframe and thus be made to bloom earlier.

Some should be sown in the open ground where the plants are to grow.

Among those that should be sown early in that way are alyssum, California-poppy, candytuft, cornflower, forget-me-not, mignonette, nemophila, Drummond phlox, sunflower, poppy, and sweet alyssum.

Among those that should be sown late in this manner after the ground is warm are the castor-bean, sorghum, milo, feterita, Indian corn, garden galsam, portulaca and four o'clock.

For August and September sowing; Forget-me-not, pansy, cornflower, pink, and snap-dragon.

Seeds that may be sown on well-prepared ground just before winter for early spring germination or on fall-prepared ground very early in the spring while the soil still freezes at night are the poppy, cornflower, cosmos, summer-cypress, larkspur, snapdragon, snow-on-the-mountain, and sweet alyssum.

Flowers that are white or with pure white varieties: 4 feet, cosmos; 3 feet, dahlia and sweet-sultan; 2½ feet, clarkia, cornflower, larkspur, and scabiosa; 2 feet, baby'sbreath, China-aster, summer chrysanthemum, lupine, balloon-flower, snapdragon, garden balsam, and poppy; 1½ feet, godetia, four-o'clock, rose everlasting, and stock; 1 foot, candytuft, Iceland poppy, petunia ageratum, lobelia, portulaca, sweet alyssum, and verbena.

Flowers having varieties mixed with white: 3 feet, dahlia; 2½ feet, salpiglossis; 1 foot, nemophila, pansy, petunia, and pink.

Flowers yellow or with yellow varieties: 4 feet, sunflower, feather cockscomb, and dahlia; 2½ feet, strawflower, sunflower, and

BLEEDING HEART.

zinnia; 2 feet, calliopsis, summer chrysanthemum, Aztec marigold, snapdragon, and four-o'clock; 1 foot, calendula, Cape-marigold, French marigold, Iceland poppy; California poppy, dwarf marigold, and portulaca.

Flowers having varieties mixed with yellow: 4 feet, dahlia; 2 feet calliopsis, rudbeckia, salpiglossis, and summer chrysanthemum; 1½ feet, four-o'clock; 1 foot, dwarf nasturtium and pansy.

Flowers of orange color or with orange varieties: 3 feet, heliopsis; 2½ feet, zinnia; 2 feet, Aztec marigold; 1 foot, calendula, Cape-marigold, French marigold, and California-poppy.

Flowers having varieties mixed with orange: 2 feet, gaillardia; 2 foot, dwarf nastrutium and French marigold.

Flowers lavender or with lavender varieties: 3 feet, basketflower and sweet-sultan; 2½ feet, larkspur, 2 feet, China-aster; 1½ feet, candytuft; 1 foot, Drummond phlox, nemophila, and pansy.

Flowers having varieties mixed with lavender: 2½ feet, salpiglossis; 1 foot, pansy.

Flowers blue or with blue varieties: 2½ feet, cornflower and larkspur; 2 feet, lupine and balloonflower; 1 foot, nemophila, ageratum, lobelia, verbena, and forget-me-not.

Flowers purple or with purple varieties: 3 feet, sweet-sultan; 2½ feet, clarkia and scabiosa; 2 feet, China-aster, 1½ feet, stock; 1 foot, verbena.

Flowers having varieties mixed with purple: 2½ feet, salpiglossis; 1 foot, pansy.

Flowers pink or with pink varieties: 4 feet, cosmos; 3 feet, dahlia; 2½ feet larkspur and zinnia; 2 feet, China-aster, garden balsam, and poppy; 1½ feet, rose everlasting; 1 foot, Drummond phlox, pinks (including carnations), portulaca, and verbena.

Flowers having varieties mixed with pink: 3 feet, dahlia; 1 foot, pinks (including carnations).

Flowers salmon or with salmon varieties: 3 feet, dahlia; 2½ feet, clarkia, 2 feet, snapdragon and poppy; 1 foot, Drummond phlox.

Flowers having varieties mixed with salmon pink: 3 feet, dahlia; 1 foot, Drummond phlox.

Flowers scarlet or with scarlet varieties: 3 feet, dahlia; 2½ feet, scarlet sage and zinnia; 2 feet, snapdragon, poppy, and four-o'clock; 1 foot, Drummond phlox, pinks (including carnations), and dwarf nasturtium.

Flowers rose or crimson or with rose or crimson varieties: 4 feet, cosmos; 3 feet, princesfeather, feather cockscomb, sweet-sultan, and spiderflower; 2½ feet, clarkia, cornflower, scabiosa, and zinnia; 2 feet, garden balsam, China-aster, cockscomb, and lupine; 1½ feet, godetia, four-o'clock, globe-amaranth, stock, and candytuft; 1 foot, Drummond phlox, petunia, and portulaca.

Flowers having varieties mixed with rose or crimson: 1 foot, Drummond phlox and petunia.

Plants used for their foliage or chiefly for it, the foliage being green unless otherwise noted: 4 feet, castor-bean (bronze and green separate), sorghum, feterita, milo, broomcorn, and Indian corn; 3 feet, Josephs-coat (red, yellow, and green mixed), love-lies-bleeding (red), summer-cypress (pea green turning crimson in late summer); 2½ feet, annual poinsettia (scarlet leaves in late summer) and snow-on-the-mountain (white-edged leaves); 1½ feet, Jobs-tears; 1 foot, mignonette (a greenish flowers grown for its sweet odor, but in its garden decorative value comparable to a plant grown for its foliage).

The obedient plant. The flower stays in any position it is turned, to the right or left. Sometimes grows six feet high. Flowers an inch long, purple, pink, lilac or white.

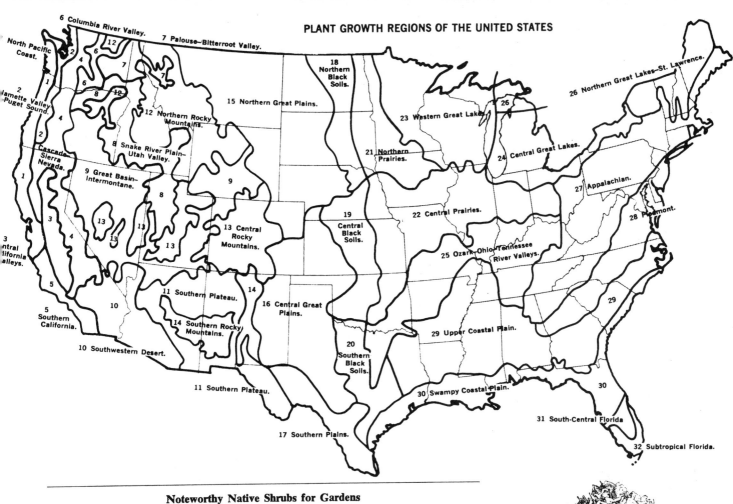

PLANT GROWTH REGIONS OF THE UNITED STATES

6 Columbia River Valley.

North Pacific Coast.

7 Palouse–Bitterroot Valley.

18 Northern Black Soils.

26 Northern Great Lakes–St. Lawrence.

Willamette Valley–Puget Sound.

2

15 Northern Great Plains.

23 Western Great Lakes.

12 Northern Rocky Mountains.

Cascade Sierra Nevada.

8 Snake River Plain–Utah Valley.

9 Great Basin–Intermontane.

26

24 Central Great Lakes.

21 Northern Prairies.

27 Appalachian.

13 Central Rocky Mountains.

19 Central Black Soils.

22 Central Prairies.

28 Piedmont.

Central California Valleys.

25 Ozark–Ohio–Tennessee River Valleys.

5

11 Southern Plateau.

14

16 Central Great Plains.

29

Southern California.

14 Southern Rocky Mountains.

29 Upper Coastal Plain.

10 Southwestern Desert.

20 Southern Black Soils.

30

11 Southern Plateau.

30 Swampy Coastal Plain.

31 South-Central Florida.

17 Southern Plains.

32 Subtropical Florida.

Noteworthy Native Shrubs for Gardens

Common name	Latin name	Growth region (see the map)	Special comment
Flame azalea	Rhododendron calendulaceum	1, 2, 3, 20, 22, 24, 25, 27–29	Flowers yellow, orange, or red, brilliant. Rated by many as the finest native ornamental.
Flannel bush	Fremontia mexicana	5	Waxy yellow flowers. Closely-related California fremontia has golden flowers, not quite as showy, but excellent. The latter can be grown in regions 3, 4, 5, 10; if seed comes from high elevations, probably can be grown in regions 1, 2, 29, 30, 31, and possibly 28. Evergreen.
Mescalbean	Sophora secundiflora	11, 16, 17, 20, 29, 30	Wisteria-like clusters of violet-blue flowers, deliciously fragrant. Forms a little tree in favorable situations. Pods hard, seeds red or carmine.
Mountain-laurel	Kalmia latifolia	1, 2, 24–30	Pink-white flowers in clusters; highly floriferous. Evergreen.
Santa Barbara ceanothus	Ceanothus impressus	5 (possibly 29 and 30)	Foliage deep green; flowers dark blue. Prolific bloomer. "Clean, tailored" shrub, often wider than tall.
Fringe-tree	Chionanthus virginica	1, 2, 3, 20, 22, 24, 25, 27–30	Lacy, white flowers; very fragrant. A large shrub or small tree.
Mountain stewartia	Stewartia ovata var. grandiflora	1, 2, 20, 22, 24, 25, 27–30	Waxy-white flowers up to 4 inches across. Orange and scarlet fall color.

BROAD LEAVED LAUREL.
(KALMIA LATIFOLIA.)

PINXTER FLOWER.
(AZALEA NUDIFLORA.)

Japanese Snowball (*Viburnum plicatum*).

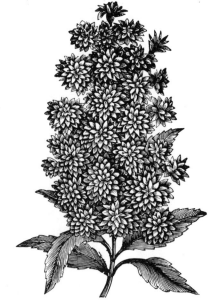

DEUTZIA CRENATA, FL. PL.

Nordsmann's Fir (*Abies Nordmanniana*).

Noteworthy Native Shrubs for Gardens—Continued

Common name	Latin name	Growth Region (see the map on page 239)	Special comment
Yaupon	Ilex vomitoria	20, 28, 29, 30 (probably 1, 2, 3 and 5)	An evergreen valuable for its profusion of red berries.
Cranberrybush	Viburnum trilobum	1, 2, 4, 12, 13, 15, 18, 21, 27	White, flat-topped flower clusters. Fruits bright red, highly attractive.
Oakleaf hydrangea	Hydrangea quercifolia	1, 2, 24, 25, 28–30 (Freezes in 27)	Large panicles of white flowers later turning copper to brown. Leaves large, oakleaf shaped. Very tolerant of shade.
Oregon-grape	Mahonia aquifolium	1, 2, 4, 6, 7, 11–16, 22, 24, 25, 27–29	Hollylike, shining green foliage. Flowers bright yellow; fruits grapelike, blue. There is a form with a dull leaf, not as good.
Creosotebush	Larrea tridentata	9, 10, 11, 16, 17	Excellent, yellow-flowered shrub for desert gardens. Foliage evergreen.
Anacahuita	Cordia boissieri	11, 17, 30; possibly 29–32	Very rare evergreen. Flowers white, with yellow centers, clustered. Fruits ivory white.
Sage brush	Artemisia tridentata	2, 4–13, 15, 27, 28	A very fine silver-white bush. Requires alkaline soil (use a little lime or crushed shells around it).

Noteworthy Native Trees for Gardens

Common name	Latin name	Growth region (see the map on page 239)	Special comment
White fir	Abies concolor	4, 5, 9–14, 27, 28	Evergreen, shapely, fine foliage
Huisache	Acacia farnesiana	5, 10, 11, 17, 20, 29, 30	Grows larger with moisture. Deciduous.
Red maple	Acer rubrum	19–30	Red fall color; rapid growing
Sugar maple	Acer saccharum	2, 15, 18, 21–29	One of our most brilliantly-colored trees in autumn.
Ohio buckeye	Aesculus glabra	22, 24, 25, 27, 28, 29	Successfully planted in recent years in region 13 at lower elevations.
Madrona	Arbutus menziesii	1–3, 5, 10	Difficult to transplant, a beauty.
Hickory	Carya spp.	20–30	Usually hard to transplant.
Catalpa	Catalpa spp.	21–23, 25–30	Leaves very large, flower clusters showy.
Hackberry	Celtis occidentalis	15–30	Drought resistant. Much planted in the Great Plains.
Paloverde	Cercidium torreyanum	10–11	Excellent in desert gardens.
Port Orford cedar	Chamaecyparis lawsoniana	1, 2, 28, 29	70 or more varieties, some exceptionally pleasing.
Flowering dogwood	Cornus florida	1, 2, 20, 22–25, 27–30	Pink, white, and double flowered forms known, also a weeping form
Pacific dogwood	Cornus nuttallii	1–5, 12	Somewhat difficult to grow; forms from region 12 will probably grow in 27 and 28.

Common name	Latin name	Growth region (see the map on page 239)	Special comment
Monterey cypress	Cupressus macrocarpa	1, 5	Growth form highly picturesque, especially along the seacoast.
American beech	Fagus grandifolia	20, 22–30	Magnificent specimen tree.
White ash	Fraxinus americana	20, 22–25, 27–30	
Red ash	Fraxinus pennsylvanica	15, 18, 20; and 12 and 17 for green ash, a variety	
Honeylocust	Gleditsia triacanthos	16, 20, 22–30	There is a thornless variety. Highly resistant to drought.
American holly	Ilex opaca	20, 25, 27–30	Many varieties available, some better than the wild form.
Walnut	Juglans spp.	18–30	
Juniper .... (Red cedar)	Juniperus spp.	Different species occur in western mountains and in the East	Eastern red cedar is rapid growing. Western species are slower.
Larch	Larix spp.	Eastern larch 22–24, 26, 27. Western larch 4, 12	The eastern species occurs in swamps, but grows quite well on dry land. Deciduous.
Incense cedar	Calocedrus decurrens	1, 4, 5, 29, 30.	Elegant evergreen foliage.
Sweetgum	Liquidambar styraciflua	2, 20, 22, 25, 27–30	Exceptionally brilliant fall color.
Tuliptree	Liriodendron tulipifera	2, 21–29	Very rapid growing. Excellent specimen tree.
Catalina ironwood	Lyonothamnus floribundus	5	Much planted in southern California.
Magnolia	Magnolia spp.	Generally 28–30, 27 for some	The evergreen magnolia is especially beautiful; planted also in 1, 2, 3, 5. Bigleaf magnolia has the largest leaves of any American tree (25, 27–30).
Red mulberry ...	Morus rubra	16–25, 27–30	Highly attractive to birds.
Blackgum	Nyssa sylvatica	20, 22, 24, 25–30	Brilliant fall color.
Sourwood	Oxydendron arboreum	25, 27–30	Very attractive in flower.
Blue spruce	Picea pungens	9, 12–14, 27–29	Many cultivated varieties. Exceptional form and color.
	(White, black and sitka spruces are also in cultivation.)		
Pines	Pinus spp.		
	(About 40 species, nearly all cultivated. Use any "good" pine native to your region. Big trees, except for the pinyon or nut pines of the Southwest.)		
Sycamore	Platanus spp.	Eastern S. 16, 20–22, 24–30. California S. 3, 4, 5. Arizona S. 10, 11	Majestic trees with "blotched" bark. Fine specimens. Best adapted to wet places, rich soil.
Douglas-fir	Pseudotsuga menziesii	The Rocky Mountain variety 9, 11, 13, 14, 16, 25, 27, 28, probably 29. The Pacific variety 1–6	The Rocky Mountain species is the only one successfully grown in the East.

JAPANESE AZALEA (*Azalea mollis*).

OAK-LEAVED MOUNTAIN ASH

JAPANESE PEA-FRUITED CYPRESS

Common name	Latin name	Growth region (see the map on page 239)	Special comment
Oaks	Quercus spp.	About 70 species, one or more in every growth region	Very slow growing, but superb trees, generally long-lived.
Black-locust	Robinia pseudoacacia	1–8, 12, 15, 16, 20–23, 25–29	
Cabbage palmetto	Sabal palmetto	30 (a related species, the Texas palm occurs in 11, 17)	
Sassafras	Sassafras albidum	2, 20, 22–30	
Redwood	Sequoia sempervirens	1	Has failed in the Eastern U.S. after many years of trial. Our tallest tree.
Sequoia	Sequoiadendron gigateum	4	Our most massive tree. Failed in the East over many years of trial.
Cypress	Taxodium spp.	17, 20, 25, 28–32	
Western red cedar	Thuja plicata	1, 2, 4, 6, 7, 12	
Basswood	Tilia spp.	Some 14 species, generally found in Eastern and Southeastern United States	Excellent shade trees.
Canadian hemlock	Tsuga canadensis	22, 25, 27–29	Excellent hedge, as well as specimen tree.
Western hemlock	Tsuga heterophylla	1, 2, 4, 6, 12	
Mountain hemlock	Tsuga mertensiana	4, 12	Slow growing. Fine specimen tree.
American elm ...	Ulmus americana	1, 2, 15, 16, 18–23, 25–30	Handsome, vase-shaped shade tree.
Yucca	Yucca spp.	Generally southwestern	Desert gardens.
Palms	Washingtonia spp.	Generally southwestern	The California species is much grown in 5.

PURPLE-FRINGE (*Rhus cotinus*)

CUT-LEAVED WEEPING BIRCH

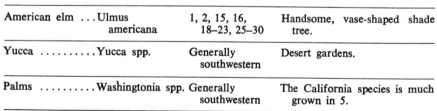

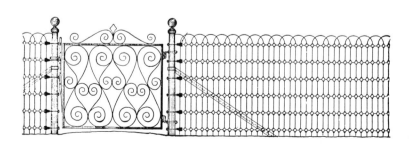

AQUATIC PLANTS

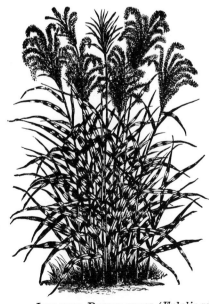

—East India Lotus (*Nelumbium roseum*).

—Purple African Water-lily (*Nymphæa Zanzibarensis*).

NYMPHÆA ZANZIBARENSIS

—Japanese Plume-grass (*Eulalia zebrina*).

TREES, SHRUBS, AND OTHER PLANTS USED NEAR WATER

Alder, Alnus spp.
American beachgrass, Ammophila breviligulata
 Fern.
Amur honeysuckle, Lonicera maacki Maxim.
Autumn olive, Elaeagnus umbellata Thunb.
Bahiagrass, Paspalum notatum Flugge
Bayberry, Myrica pensylvanica Lois.
Beachplum, Prunus maritima Marsh.
Bentgrasses, Agrostis spp.
Bermudagrass, Cynodon dactylon (L.) Pers.
Big bluestem, Andropogon gerardii Vitman
Boxelder, Acer negundo L.
Coralberry, Symphoricarpos orbicularis Michx.
Cornelian-cherry, Cornus mas L.
Creeping meadow foxtail, Alopecurus arundin-
 aceus Poir.
Creeping red fescue, Festuca rubra L.
Daylily, Hemerocallis fulva L.
European beachgrass, Ammophila arenaria
 (L.) Link
Inkberry, Ilex glabra (L.) Gray
Intermediate wheatgrass, Agropyron intermedium
 (Host) Beauv.
Lilyturf, Liriope spicata Lour., and Ophiopogon
 japonicus Ker-Gawl.
Orchardgrass, Dactylis glomerata L.
Poplar, Populus spp.
Purple-osier willow, Salix purpurea L.
Red-osier dogwood, Cornus stolonifera Michx.
Reed canarygrass, Phalaris arundinacea L.
Ribbongrass, Phalaris arundinacea v. picta L.
Rugosa rose, Rosa rugosa Thunb.
Saltmeadow cordgrass, Spartina patens (Ait.) Wood
SAnd lovegrass, Eragrostis trichodes (Nutt.) Wood
Sandbar willow, Salix interior Rowlee
Sericea lespedeza, Lespedeza cuneata (Dumont)
 G. Don.
Shrub lespedezas, Lespedeza bicolor Turcz., and
 Lespedeza japonica Bailey
Siberian dogwood, Cornus alba sibirica Loud.
Silky dogwood, Cornus amomum Mill.
Smooth bromegrass, Bromus inermis Leyss.
Switchgrass, Panicum virgatum L.
Tall fescue, Festuca arundinacea Schreb.
Weeping forsythia, Forsythia spp.
Western sand cherry, Prunus besseyii Bailey
Western wheatgrass, Agropyron smithii Rydb.
Wichura rose, Rosa wichuraiana Crep.
Willows, Salix spp.

TRANSPLANTS

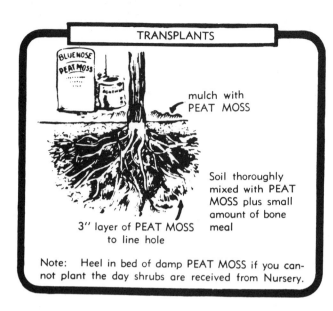

mulch with PEAT MOSS

3" layer of PEAT MOSS to line hole

Soil thoroughly mixed with PEAT MOSS plus small amount of bone meal

Note: Heel in bed of damp PEAT MOSS if you cannot plant the day shrubs are received from Nursery.

SEED FLATS

water by immersing

PEAT MOSS is the ideal medium for seed germination. It eliminates damping off, can stand over-watering. After seeds are planted in PEAT sprinkle thin layer of fine PEAT over seeds & cover with pane of glass

RENOVATING OLD LAWNS

SPRING { Rake old grass & scratch hard crust to pierce it.
Mix a good complete garden fertilizer (4 lbs. per 100 sq. ft.) with fine dry PEAT MOSS & top dress about ½" thick.

AUTUMN { Repeat, using bonemeal. When ground heaves in winter the fine PEAT enters cracks & keeps roots covered & alive.

PEAT MOSS

HOUSEPLANTS

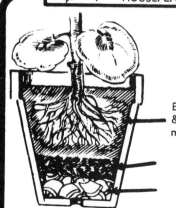

Equal parts of sand, soil & PEAT MOSS plus bonemeal

layer of PEAT MOSS

broken crockery

The same procedure may be used for window boxes

ACID LOVING PLANTS

AZALEAS	RHODODENDRONS
DOGWOOD	LILY
HEATHER	PRIMROSE
MOUNTAIN HOLLY	PHLOX
LILY of the VALLEY	TRAILING ARBUTUS
IRIS	COLUMBINE
LADY SLIPPER	GENTIAN
PAINTED TRILLIUM	WILD INDIGO
WHITE ELDER	MARSH MARIGOLD
MAGNOLIA	BEGONIAS
BLACKBERRY	RASPBERRY

ALL THESE DO ESPECIALLY WELL IN SOILS CONSISTING OF 50% OR MORE PEAT MOSS

CUTTINGS

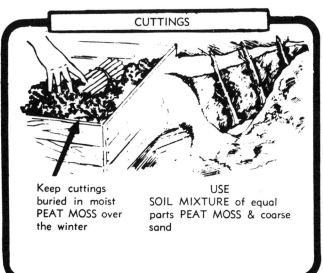

Keep cuttings buried in moist PEAT MOSS over the winter

USE SOIL MIXTURE of equal parts PEAT MOSS & coarse sand

ROSES

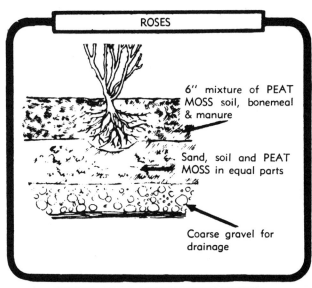

6" mixture of PEAT MOSS soil, bonemeal & manure

Sand, soil and PEAT MOSS in equal parts

Coarse gravel for drainage

HOT BED

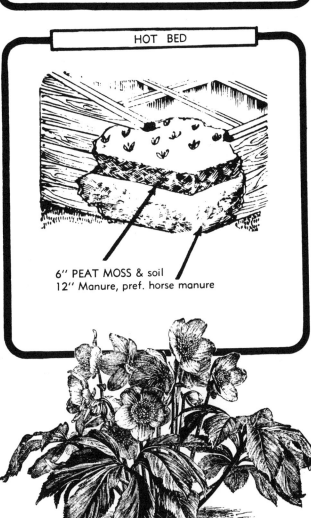

6" PEAT MOSS & soil
12" Manure, pref. horse manure

BULBS & TUBERS

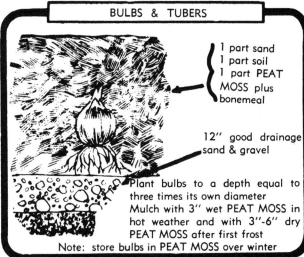

1 part sand
1 part soil
1 part PEAT MOSS plus bonemeal

12" good drainage sand & gravel

Plant bulbs to a depth equal to three times its own diameter
Mulch with 3" wet PEAT MOSS in hot weather and with 3"-6" dry PEAT MOSS after first frost
Note: store bulbs in PEAT MOSS over winter

FLOWERBEDS & BORDERS

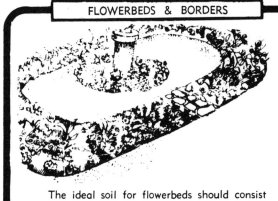

The ideal soil for flowerbeds should consist of equal parts loam, sand and PEAT MOSS.

Add to this slow acting organic fertilizers such as bonemeal, dried blood & wood ashes.

NEW LAWNS

1. Remove debris and level.
2. Spread 2" layer of **wet** PEAT MOSS over soil; add bonemeal and lawn fertilizer (4 pounds of each per 100 square feet.)
3. Mix thoroughly with top 4" of soil, then level.
4. Rake smooth, roll, rake again.
5. Broadcast seed, roll lightly once more.
6. Cover with ¼" layer of fine dry BLUENOSE PEAT MOSS then sprinkle.
7. Keep moist continuously.

Some plants that will grow in shade
Deciduous shrubs
Abelia grandiflora (Glossy Abelia)
Amelanchier (Juneberry)
Berberis thunbergii (Japanese Barberry)
Calycanthus floridus (Carolina Allspice)
Cercis canadensis (Redbud)
Cornus (Dogwood)
Hydrangea quercifolia   (Oakleaf Hydrangea)
Ilex verticillata (Winterberry)
Ligustrum (Privet)
Symphoricarpos (Snowberry)
Viburnum
Evergreen shrubs
Aucuba japonica (Gold Dust Tree)
Berberis julianae (Barberry)
Buxus (Boxwood)
Camellia
Euonymus fortunei vegetus
Fatsia japonica
Ilex (Holly)
Kalmia latifolia (Mountain Laurel)
Leucothoe
Mohonia aquifolium (Holly Mahonia)
Namdina domestica
Photinia serrulata
Pieris
Taxus (Yew)
Vines
Aristolochia durier   (Dutchman's Pipe)
Gelsemium sempervirens   (Carolina Yellow Jess.)
Hedera canariensis (Algerian Ivy)
Hedera helix (English Ivy)
Lonicera (Honeysuckle)
Pathenocissus (Boston Ivy)
Vitis labrusca (Fox Grape)
Flowering annuals
Begonia semperflorens (Wax Begonia)
Coleus
Impatiens holstii
Lobelia ermus)
Nicotiana (Flowering Tobacco)
Torenia fournieri (Wishbone Flower)
Vinca rosea (Madagascar Periwinkle)
Flowering perennials
Ajuga (Bugleweed)
Anemone japonica
Aquilegia (Columbine)
Astilbe (Spirea)
Campanula (Bellflower)
Convallaria majalis (Lily of the Valley)
Dicentra (Bleeding Heart)
Digitalis (Foxglove)
Helleborus
Heuchera (Coralbells)
Hosta (Plantain Lily)
Hypericum calycinum (St. Johnswort)
Lunaria biennis (Honesty)
Mertensia virginica (Virginia Bluebell)

Myosotis (Forget Me Not)
Trollius (Globeflower)
Viola (Violet)
Bulbs
Begonia
Caladium
Chionodoxa luciliae (Glory of the Snow)
Colchicum (Autumn Crocus)
Colocasia antiquorum (Elephant's Ear)
Galanthus nivalis (Snowdrop)
Leucojum aestivum (Summer Snowflake)
Lilium (Lily)
Muscari (Grape Hyacinth)
Narcissus
Ornithogalum (Star of Bethlehem)
Scilla hispanica (Spanish Bluebell)

Plants Resistant to Photochemical Smog
Shrubs and trees
Acacia
Aralia
Arbutus
Buxus (Boxwood)
Camellia
Cedrus
Cistus
Cotoneaster
Cupressus (Cypress)
Fraxinus (Ash)
Ginkgo (Maidenhairtree)
Prunus
Pittosporum
Pyracantha (Firethorn)
Quercus (Oak)
Spiraea (Bridal Wreath)
Syringa (lilac)
Viburnum
Yucca
House Plants
Dieffenbachia
Dracacaena
Fatsia
Philodendron
Pittosporum

Plants Sensitive to Photochemical Smog
Shrubs and trees
Acer (Maple)
Alnus (Alder)
Calycanthus (Carolina Allspice)
Ficus (Fig)
Gleditsia (Locust

BRANCHING HABITS OF TREES
1. Trunk Dividing, Branches Spreading, Elm
2. Branches Pendulant, Willow
3. Branches Ascending, White Oak
4. Trunk Single, Branches Horizontal, White Pine

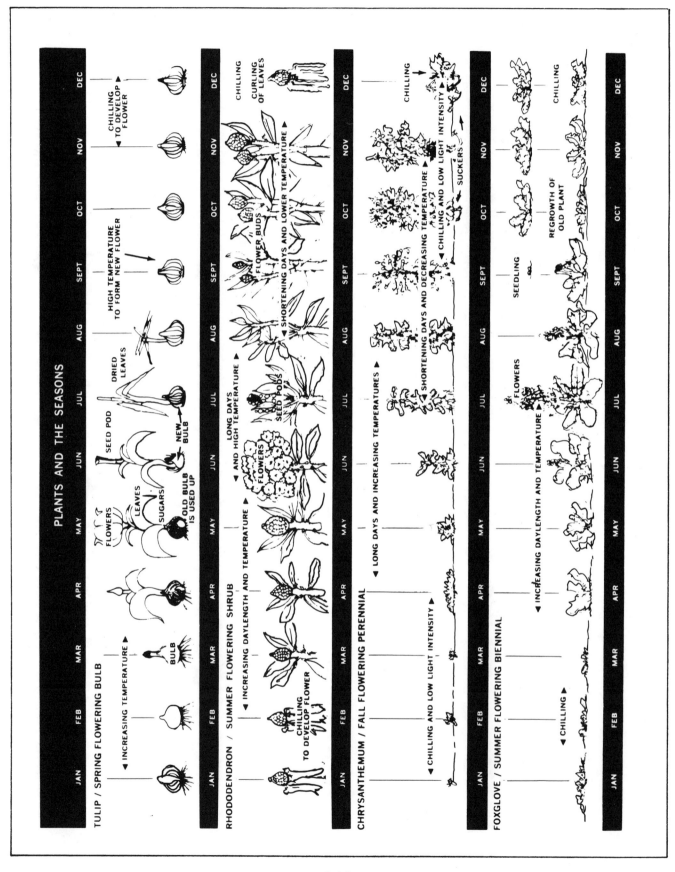

PLANTS AND THE SEASONS

TULIP / SPRING FLOWERING BULB

JAN · FEB · MAR · APR · MAY · JUN · JUL · AUG · SEPT · OCT · NOV · DEC

◄ INCREASING TEMPERATURE ►

BULB

FLOWERS

LEAVES

SUGARS

SEED POD

DRIED LEAVES

NEW BULB

OLD BULB IS USED UP

HIGH TEMPERATURE TO FORM NEW FLOWER

CHILLING TO DEVELOP FLOWER ►

RHODODENDRON / SUMMER FLOWERING SHRUB

JAN · FEB · MAR · APR · MAY · JUN · JUL · AUG · SEPT · OCT · NOV · DEC

◄ INCREASING DAYLENGTH AND TEMPERATURE ►

◄ CHILLING TO DEVELOP FLOWER

◄ LONG DAYS AND HIGH TEMPERATURE ►

FLOWERS

SEED PODS

FLOWER BUDS

SHORTENING DAYS AND LOWER TEMPERATURE ►

CHILLING

CURLING OF LEAVES

CHRYSANTHEMUM / FALL FLOWERING PERENNIAL

JAN · FEB · MAR · APR · MAY · JUN · JUL · AUG · SEPT · OCT · NOV · DEC

◄ CHILLING AND LOW LIGHT INTENSITY ►

◄ LONG DAYS AND INCREASING TEMPERATURES ►

◄ SHORTENING DAYS AND DECREASING TEMPERATURE ►

CHILLING AND LOW LIGHT INTENSITY ►

SUCKERS

CHILLING

FOXGLOVE / SUMMER FLOWERING BIENNIAL

JAN · FEB · MAR · APR · MAY · JUN · JUL · AUG · SEPT · OCT · NOV · DEC

◄ CHILLING ►

◄ INCREASING DAYLENGTH AND TEMPERATURE ►

FLOWERS

SEEDLING

REGROWTH OF OLD PLANT

CHILLING

VINES
Actinidia arguta, Bower Actinidia
Campsis radicans, Trumpet Vine
Celastrus orbiculatus, Oriental Bittersweet
Celastrus scandens, Amer. Bittersweet
Clematis virginiana, Virgin's Bower
Hedera helix, English Ivy
Lonicera sps., Honeysuckle
Parthenocissus quinquefolia, Virginia Creeper
Parthenocissus tricuspidata, Boston Ivy
Vitis labrusca, Fox Grape
Wisteria sinensis, Chinese Wisteria

GROUND COVERS
Arctostaphylos uva-ursi, Bearberry
Cotoneaster horizontalis, Rock Spray
Hedera helix, English Ivy
Juniperus chinensis sargenti, Sargent's Juniper
Juniperus conferta, Shore Juniper
Juniperus horizontalis, Creeping Juniper
Lonicera japonica halliana, Hall's Honeysuckle
Lonicera sempervirens, Trumpet Honeysuckle
Phlos subulata, Moss Pink
Vinca minor, Periwinkle

WISTARIA SINENSIS.

DWARF SHRUBS 1' to 3'
Aronia melanocarpa, Black CHokeberry
Calluna vulgaris, Heather
Cotoneaster horizontalis, Rock Spray
Hydrangea arborescens grand., Hills of Snow
Hudsonia tomentosa, Beach Heather
Juniperus communis, Common Juniper
Juniperus conferta, Shore Juniper
Pinus mugo mughus, Mugho Pine
Rhus aromatica, Fragrant Sumac

FOUR GOOD CLEMATISES.

SMALL SHRUBS 4' to 6'
Aronia arbutifolia, Red Chokeberry
Baccharis halimifolia, Groundsel Bush
Berberis julianae, Wintergreen Barberry
Cotoneaster divaricata, Spreading Cotoneaster
Cytisus scoparius, Scotch Broom
Lonicera fragrantissima, Winter Honeysuckle
Lonicera Morrowi, Morrow Honeysuckle
Prunus maritima, Beach Plum
Rhododendron carolinianum Carolina Rhodo.
Rosa rugosa, Rugosa Rose
Spiraea sps., Spirea

SHRUBS 6' to 10'
Clethra alnifolia, Summersweet
Euonymus alatus, Winged Euonymus
Ilex verticillata, Winter Berry
Juniperus chin. pfitzeriana, Pfitzer's Juniper
Ligustrum obtusifolium, Border Privet
Lonicera Tatarica, Tatarian Honeysuckle
Myrica pensylvanica, Bayberry
Rhododendron catawbiense, Catawba Rhodo.
Rhus sps., Sumac
Rosa sps. (own root), Rose
Vaccinium corymbosum, Highbush Blueberry
Viburnum (native sps.), Viburnum

ERIANTHUS RAVENNÆ.

JAPAN IRIS.

(IRIS KÆMPFERI.)

FESTUCA GLAUCA.

GERANIUM

SHRUBS 10' AND OVER

Alnus sps., Alder
Amelanchier sps., Serviceberry
Elaeagnus angustifolia, Russian Olive
Elaeagnus umbellata, Autumn Elaeagnus
Hibiscus syriacus, Shrub Althea
Hippophae rhamnoides, Sea Buckthorn
Ilex crenata, Jap. Holly
Ilex glabra, Inkberry
Ligustrum amurense, Amur Privet
Ligustrum ovalifolium, California Privet
Ligustrum vulgare, Common Privet
Lonicera maacki, Amur Honeysuckle
Rhododendron maximum, Rosebay Rhododendron
Rosa sps. (own root), Rose
Sambucus canadensis, Amer. Elder
Tamarix sps., Tamarisk
Taxus sps., Yew
Viburnum (native sps.), Viburnum

TREES

Acer pseudoplatanus, Sycamore Maple
Aesculus hippocastanum, Horse Chestnut
Ailanthus altissima, Tree-of-Heaven
Fagus sylvatica, European Beech
Fraxinus americana, White Ash
Gleditsia triacanthos, Honey Locust
Ilex opaca, American Holly
Juniperus virginiana, Red Cedar
Malus sps., Crabapple
Nyssa sylvatica, Tupelo
Picea polita, Tigertail Spruce
Pinus nigra, Austrian Pine
Pinus sylvestris, Scotch Pine
Pinus thunbergi, Jap. Black Pine
Platanus acerifolia, London Planetree
Populus alba, White Poplar
Prunus serotina, Black Cherry
Quercus alba, White Oak
Robinia pseudoacacia, Black Locust
Salix alba, White Willow
Salix blanda, Weeping Willow
Tilia americana, Amer. Linden
Tilia cordata, Littleleaf Linden
Ulmus pumila, Siberian Elm

EUROPEAN PASQUE-FLOWER.

(ANEMONE PULSATILLA.)

FLOWERS

Ageratum
Anemones
Candytuft
Chrysanthemums
Coleus
Coreopsis
Cornflower
Cosmos
Day-lilies
Gaillardia
Geranium
Gladiolus
Globe Amaranth
Iresine
Iris
Larkspur
Lunaria
Marigold
Pansy
Periwinkle
Petunia
Phlox
Pinks
Portulaca
Slavia
Snowdrops
Straw-flower
Sweet Alyssum
Trilliums
Zinnia

TURK'S-CAP LILY.

(LILIUM SUPERBUM.)

250

QUESTIONS AND ANSWERS ABOUT COMPOSTING

In great gardening countries like England and Japan no garden is complete without a compost pile, made from garden and kitchen wastes to condition and feed the soil. In the United States gardeners will seem to be learning about the benefits of composting, and according to the experience of Rotocrop (USA) Inc. manufacturers of compost bins, there are ten questions most often asked about composting and compost piles.

Here they are, the ten most-often-asked questions about composting:

Does compost have any value as a fertilizer? Yes, if it is made from materials that contain essential plant nutrients. Animal manures and green wastes such as grass clippings and green leaves are a source of nitrogen; bone meal and rock phosphate are a source of phosphorus and wood ashes are an excellent source of potash. Compost also conditions the soil, improving the moisture holding capacity of sandy soils and breaking up sticky, cold clay soils.

What materials are best for composting? From the house: fruit and vegetable peelings, shredded newspapers, eggshells, coffee grounds, tea bags, wood ashes, cotton and wool rags; from the garden: grass clippings, hedge trimmings, weeds, shredded leaves, animal manures (including dog, cat, rabbit and poultry). Leaves and fibrous weed roots are best shredded with a lawn mower to speed decomposition.

How long does it take to make compost? That depends on the method used and time of year (warm temperatures hasten decomposition). With a compost bin, which prevents waste materials from dying out or becoming waterlogged, it's possible to have useful compost within six weeks.

Is it necessary to add chemicals to a compost pile to help it decompose? No, but what a compost pile often needs is an "activator", which is an additional source of nitrogen to speed decomposition. Nitrogen is obtainable in chemical form but it is also widely available organically. Animal manures, bone meal and fish meal make excellent natural "activators".

Do compost piles attract vermin? Not if the compost is made in a compost bin and the mixture contains no meat scraps. A properly made and well ventilated compost pile bcomes too hot, dense, and moist for the comfort of vermin.

Do compost piles have offensive odors? Not if the compost is made in a bin with adequate ventilation. As decomposition occurs the mixture will give off a pleasant "yeasty" odor, but it is not offensive.

Do compost heaps need turning? With an exposed compost pile the sides have a tendency to dry out and so turning the heap will ensure thorough decomposition. Turning an exposed heap also aids aeration. With an enclosed bin, ventilation from below and along the sides provides adequate aeration without the need for turning. Also the protection provided by a bin extends fermentation to all areas of the heap.

How can you tell when compost is ready? Well made compost has the appearance of moist, dark, crumbly earth with a pleasant "earthy" odor. It can be shovelled into a wheelbarrow and spread directly onto the garden in spring or fall, or at any time during the growing season as a mulch.

Can compost feed lawns? Yes, and the time to apply it is in fall. Spread it evenly over lawn areas and during winter the compost will work its way into the existing soil. By spring it will be all gone, absorbed into the upper soil surface helping the grass to grow thick and healthy.

Where do I obtain a compost bin? The most widely used compost bin is an Accelerator, made from interlocking green panels with aeration holes in the side and an inflatable cover. For information write: Rotocrop (USA) Inc., 58 Buttonwood St., New Hope, Pa. 18938.

GREEN-LEAVED BAMBOO.

(ARUNDO DONAX.)

BUSHES
FOR BIRDS

BUSHES FOR BIRDS

Autumn-olive—Elaeagnus umbellata
Bird use: 15 species
Ornamental value: Large, spreading shrub with gray-green foliage, fragrant, small, yellowish blooms; abundant red fruits.
Adaptation: Moist to dry soil; sun to light shade; Cardinal variety, winter hardy.
In bloom: May-July. In fruit: September-Dec.
Height: 8 to 15 ft.
Sources: Commercial nurseries, several State nurseries.

Dogwood—Cornus spp.
Bird use: 47 species
Ornamental value: Variable forms: small to large shrubs, small trees; leaves strongly veined, red to bronze in the fall; whitish to yellowish blooms; fruits bunched or clustered—red, blue, or white.
Adaptation: Moist to well-drained soil; sun to shade.
Height: shrub, 5 to 8 ft.; tree, 20 to 30 ft.
In bloom: April-June. In fruit: Aug.—Feb.
Sources: Commercial and State nurseries, wild transplants, cuttings.

Mountain-ash—Sorbus spp.
Bird use: 20 species
Ornamental value: Medium-size trees with compound leaves; flat, white flower clusters; bright red to orange berry clusters.
Adaptation: Moist to dry soil; sun; cool climate.
In bloom: May-June. In fruit: Aug.-March
Height: 20 to 40 ft.
Sources: Commercial nurseries, wild transplants.

Russian-olive—Elaeagnus angustifolia
Bird use: 31 species
Ornamental value: Large shrub to small tree; introduced species widely established in dry alkaline sites in West; silvery yellow to pink fruits persist nearly all winter; narrow green leaves silvery below.
Adaptation: Well-drained to dry soil; sun.
In bloom: June-July. In fruit: Sept.-Feb.
Height: 15 to 25 ft.
Sources: Commercial nurseries and wild transplants.

Firethorn—Pyracantha spp.
Bird use: 17 species
Ornamental value: Medium to large shrubs; white blooms; showy, orange to red fruits.
Adaptation: Moist to well-drained soil; sun to partial shade.
In bloom: June. In fruit: Sept.-March
Height: 6 to 12 ft.
Sources: Commercial nurseries

Sunflower—Helianthus spp.
Bird use: 52 species
Ornamental value: Tall annual plant; has large yellow flowers.
Adaptation: Well-drained soil; sun.
In bloom: June-August. Ripe seed: Aug.-Sept.
Height: 4 to 8 ft.
Sources: Commercial seed stores and mail order nurseries.

Crabapple—Malus spp.
Bird use: 29 species
Ornamental value: Small to medium-size trees; showy, white to pink blooms; red, purple, orange, or yellow fruits.
Adaptation: Well-drained soil; sun and light shade.
In bloom: April-May. In fruit: Sept.-April
Height: 10 to 30 ft.
Sources: Commercial nurseries, grafting, budding.

NOTE: In many areas wild transplants are subject to local regulations. Check your state rules.

Elderberry—Sambucus spp.
Bird use: 50 species
Ornamental value: Tall shrubs; flat, whitish flower clusters; red to purple-black fruits.
Adaptation: Moist to well-drained soil; sun to shade.
In bloom: May-July. In fruit: July-Oct.
Height: 5 to 8 ft.
Sources: Commercial nurseries.

American Cranberrybush—Viburnum trilobum
Bird use: 28 species
Ornamental value: Tall upright shrub; showy flat clusters of whitish flowers; glossy scarlet fruit clusters.
Adaptation: Deep, moist to well-drained soil; sun to light shade.
In bloom: May-June. In fruit: Sept.-May
Height: 8 to 12 ft.
Sources: Commercial nurseries, some State nurseries, wild transplants or cuttings.

Cherry—Prunus spp.
Bird use: 49 species
Ornamental value: Variable forms; shrubs, small
    to large trees; small fine-toothed leaves, yellow
    in fall; showy white flower clusters or drooping
    spikes; small, bright-red to black fruits.
Height: shrub, 5 to 15 ft.; tree, 20 to 75 ft.
Adaptation: moist to dry soil; sun to light shade.
In bloom: April-June. In fruit: Variable with
    species, June—November.
Sources: Commercial nurseries, wild transplants.

Wild Plum-Prunus americana
Bird use: 16 species
Ornamental value: Large shrub to small tree;
    suited to large yards or fields; spreads by
    suckers to form clumps; fragrant pink and white
    flowers; hardy red or yellow fruits.
Adaptation: Moist to well-drained loamy soil; sun.
In bloom: April-May. In fruit: July-October
Height: 10 to 30 ft.
Sources: Commercial nurseries, wild transplants.

Cotoneaster—Cotoneaster spp.
Bird use: 6 species
Ornamental value: Medium-size shrub; usually
    planted as a hedge but also as ground cover;
    dark-green leaves turning red-gold in fall;
    small pink or white flowers; showy red,
    orange, or black fruits.
Adaptation: Moist to well-drained soil; sun.
In bloom: May-June. In fruit: Sept.-Nov.
Height: 2 to 10 ft.
Sources: Commercial nurseries.

THE DOUBLE-FLOWERING CHERRY. (PRUNUS CERASUS, FL. PL.)

Tatarian Honeysuckle—Lonicera tatarica
Bird use: 18 species
Ornamental value: Large shrub; pink to
    yellow-white blooms; yellow to red fruits.
Adaptation: Well-drained to dry soil; sun to
    light shade.
In bloom: May-June. In fruit: July-Sept.
Height: 5 to 15 ft.
Sources: Commercial nurseries.

Redcedar—Juniperus virginiana
Bird use: 25 species
Ornamental value: Medium-size coniferous
    tree (many varieties); dense, green to
    blue-green needles; small, dusty-blue,
    berry-like cones.
Adaptation: Moist to dry soil; sun to light shade.
In bloom: April-May. In fruit: Sept.-May
Height: 15 to 40 ft.
Sources: Commercial nurseries, some State
    nurseries.

Bittersweet—Celastrus scandens
Bird use: 12 species
Ornamental value: Twining vine; pale-green
    flowers; bright-red berries in yellow or
    orange husks.
Adaptation: Well-drained to dry soil; light shade.
In bloom: May-June. In fruit: Sept.-Dec.
Height: Climbs to 25 ft.
Sources: Commercial nurseries, some State
    nurseries, cuttings.

Holly—Ilex spp.
Bird use: 20 species
Ornamental value: Variable forms: upright
    rounded shrubs, small to medium-size trees;
    many varieties; dark green foliage, evergreen
    or deciduous; small whitish blooms, bright-
    red, black, or yellow fruits (very persistent).
Adaptation: Moist to well-drained soil; sun to
    shade.
In bloom: April-June. In fruit: Sept.-May
Height: Shrub, 5 to 15 ft.; tree, 30 to 50 ft.
Sources: Commercial nurseries, cuttings.

Hawthorn—Crataegus spp.
Bird use: 19 species
Ornamental value: Small trees; pale-green
    toothed leaves; abundant, clustered, white
    flowers; orange to red fruits (very persistent).
Adaptation: Deep, moist to dry soil; sun to shade.
In bloom: May-June. In fruit: Oct.-March
Height: 15 to 30 ft.
Sources: Commercial nurseries.

255